The Classical Ideal
English Silver, 1760–1840

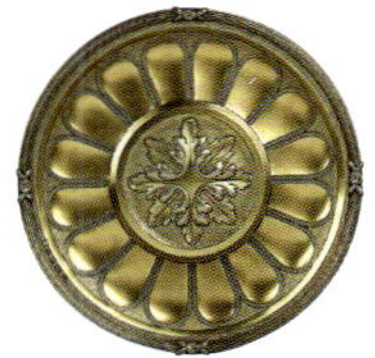

A loan exhibition at Koopman Rare Art

The Classical Ideal

English Silver, 1760–1840

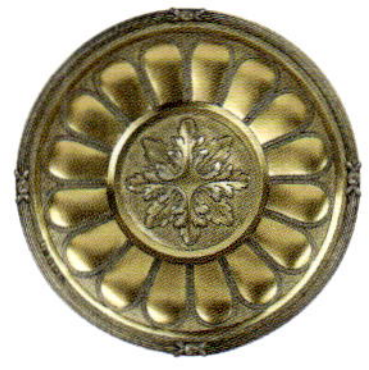

Christopher Hartop

Foreword by Tim Knox
Director, Sir John Soane's Museum

John Adamson • *Cambridge*
for Koopman Rare Art

Published in conjunction with the exhibition

The Classical Ideal
English Silver, 1760–1840

3–25 June 2010

at Koopman Rare Art
53–64 Chancery Lane
London WC2A 1QS
T. 020 7242 7624
www.koopmanrareart.com

Proceeds from the sale of this catalogue will benefit Sir John Soane's Museum and its Adam Drawings On-line Project.

Edited and produced by John Adamson

British Library cataloguing in publication data
A catalogue record for this book is available from the British Library.

Published by John Adamson
90 Hertford Street, Cambridge CB4 3AQ, England

First published 2010

ISBN: 978-0-9524322-9-6

Designed by Chris Jones, Design4Science Ltd
Printed on 170 gsm Burgo R400 paper by Conti Tipocolor, Florence, Italy

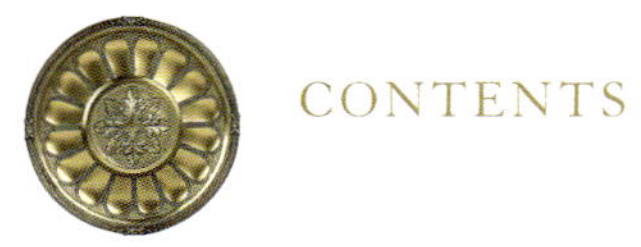

CONTENTS

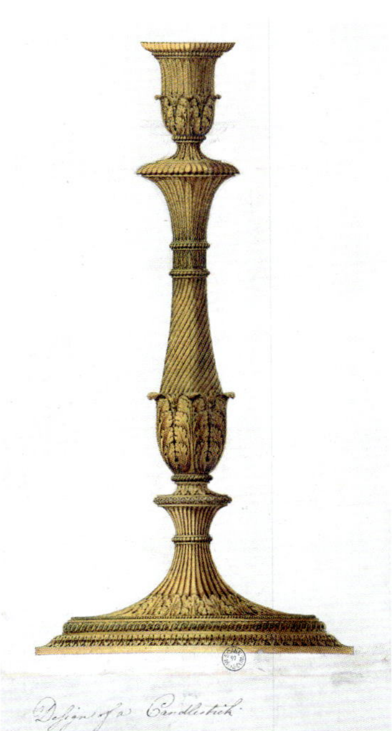
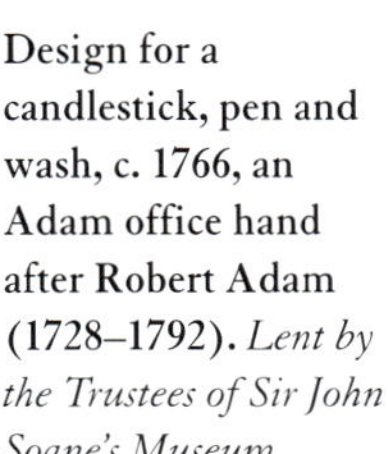

Design for a candlestick, pen and wash, c. 1766, an Adam office hand after Robert Adam (1728–1792). *Lent by the Trustees of Sir John Soane's Museum.*

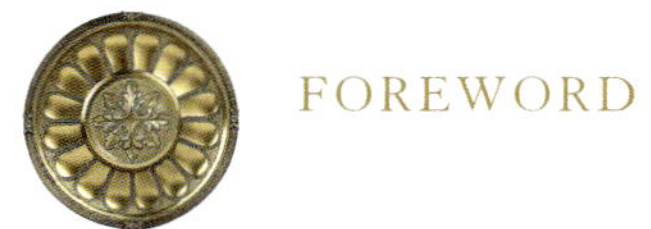

The purchase by John Soane in June 1833 of nearly 9,000 drawings by Robert and James Adam, the surviving collection of the architectural drawings from their busy London and Edinburgh offices, was indeed a momentous event. The Adam family had unsuccessfully attempted to sell the collection to Soane the previous year, and it was only after the drawings failed to sell at auction in Edinburgh that the family capitulated to Soane's original offer of £200. The drawings arrived at Lincoln's Inn Fields in July 1833 after being brought from Leith to the Pool of London in wooden boxes covered with tarpaulins lashed to the deck of the *Soho Steamer*.

What a bargain it was! The fifty-seven albums of Adam drawings Soane had acquired contained not only the brothers' designs for buildings, interiors and furniture, but also a whole treasury of designs for silver – among them drawings for the Dundas Race Cup and for the table silver commissioned by Sir Watkin Williams-Wynn. These drawings, combined with Soane's collection of plaster models for sculpture and plate by John Flaxman, another noted designer of silver, give Sir John Soane's Museum a special place in the study of the arts of the neo-classical era.

The Soane Museum is proud to be associated with this exhibition on the classical ideal mounted by our distinguished neighbours, Koopman Rare Art. The first ever to have been held on the subject of neo-classical silver, the exhibition follows on from the success of their Rundell and Bridge show in 2005, also curated by Christopher Hartop, one of the most knowledgeable and eloquent specialists on the silver of this era. We are grateful to Christopher, and to Lewis Smith and Timo Koopman of Koopman Rare Art, for their generous idea of making Sir John Soane's Museum the beneficiary of the sales of the magnificent catalogue which accompanies this exhibition. All proceeds from catalogue sales will go towards the current project to catalogue all the Adam drawings and make them freely available on line via the museum's web site.

Tim Knox
Director
Sir John Soane's Museum
Lincoln's Inn Fields

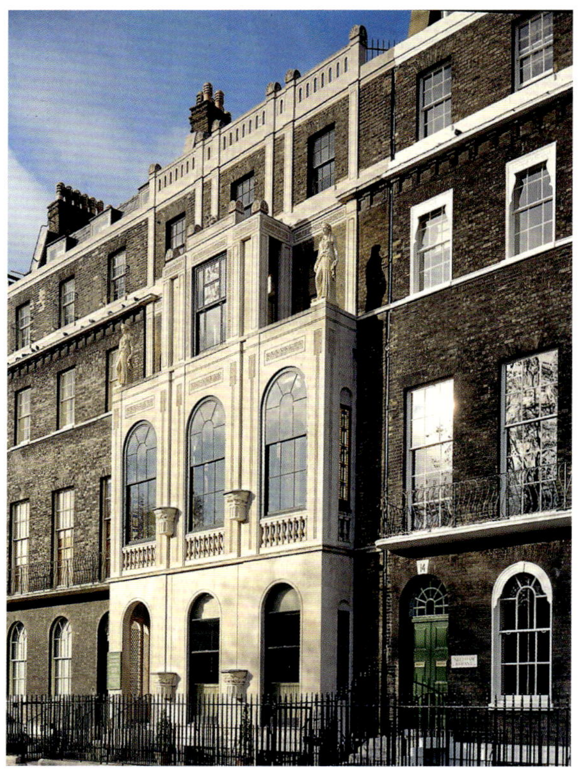

Silver scholarship has long blown hot and cold over neo-classical silver. After the late Robert Rowe's landmark book, *Adam Silver*, appeared in 1965, there followed a flurry of interest, much of it in the wake of the great Royal Academy exhibition on neo-classicism in 1972. Although Rowe's groundwork, not to mention Sven Eriksen's and David Udy's, was assiduously built upon by Frances Fergusson, Kenneth Quickenden and Hilary Young, interest has waned over the last twenty years. Exhibitions have addressed neo-classical silver in the context of major figures for whom silver was just one facet of a varied career, notably Matthew Boulton, John Flaxman, Thomas Hope and James "Athenian" Stuart, and although Adam as designer and architect continues to be a rich vein his silver has, with the exception of Michael Snodin's perceptive analyses and Oliver Fairclough's researches, attracted almost no new scholarship. It has been up to Snodin to produce a steady stream of articles and catalogue essays on virtually every aspect of the subject, and James Lomax and Timothy Schroder have written elegantly on neo-classical silver in the general context. It is my hope that this catalogue may bring together many of the ideas and information that all this scholarship has produced during the last few decades.

The opportunity to gather a broad selection of silver objects in this exhibition, thanks to Koopman Rare Art, means that silver can be studied at first hand alongside designs, and the different, and often quite diverse, strands that make up English neo-classical silver can be compared. I hope the exhibition also provides a chance to turn the spotlight on individuals who have not been studied in this context, such as Humphry Repton and Digby Scott. Pieces like the Castle Corporation Vase (figs. 90–2), designed by a member of the committee which commissioned it, show how widespread the understanding and use of the classical vocabulary were.

Our loan requests received a most enthusiastic response. Her Majesty The Queen graciously agreed to lend five items. I am also very grateful to His Excellency Mohamed Mahdi Altajir, Viscount Coke, Lord and Lady Harewood and Alan and Simone Hartman for generously placing objects at our disposal. Many collectors were kind in not only agreeing to lend items from their collections but also in offering help and advice in their particular field, notably Simon and Cathlyn Davidson, David Needham and Timothy Schroder.

Many are those to whom I owe a debt of gratitude, including Derek Adlam, Catherine Arminjon, David Beasley, Peter Bentley. Eleni Bide, Georgia Bottinelli, Alan Brown, Nigel Bumphrey, George Carter, Harry Charteris, Michael Daley, Aileen Dawson, Alastair Dickenson, Rachel Elwes, Oliver Fairclough, Kaveh Ghaharian, Philippa Glanville, Ian Graves, Caroline de Guitaut, Louise Hofman, Kathryn Jones, Heidi Kucker, Lesley Leader, John Lumley, Jet Pijzel-Dommisse, Rosemary Ransome-Wallis, Sir Hugh Roberts, Anna Robinson, Colin Shearer, Ruth Shrigley, Charles Truman, Richard Vander, Francesca Vanke, Annette de Vries, James Yorke and Heike Zech.

A special word of thanks must go to Philip Hewat-Jaboor, James Lomax, Tessa Murdoch, James Rothwell and Judy Rudoe, all of whom have been great supporters of the project, while at the Soane Museum I have received help and encouragement not only from its director, Tim Knox, but also from Stephen Astley, Mike Nicholson and Susan Palmer. Sotheby's most generously helped with promotion and thanks for this are particularly due to Cynthia Harris in London and John Ward in New York.

The staff of Conti Tipocolor in Florence have worked their customary magic, and Chris Jones has provided superb design under pressure. At Koopman Rare Art, Lewis Smith and Timo Koopman have been enthusiastic leaders of the project, and their colleagues Michael Ace, Niamh Coghlan, Peter Nolan, Daniel Palmer, Chiara Scotto, Anthony Sefton and Carole Weaver have worked tirelessly and cheerfully to make it all happen. Once again I have had the benefit of a congenial partnership with John Adamson as catalogue project manager, and the great support and sage counsel of my wife Juliet.

Christopher Hartop

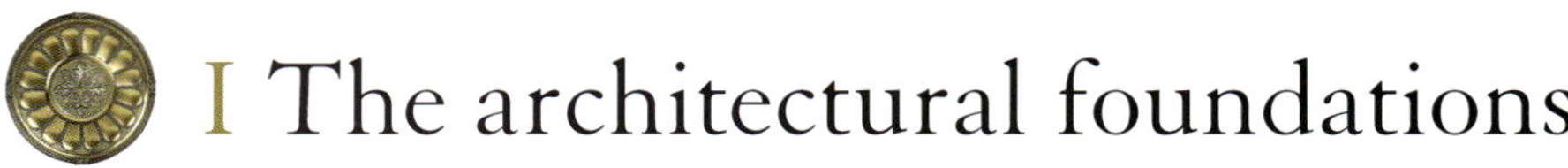

I The architectural foundations

Within neo-classicism two notions seem at odds with each other. On the one hand there is a desire for a return to the rational order and morality of the ancient world and on the other a romantic quest for lost civilizations. Yet both seem to sit happily together, for example, in the work of Robert Adam. When we look at his sideboard arrangement at Kedleston (fig. 21) we see that it represents order, proportion and balance, creating what Vitruvius had described as, "a pleasing and elegant appearance", but the arrangement is also an altar, dedicated to an idealized past, the fumes from its tripod perfume burner adding to the theatricality. The historian Sir John Plumb saw this love of the antique as an escape from the reality of the Georgian environment. If houses could be conceived as temples of the arts, as Holkham had been (see pp. 41–5), they could also be theatres.

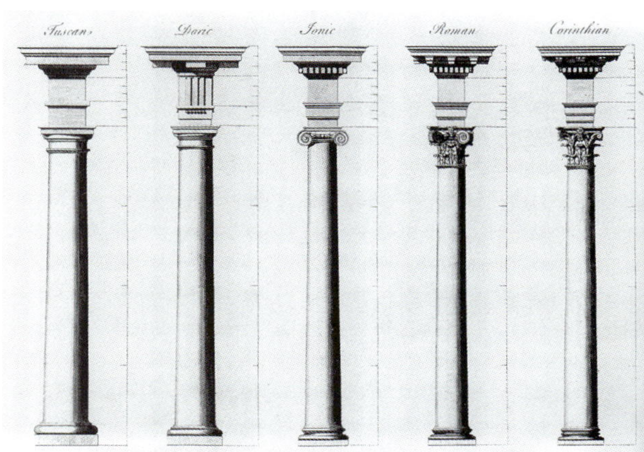

1

The Orders of the Ancients, **Pierre Fourdrinier after Thomas Gandon, engraving from William Chambers,** *A Treatise on the Decorative Part of Civil Architecture*, **1759. To the Greeks' three forms of architectural column, or orders as they were known, the Romans added two of their own. The five orders formed the basic vocabulary of virtually all architecture in the ancient world. They were revived in Renaissance times, but it was in the eighteenth century that their proportions were scientifically analyzed and codified to provide a discipline not only for architecture, but for decorative arts.**

2

The Gibbon Salt, silver, silver-gilt, rock crystal, London, 1576–7, maker's mark three trefoils. In England John Shute's book *The First and Chief Groundes of Architecture*, **which appeared in 1563, included detailed engravings of the five orders. But the Elizabethans often used the column out of context, as with these Ionic columns. Although in the form of a small temple, the salt's overall proportions owe little to classical architecture.** *The Worshipful Company of Goldsmiths, London.*
Cat. no. 1

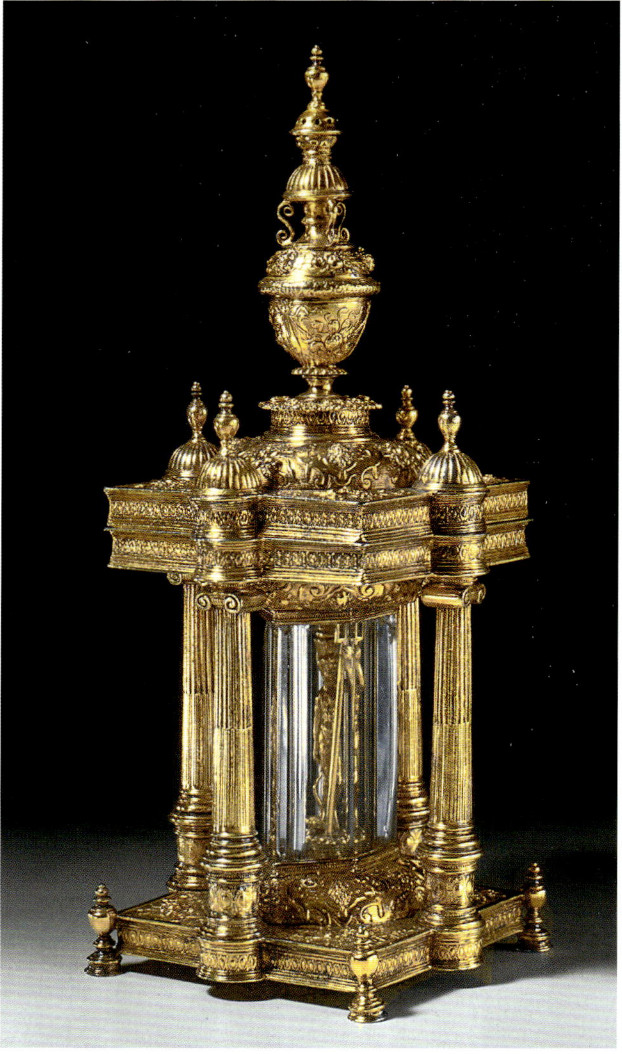

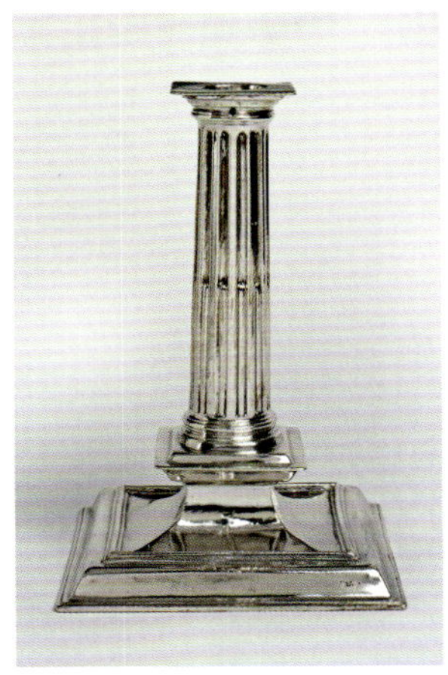

3
Candlestick, silver, London, c. 1682, maker's mark RM or RA in monogram.
In the form of small Doric columns, "monument" candlesticks enjoyed a vogue during the Restoration period. Said to have been named after the Monument, the stone column commemorating the Great Fire of London that was completed in 1677, they are made from thin sheet silver and are relatively flimsy. *Lent by the Trustees of the Victoria and Albert Museum.*
Cat. no. 2

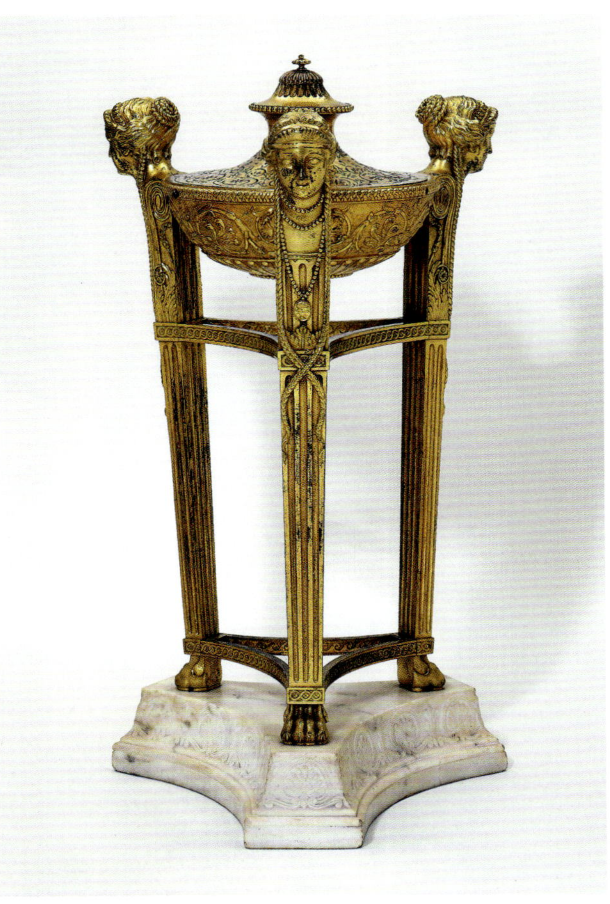

4
Perfume burner, gilt-bronze, marble, probably made by Diederich Nicolaus Anderson, c. 1760 and designed by James "Athenian" Stuart (1713–1788). The tripod was revived by Stuart with his reconstruction of the one that had surmounted the Choragic Monument of Lyscrates in Athens. The design was used to make perfume burners such as this one commissioned by Charles, 2nd Marquess of Rockingham (1730–1782) for his house, Wentworth Woodhouse in Yorkshire. *Lent by the Trustees of the Victoria and Albert Museum.*
Cat. no. 69

One of the problems facing a designer of neo-classical silverware was the lack of authentic ancient examples to use as models, and those examples which did survive were relics of completely obsolete ways of drinking and dining. Prototypes for the Georgian dining table's soup tureens, sauce boats, condiment pots and candlesticks had thus to be found elsewhere. The essential vessel forms of neo-classical silver were the vase, which had developed gradually during the sixteenth and seventeenth centuries and had only a vague ancestry in the ancient world,[1] and the column, the basic element of all ancient architecture.

The classical column had never gone away but had been immersed in other styles during the intervening centuries. The five orders of ancient column were codified, engraved and studied during the Renaissance, allowing them to be used somewhat awkwardly on the Gibbon Salt, for example, made in London in 1576–8.[2] The Ionic columns that support the salt's entablature lend dignity to the design, but they do more than that for they are part of a *lingua franca* that was intelligible to any educated patron in Europe. In a way the columns declared the upbringing and interests of the salt's owner. The use of such vocabulary harked back to the world of the ancient authors,

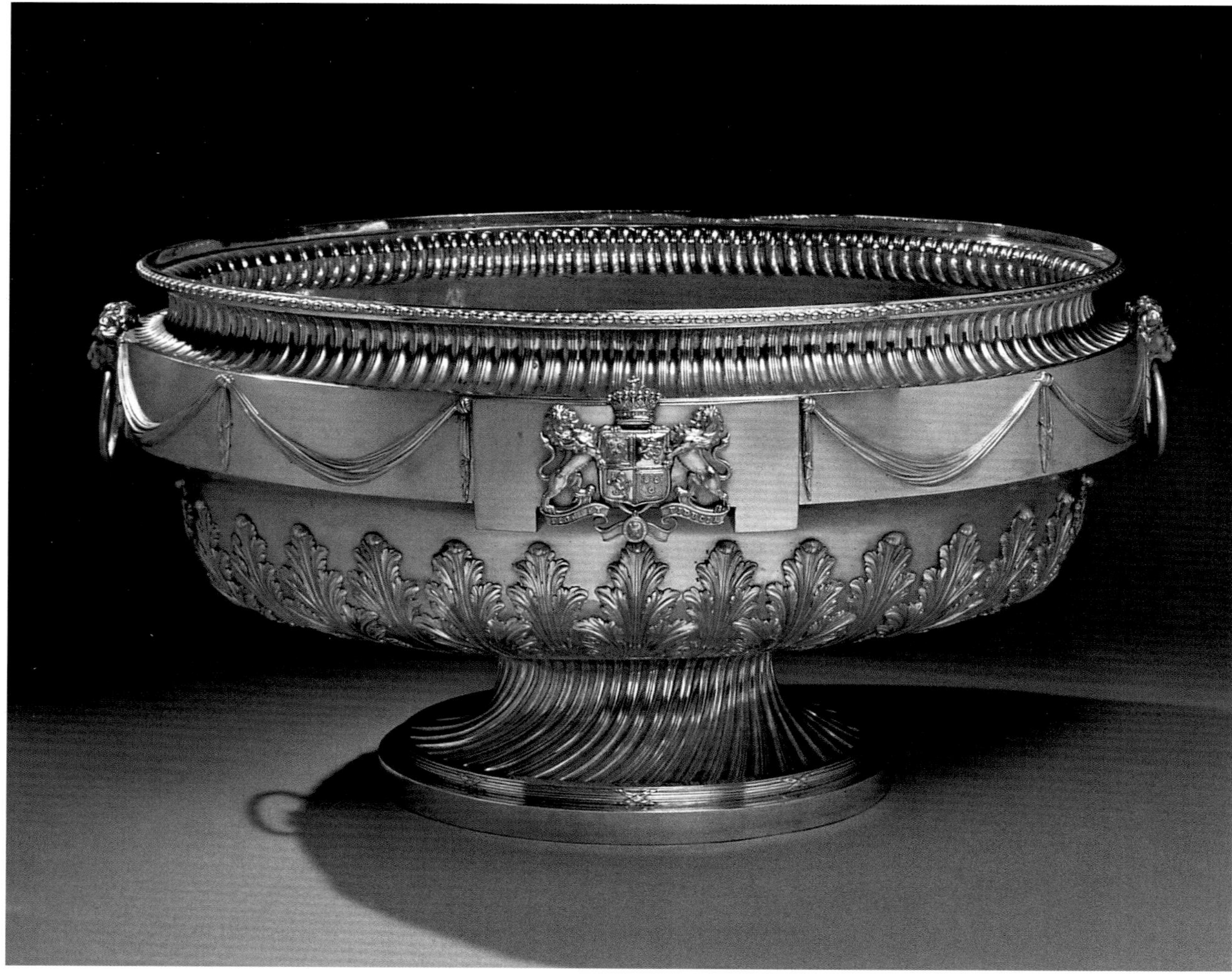

5
Wine cistern, silver, London, 1773–4, maker's mark of Daniel Smith & Robert Sharp. The monumental form of this vessel has classical decoration in the form of lion-head ring handles as well as architectural dentilation but the elliptical shape is a product of the Renaissance. Although the ellipse was known to classical authorities, it was not until the seventeenth century that a practical means of drawing the shape was published. *Lent by His Excellency Mohamed Mahdi Altajir.*
Cat. no. 19

who were essential reading. From these hesitant beginnings classical art supplied the ornamental repertory for the next two hundred years. However, it was not until the mid eighteenth century that an analytical study of ancient buildings allowed for their proportions to be standardized in the quest for balance and ideal beauty – or "noble simplicity and calm grandeur" as Johann Joachim Winckelmann was to put it.

In the middle years of the eighteenth century, neo-classicism began with the careful measurement and accurate recording of ancient buildings in Asia Minor and Greece. As David Udy observed, "based on the direct study of antiquity in place of academic theory, neo-classicism was a rejection of *a priori* assumptions in favour of the study of original evidence".[3] And what a treasure trove it turned out to be, as the whole of antiquity was ransacked for ornament. With the exception of sculpture, buildings were the only relics of the ancient world known to the artists and designers who sought the antique, and so borders of decoration such as the Greek key and the Vitruvian scroll, originally intended to be rendered in stone, found their way inside the house in the form of decoration on furniture and on silver for the table top. James "Athenian" Stuart's tripod perfume burners (fig. 4), based on the finial of an ancient monument in Athens, went on to provide the form for miniature examples in silver some twenty-five years later (fig. 6).

The basic vocabulary of ornament – the goat's heads, the bands of scrolls, the stiff

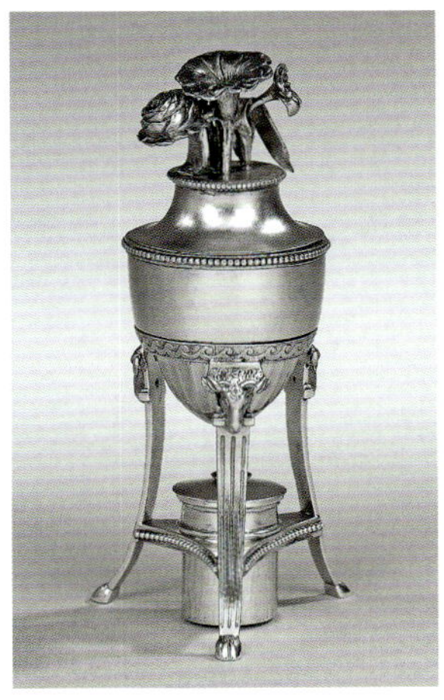

6

Perfume burner, silver, London, 1785–6, maker's mark of Andrew Fogelberg & Stephen Gilbert. "Athenian" Stuart's revival of the classical tripod has inspired this silver example for use on a table top. *Lent by a private collector*.
Cat. no. 41

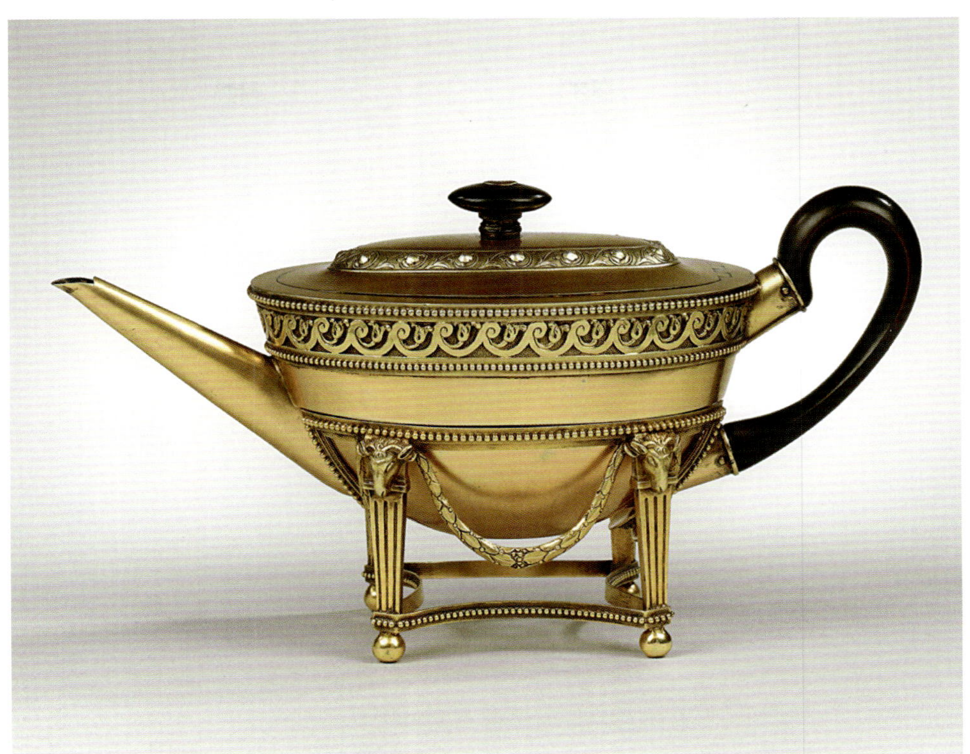

7

Teapot and stand, silver-gilt, ebony, London, 1785–6, maker's mark of Andrew Fogelberg & Stephen Gilbert. Straight legs headed by animal masks support an elliptical removable pot. The overall concept is based on an ancient sarcophagus but the shape is a Renaissance one. *Lent by Koopman Rare Art*.
Cat. no. 42

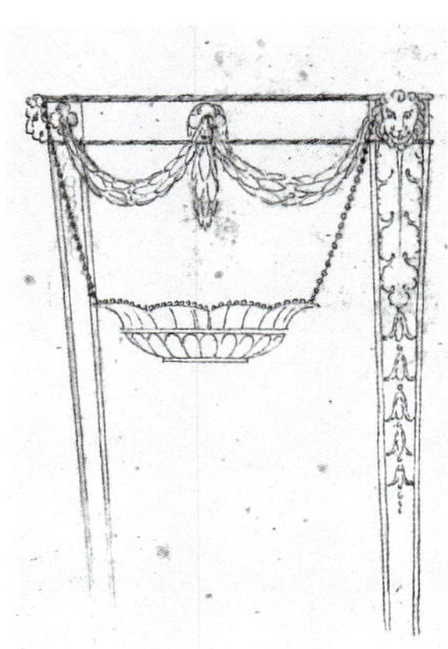

8

Design for a tripod, pencil and wash, James Wyatt (1746–1813). Wyatt enthusiastically took up the tripod form and used it for furniture as well as for silver. *V&A Images*.

stylized leaves – was used over and over again. "No man should be ashamed of copying the Ancients," advised Sir Joshua Reynolds in 1774, an attitude that was to live on for the next hundred years. Charles Heathcote Tatham, writing in 1810, declared that "the works of the Ancients are A MAP TO THE STUDY OF NATURE".[4]

The educated patron spoke the same language as the professional, demanding silverware in the "antique" or "true style". The business ledgers of the fashionable retailers Parker & Wakelin record "a pair of Goat's head Candlesticks" purchased by Lord Digby in 1771, "an Antique Tea Vase with water leaves & Vetruvia foot" (William Fellowes, 1773) and "a fine Antique Coffee Pot with festoons and water leaves" (Sir Thomas Burdett, 1776). It was to be later, with the publication of the discoveries at Pompeii and especially at Herculaneum, that household items were unearthed in sufficient quantities to be used as models for silverware (see Chapter VII).

[1] Joshua Wedgwood spoke of "violent vase madness" in the 1770s; see also McCormick and Ottomeyer, *passim*.
[2] In 1558–9 the English protestant congregation in exile in Frankfurt presented that city with an Antwerp-made beaker in the form of a Doric column (Historisches Museum, Frankfurt).
[3] Udy, "Adam's Vase", p. 193.
[4] Reynolds, 6th Discourse; C.H. Tatham, *Etchings representing the Best Examples of Ancient Ornamental Architecture*, London, 1810, p. 6.

II "Le goût grec" and the influence of France

Reaction against the rococo was more than an argument for plain rather than fancy, or for beauty of line rather than ornament. It was also about a perceived need for balance, proportion and moderation. It was an argument that went back to ancient times when the need for a balance between the humours was seen as the key to health. The rococo was regarded not merely as excessive but anarchic, a style without rules. In 1754 Charles-Nicolas Cochin had attacked the silversmiths in the columns of the *Mercure de France*, fulminating against soup-tureen covers adorned with models of vastly different proportions – "a hare as big as a finger" amongst life-size carrots. A "retour à l'Antique" was, once again, deemed the solution, providing rules as well as models in the pursuit of balance and proportion. But, at least in its early manifestations, French neo-classicism was not averse to playing with scale and surface in the best baroque tradition: Vien's *Suite de Vases Composée dans le Goût de l'Antique* of 1760 set preposterously heavy swags against plain surfaces. The tension between ornament and surface was still a necessary element.

With the artistic winds blowing, as always, from France across the Channel, and helped by a short interlude of peace between the two countries, "le goût grec", as it came to be known, was enthusiastically taken up in England. As they had done with the rococo, London silversmiths directly copied French prototypes, such as the "lyon-faced" candlesticks promoted by Matthew Boulton and others (fig. 9),[1] and Durand's classical tea urn, copied by Heming for Queen Charlotte (fig. 15).[2] Nevertheless, designers such as Sir William Chambers, although with direct experience of the latest

9

Pair of two-light candelabra, silver, London, 1774–5, maker's mark of Thomas Heming. 'Lyon-faced' candlesticks of this form were first made in ormolu in the Paris workshop of Pierre Gouthière, the most famous *ciseleur-doreur* of his time. Matthew Boulton enthusiastically began producing cheap silver versions in the late 1760s, hoping to compete with the London manufacturers. These examples are from the workshop of Thomas Heming, the Royal Goldsmith. *Lent by the Earl and Countess of Harewood and the Trustees of the Harewood House Trust.*
Cat. no. 25

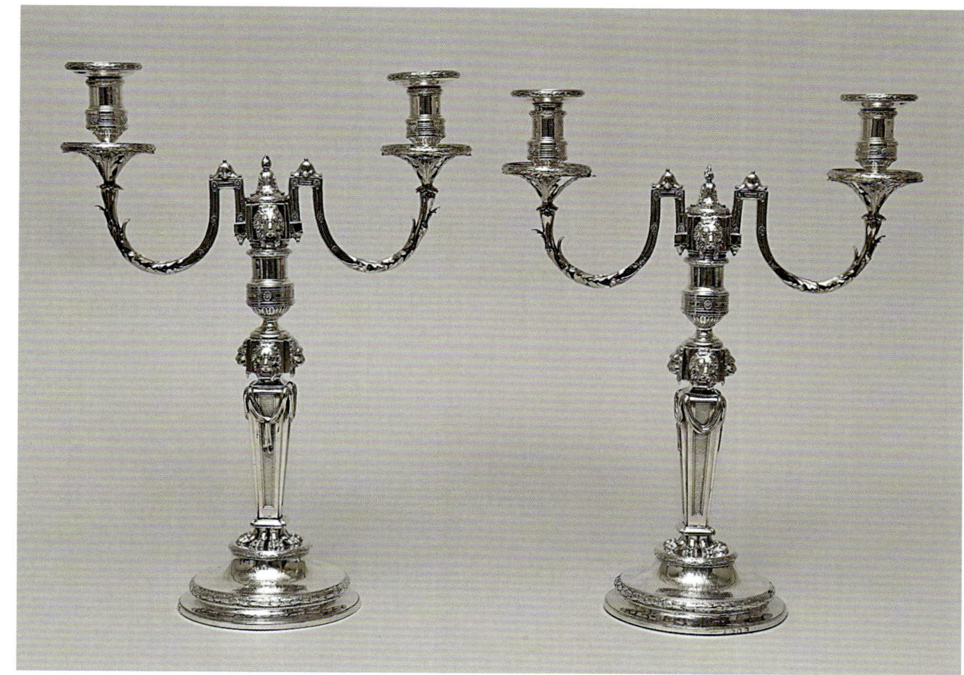

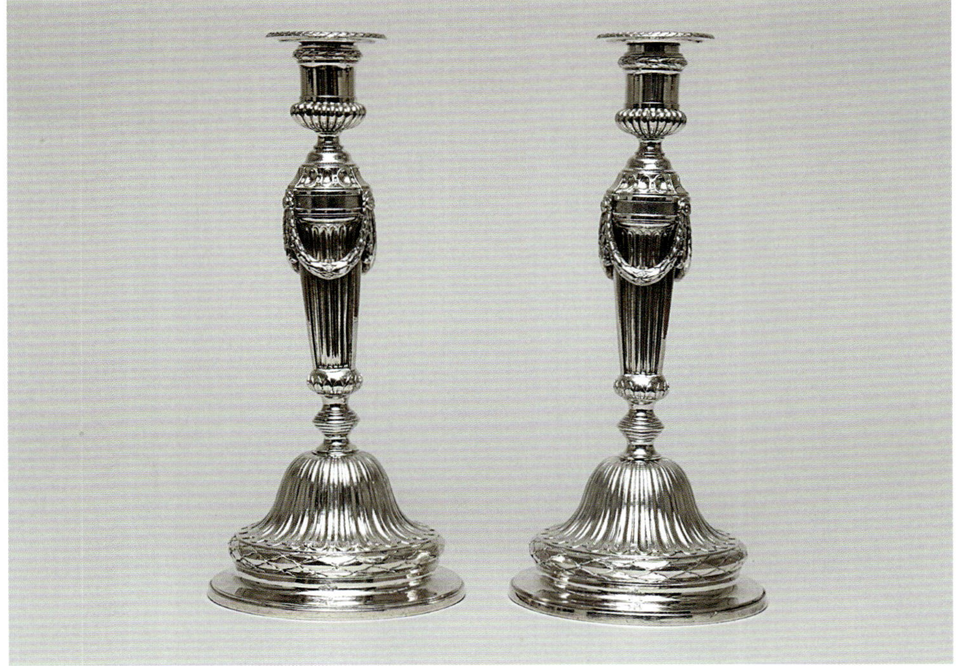

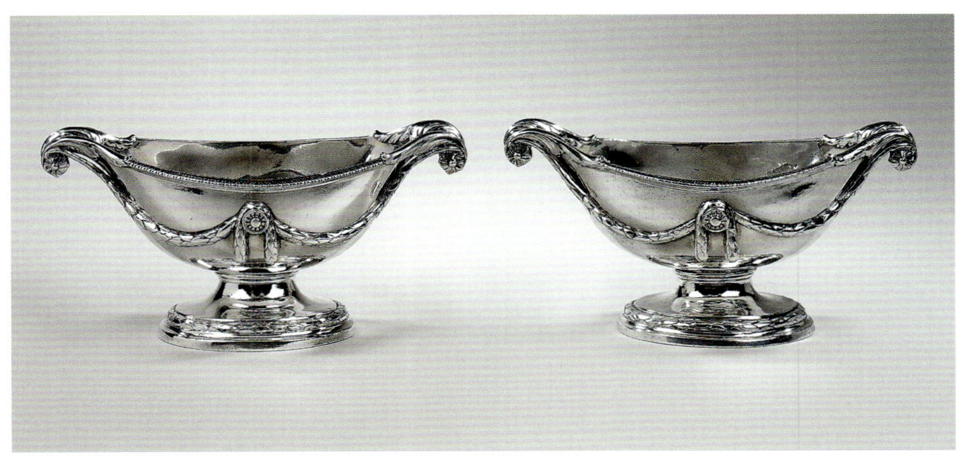

French motifs, tended to produce somewhat watered down versions of Gallic prototypes, especially when designing native forms such as the two-handled cup (fig. 14) or a wine cistern.[3] The more extreme devices of French makers like Jean-Charles Delafosse and others, such as heavy vertical fluting and the superimposition of circles on squares, do not appear to have found much favour in London. On the other hand, the elegance of much of French silver of that time was often lacking. Take, for example, Chambers's sauce boats and other pieces that he had made for the 4th Duke of Marlborough. They have a bold heaviness in keeping with the militaristic masculinity

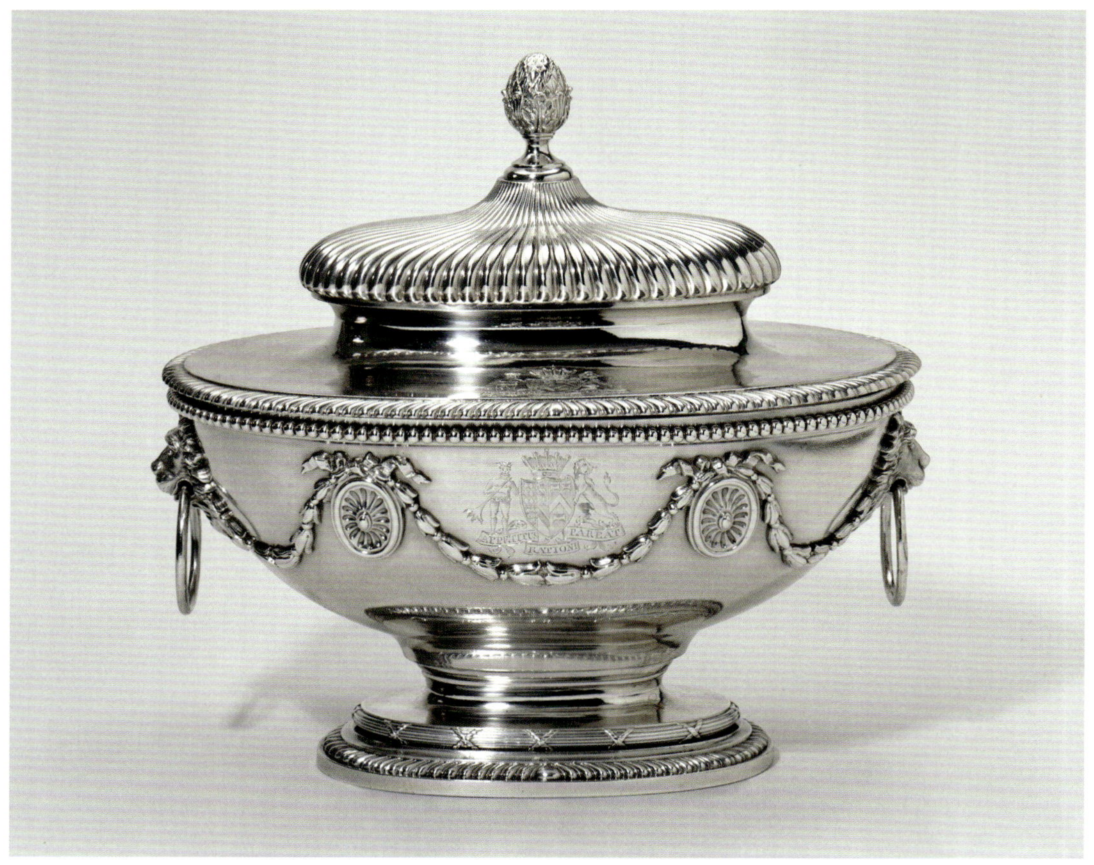

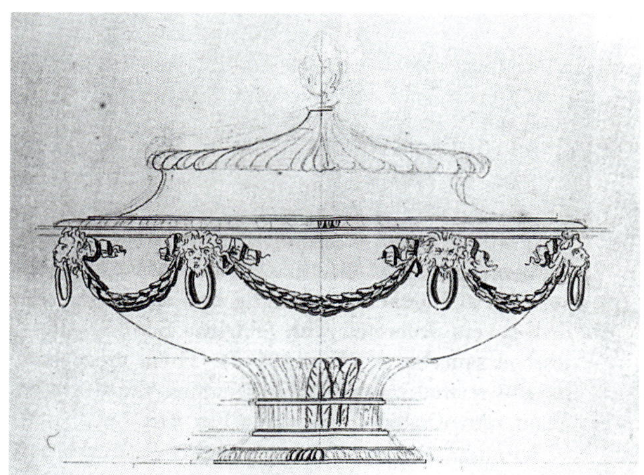

of Blenheim, the duke's seat, rather than a gracefulness of style. We know from the
Parker & Wakelin ledgers that it was Chambers who placed the order, for he is named
as the client in Ansill & Gilbert's account for supplying the finished items to them. It is
most likely therefore that he provided the designs too.[4] Chambers's tureen design of the
early 1770s for Lord Fitzwilliam (figs. 12–13) has a simple dignity that is enhanced by
the fact that it lacks the stand regarded as *de rigueur* in France (they would become
popular in England later in the decade).

A strand of naturalism was always evident in French art. While Vien and Delafosse
produced more and more monumental yet austere classical designs, it often seems that

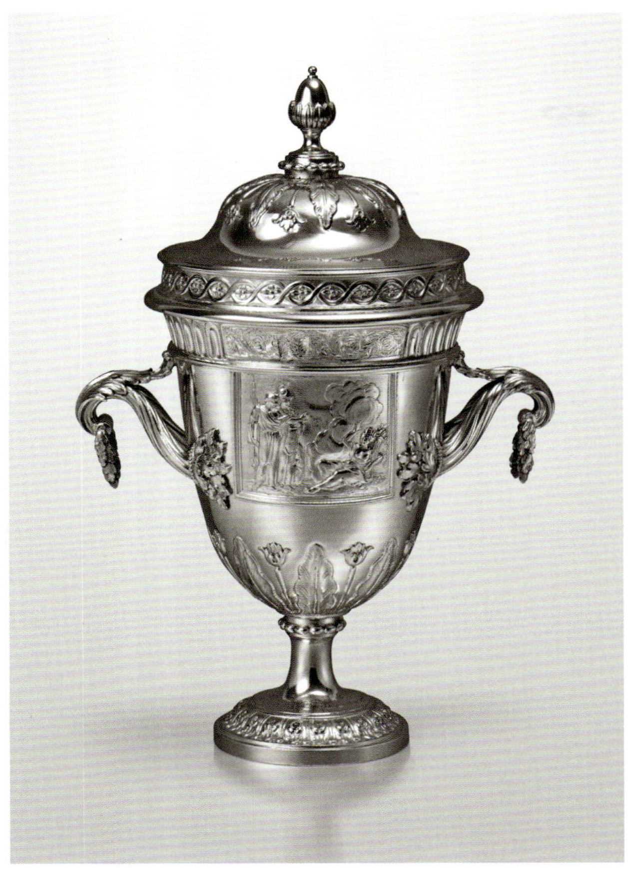

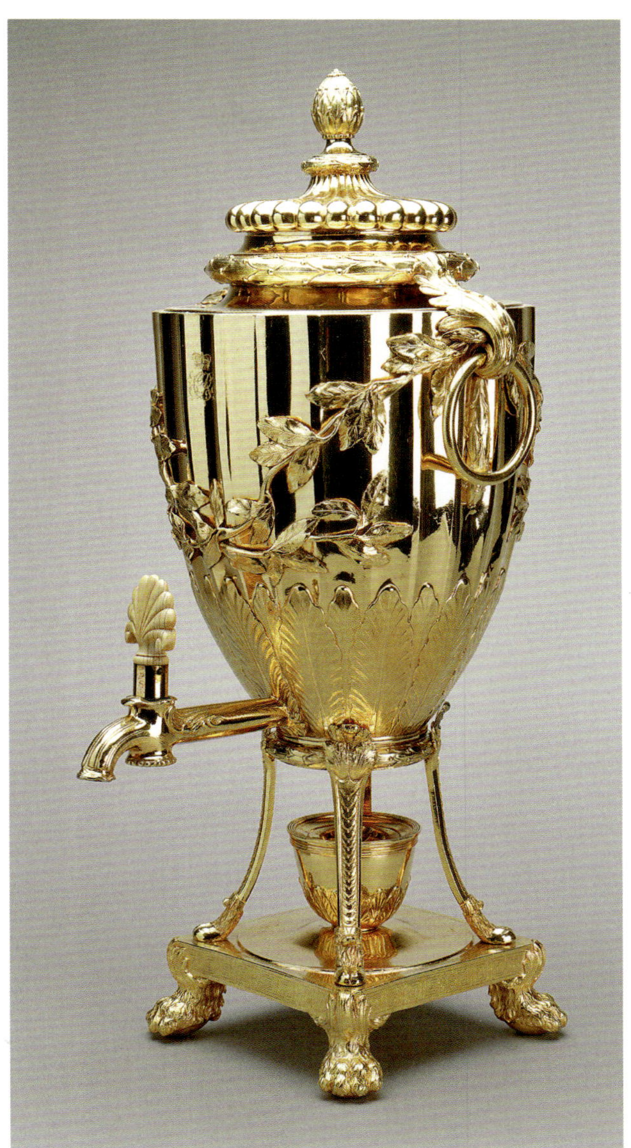

14

Cup and cover, silver, London, 1770–1, maker's mark of Louisa Courtauld & George Cowles. A similar cup with two volute handles, from the same workshop and of the same date, is part of a set of communion plate at Blenheim probably designed by Sir William Chambers. On this cup, the naturalism of the handles and the interlaced band are typical of Chambers's distinctive form of classicism. *Lent by the Azko Nobel Corporation, on loan to the Courtauld Institute of Art.*

15

Tea urn, silver-gilt, ivory, London, 1768–9, maker's mark of Thomas Heming. Supplied to Queen Charlotte, consort of George III, by the Royal Goldsmith Thomas Heming, this tea urn is virtually identical to one made in Paris in 1765–6 in the workshop of Antoine-Sébastien Durand (now minus its spigot). They are both based on engraved designs for urns by Joseph-Marie Vien published in Paris in 1760. *Lent by Her Majesty The Queen.*

the most popular designs were those where austerity was tempered with a band of leaves, or some piece of foliage. As the Marquis de Marigny, *Directeur général des Bâtiments*, brother of Madame de Pompadour and chief exponent of the new style, had declared in 1760, "I do not want any of those modern chicory leaves, nor do I want any of that classical austerity; I seek a happy medium". Perhaps what he had in mind was a tea urn similar to the one in fig. 15.

It was rare for an English client or his agent to supply his own design. The retailer had to fall back upon his own staff, or presumably buy in or borrow drawings. The output of Thomas Heming, in the 1770s probably the largest retailer in London, largely

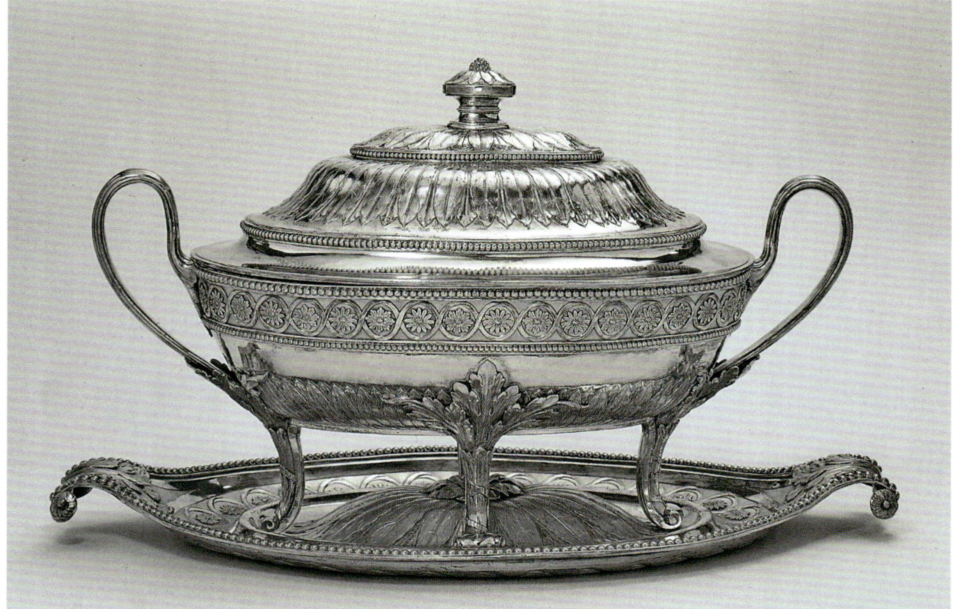

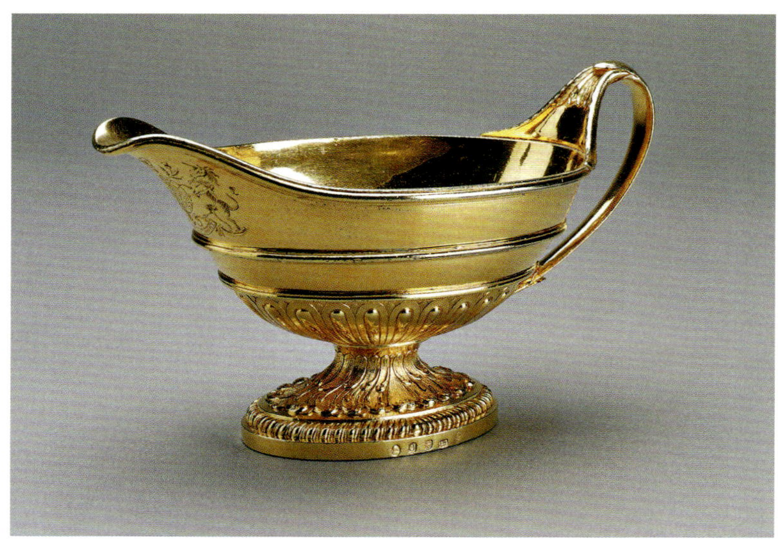

on account of his role as Royal Goldsmith, includes pieces of varying degrees of classicism. Just as with his rococo products, much of his output relies heavily on French printed sources, and suggests a workshop synthesis rather than the presence of one forceful artist in his employ, producing what Timothy Schroder has described as a "distinctive brand of neo-classicism". The soup tureen in fig. 16, supplied to an unknown client by Heming in 1776–7, has a host of French elements such as the presence of a stand, the position of the legs in the centre of the sides, and the composition's horizontality, but the ultimate appearance is decidedly un-French and betrays a certain lack of confidence in such a ponderous blend of classical components.

After the suppression of the Jewel House in 1782 and the dismissal of Heming from his royal post, other retailers had the opportunity to work up large commissions. In 1789, Wakelin & Tayler, the successors to Parker & Wakelin, secured the commission for a large dinner service (figs. 17–18) to commemorate the King's recovery from

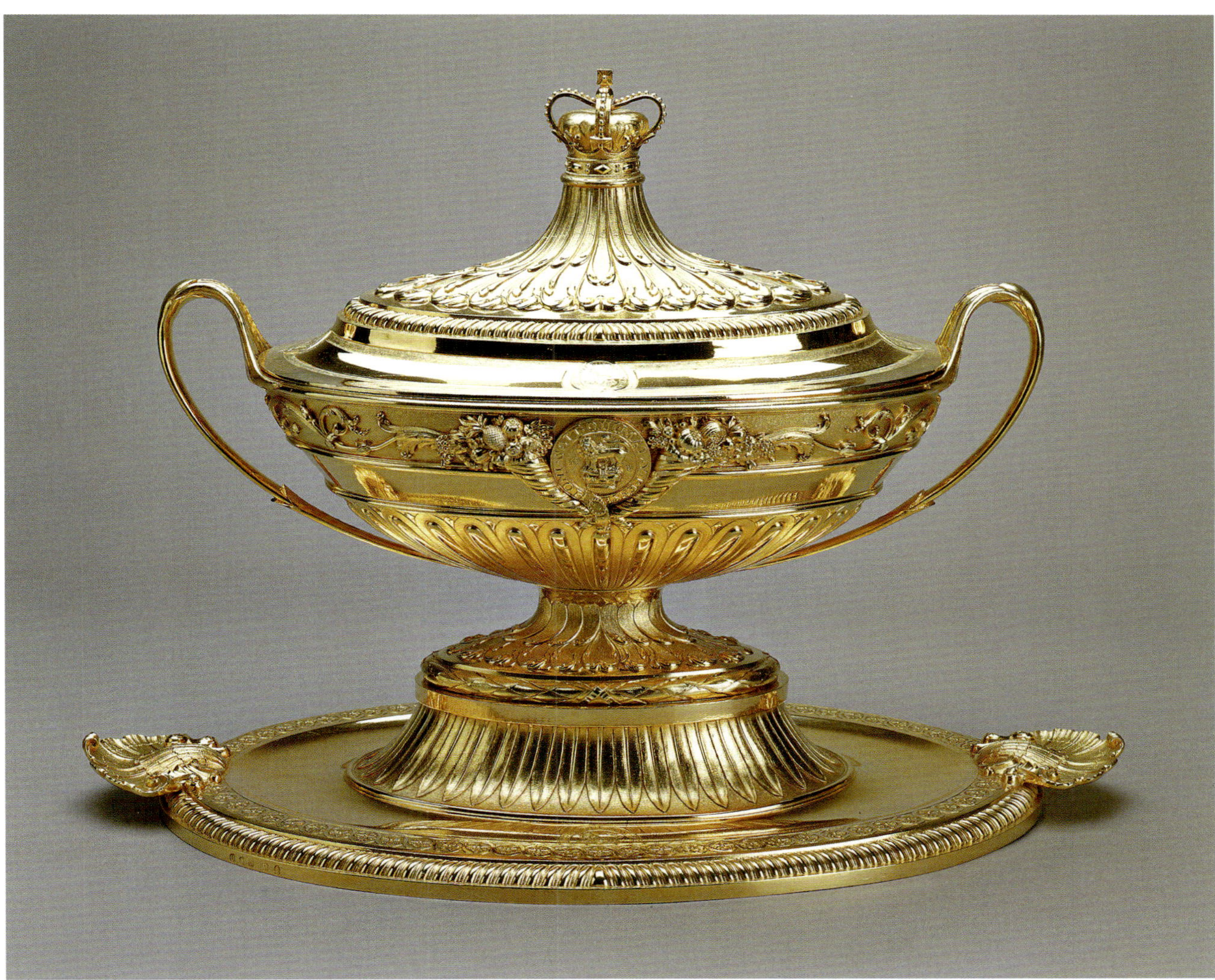

illness, believed at the time to be insanity. Of the small group of surviving components, the sauce boats and soup tureen show an elegant use of bold ornament tempered with naturalism. The tureen is one of "2 fine chased tureens, covers and stands" supplied by Sebastian & James Crespel for £110 10s and sold on by Wakelin & Tayler to the King for £136 8s 3d.[5]

1 Quickenden, "Lyon", pp. 196–210.
2 The French prototype is illustrated in James Lomax, "Neo-classicism" in C. Blair, ed., *The History of Silver*, New York, 1987, p. 143.
3 The wine cistern bearing Abraham Portal's mark, London, l764, now in the Dallas Museum of Art, shows many Chambers characteristics.
4 Young, "Marlborough", pp. 396–400.
5 Luke Schrager, "The royal and aristocratic patronage of Wakelin & Tayler, 1776–92", *Silver Studies: The Journal of the Silver Society*, 21 (2006), p. 90.

18
Soup tureen, cover and stand, silver-gilt, London, 1789–90, maker's mark of John Wakelin & William Tayler but made by Sebastian & James Crespel. As a result of Burke's Economical Reform Act of 1782, the Jewel House had been abolished and Thomas Heming lost his monopoly of royal commissions. The restrained classicism of this tureen, like that of the sauce boat in fig. 17, shows a confidence that was lacking in much of Heming's output in the classical style. *Lent by Her Majesty The Queen*. Cat. no. 49

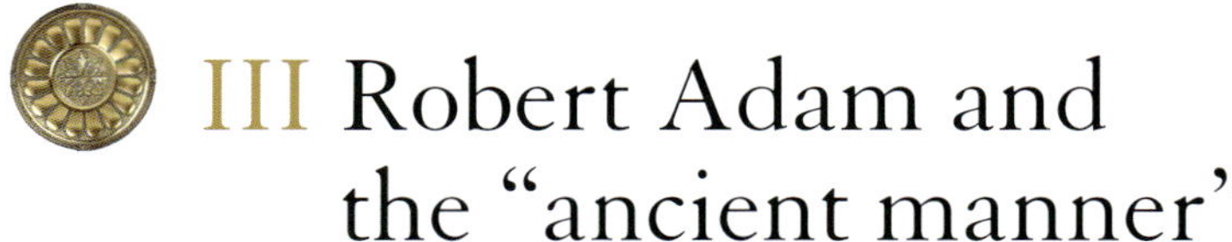

III Robert Adam and the "ancient manner"

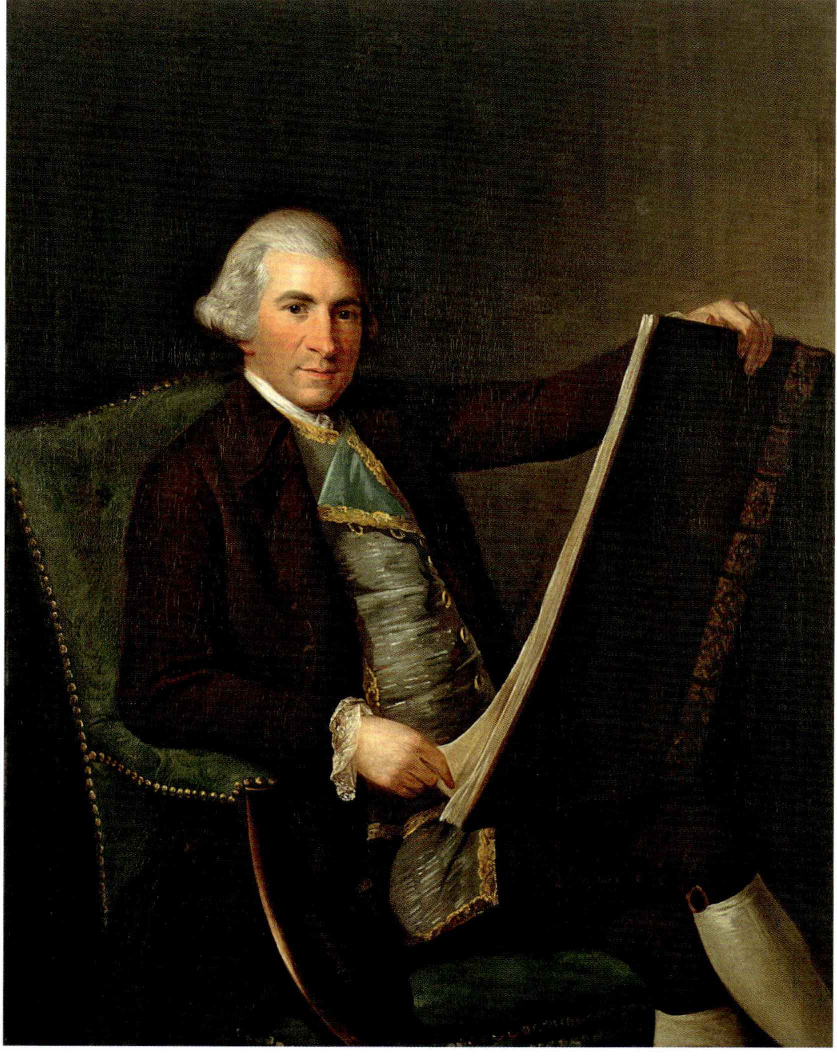

19

Robert Adam (1728–1792), oil on canvas, attributed to George Willison (1741–1787). Adam's designs for silver utilize baroque features and conventional English forms, such as the two-handled cup, to create a distinctive version of neo-classicism that owes little to France. But he was the first to bring together a visual vocabulary for the style in Britain. *The National Portrait Gallery.*

"Manufacturers of every kind felt the electric power of his revolution in art"

Sir John Soane, 1812

The name Adam has for so long been synonymous with neo-classicism in England that we tend to view the work of others through his eyes. In silver, we see Chambers's designs as "ponderous" and "very French", and we regard Wyatt's as light and flimsy. Surely it was Wyatt and not Adam who was responsible for the "insignificant" forms against which the next generation would rail? Even Horace Walpole's jibe about "sippets of embroidery" is hard to apply to Adam's silver designs, which have a solidity as well as a crispness of detail that one would never apply to mere needlework.

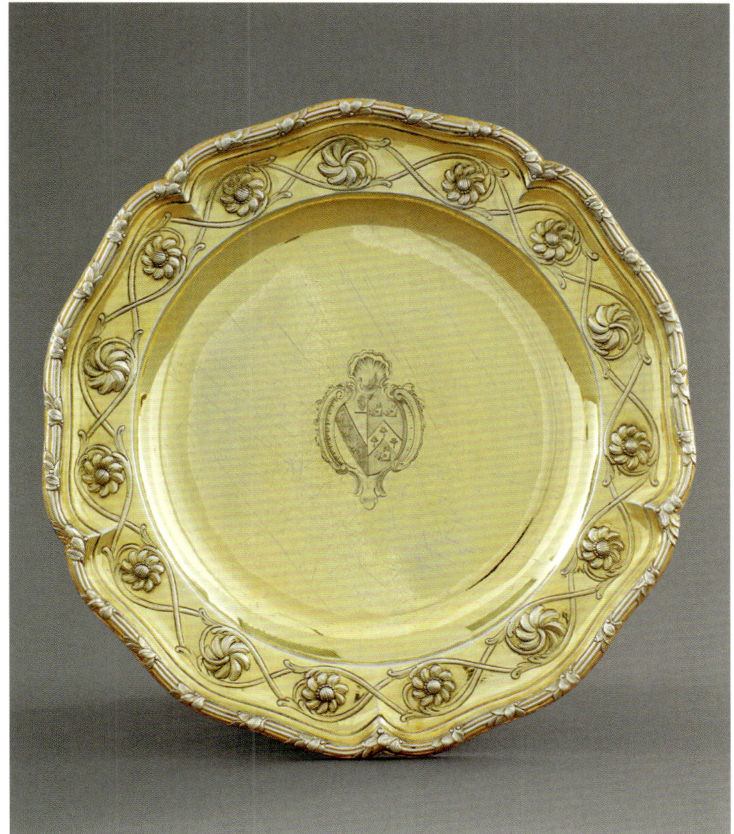

Plate, silver-gilt, London, 1758–9, maker's mark of William Cripps for Philips Garden. This plate is part of a large set supplied by the retailer Philips Garden to Sir Nathaniel Curzon (1726–1804) of Kedleston Hall, Derbyshire, in March 1759. The interlaced border of stylized flowerheads is one of the first instances of classicism in English silver of the Georgian period. A pair of soup tureens from the same order shares the same decoration. At the time, Curzon was employing James Stuart, Matthew Brettingham and John Linnell at Kedleston. The design of these plates could be by either Stuart or Linnell, both of whom are known to have designed silver. Shortly after these plates were delivered, Robert Adam started work on his transformation of the dining-room, incorporating classical features already in place. *Lent by the National Trust, Kedleston Hall, the Scarsdale Collection.*
Cat. no. 3

Nowadays, thanks to the lucky survival of so many of the drawings from his workshop, now in the Soane Museum, we have to regard Robert Adam in a different light from his contemporaries. These, some two hundred of them, offer us an unparalleled opportunity to look at his design process, and the way he experimented with new forms as well as with decoration. Moreover, with the survival of many of the objects themselves, we may study the development of his designs for silver, from paper to finished silverware.

Adam spent four years in Italy absorbing the fomenting ideas of neo-classicism, returning in 1758. These ideas, combined with his direct experience of ancient ruins themselves, gave him a confident and direct approach to the classical vocabulary that contrasts, for example, with the Francophile classicism of Chambers. Indeed, it may be said that there is very little French influence at all in Adam's work; it is in an entirely British vein, bringing together a miscellany of classical forms and decorative motifs. Moreover, his use of baroque features, and his "smallness of scale, through sub-division (sometimes excessive) of parts and sub-enrichment of enrichments", as Sir John Summerson put it, makes his a decidedly idiosyncratic form of neo-classicism. Adam's silver designs have many features, such as a *horror vacui*, that are not normally associated

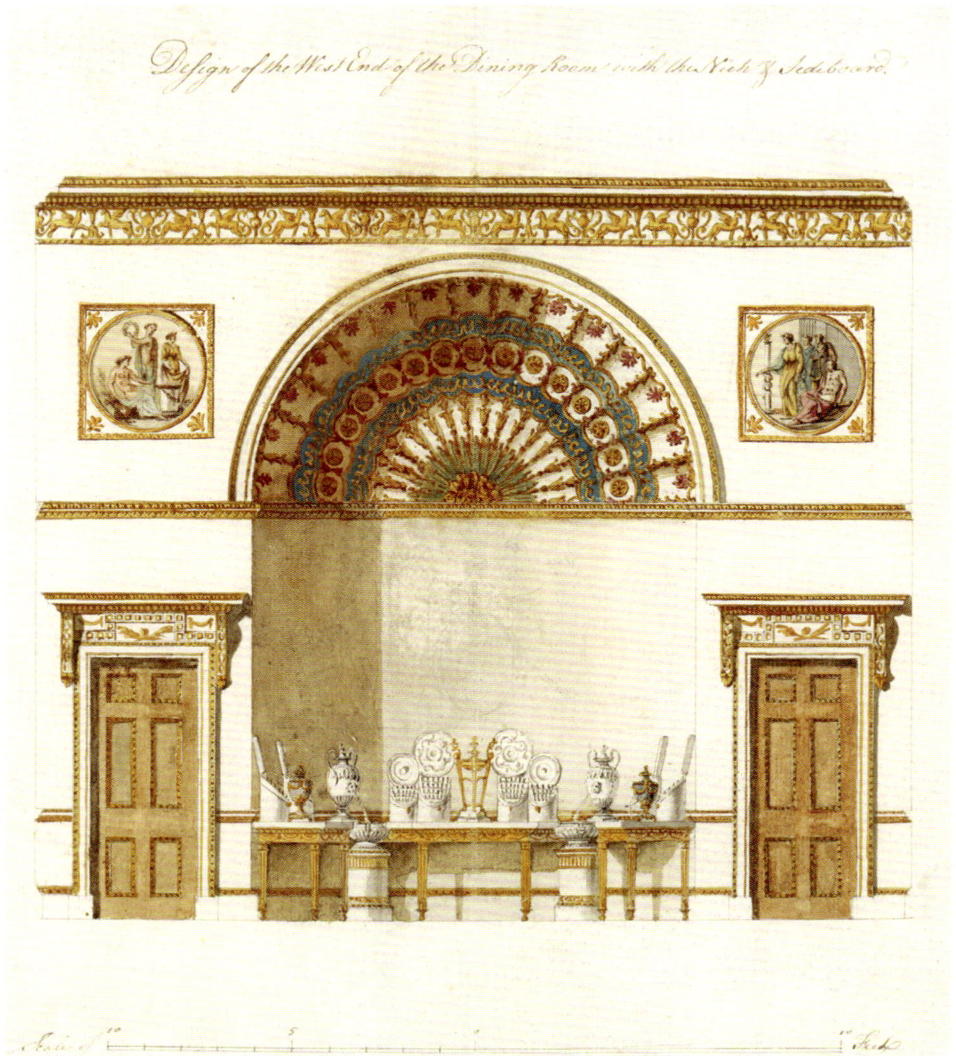

21

Design for the West End of the Dining Room with the Nich & Sideboard, pen, ink, watercolour with pencil additions, 1762, Robert Adam (1728–1792). Adam supplanted "Athenian" Stuart and Matthew Brettingham at Kedleston and created this arrangement utilizing Stuart's tripod and chestnut warmers as well as pieces of seventeenth-century silver. His involvement in the project came too late for the design of the plates (see fig. 20) to be attributed to him. *The National Trust, Kedleston Hall, the Scarsdale Collection.*

with the style. All this makes it all the more curious that his name has traditionally been assigned to so much neo-classical silver – often to objects with little more than a vase shape, or with high loop handles, that hint at neo-classicism.[1]

Much of this is owing to Adam's method of work. He relentlessly pursued prospective clients and once an introduction had been secured, as with Nathaniel Curzon at Kedleston, he peremptorily pushed aside any competition. More than that, Adam's work in the dining-room there shows his ability to assimilate the work of others, in this case James "Athenian" Stuart. He moved swiftly, but unlike his great rival James Wyatt, with great efficiency, from client to client. As has been observed, he "showed that it was not necessary for a creative person to remain under the wing of a patron, as William Kent had done, but he could, through assiduous self-promotion, sell his talents literally to the highest bidder".

Adam's work itself reflected the brimming enthusiasm for the classical ideal with which he had come back from Italy. This is well exemplified in his arrangement of the sideboard in the west end of the dining-room at Kedleston. Using Stuart's recently delivered gilt-bronze and marble tripod based on the Choragic Monument of Lyscrates in Athens as the centrepiece, he skilfully arranged the silver fountains and cisterns

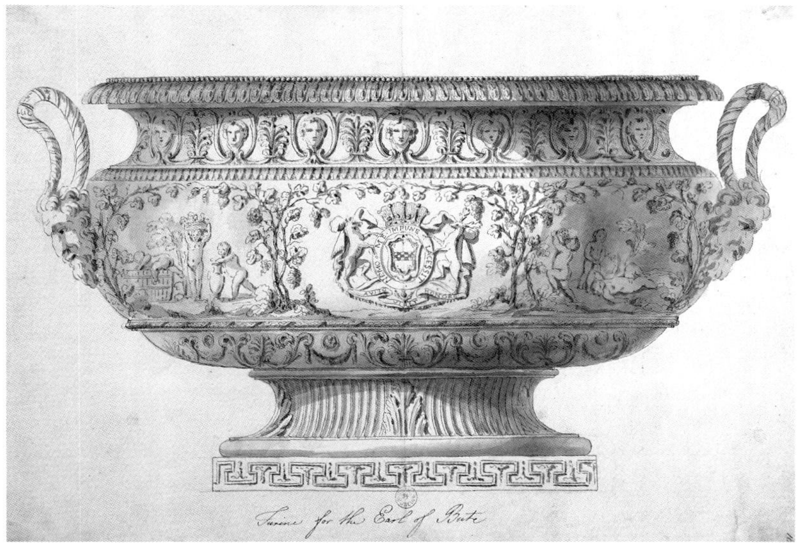

22
Terrine for the Earl of Bute, pen and wash, c. 1761–3, Robert Adam (1728–1792). One of a series of designs, presumably never executed, for George III's favourite, the Earl of Bute, it shows Adam's use of naturalism and baroque forms (the elliptical bellied basin) which, combined with his crowded bands of ornament, create his particular style. The drawing has been mislabelled as a "terrine" at a later date but it is clearly a wine cistern. *Lent by the Trustees of Sir John Soane's Museum.*

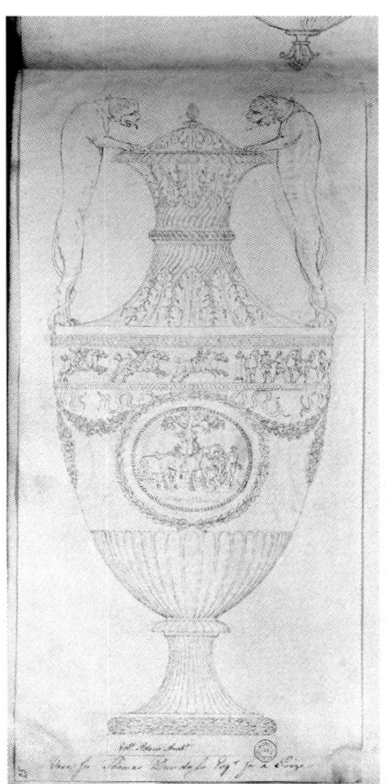

23
Design for a race cup, pen and pencil, c. 1763, Robert Adam (1728–1792). According to the inscription this drawing was done for Thomas Dundas "for a Prize" but it does not appear to have been carried out, and was superseded by another (fig. 24). Dundas was the son of Sir Lawrence Dundas, one of Adam's chief patrons during the 1760s. Adam billed Sir Lawrence £5 5s for '2 Drawings of Cups for Richmond Races". *Lent by the Trustees of Sir John Soane's Museum.*

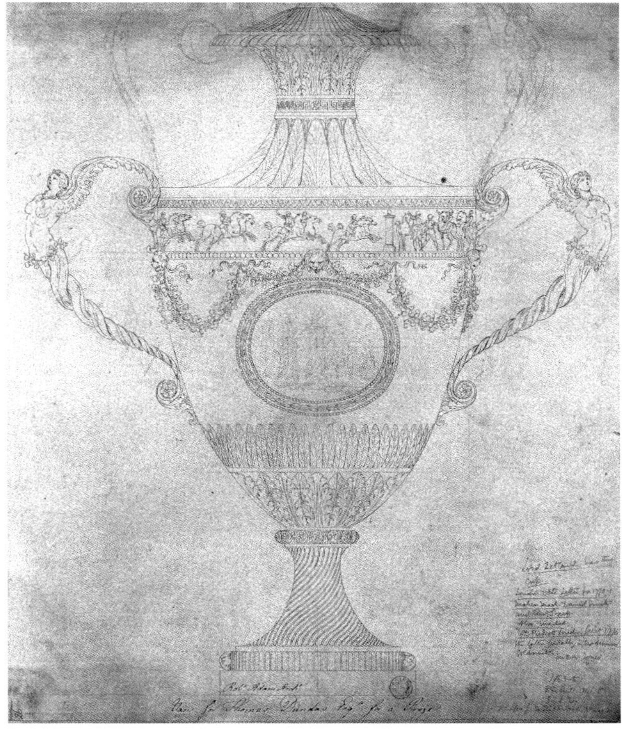

24
Design for a race cup, pen and pencil, c. 1763, Robert Adam (1728–1792). The design was used for the Richmond Race Cup of 1764, for which Thomas Dundas was one of the stewards. Like Adam's other, and presumably rejected, design (fig. 23), the cup is a complex mixture of classical and baroque features. *Lent by the Trustees of Sir John Soane's Museum.*

dating from the end of the previous century that Curzon's ancestor had acquired, with open modern cutlery boxes daringly surmounted by newly purchased plates with interlaced borders. The result was pure theatre. The gods of the ancients – those of peace, wisdom and justice as well as the traditional dining-room ones of wine, food and love – were celebrated not with sculpture as before but with an altar set within an apse. As David Udy observed: "essentially a decorative artist, he leaned heavily on decoration to create that evocative aura of romantic antiquity which was the source of his success".[2]

Adam was given a boost by Lord Bute, whom he met shortly after his return to England. A number of silver designs for this nobleman, whose political career was to be short-lived, are in the Soane collection. One of these, for a wine cistern, but erroneously

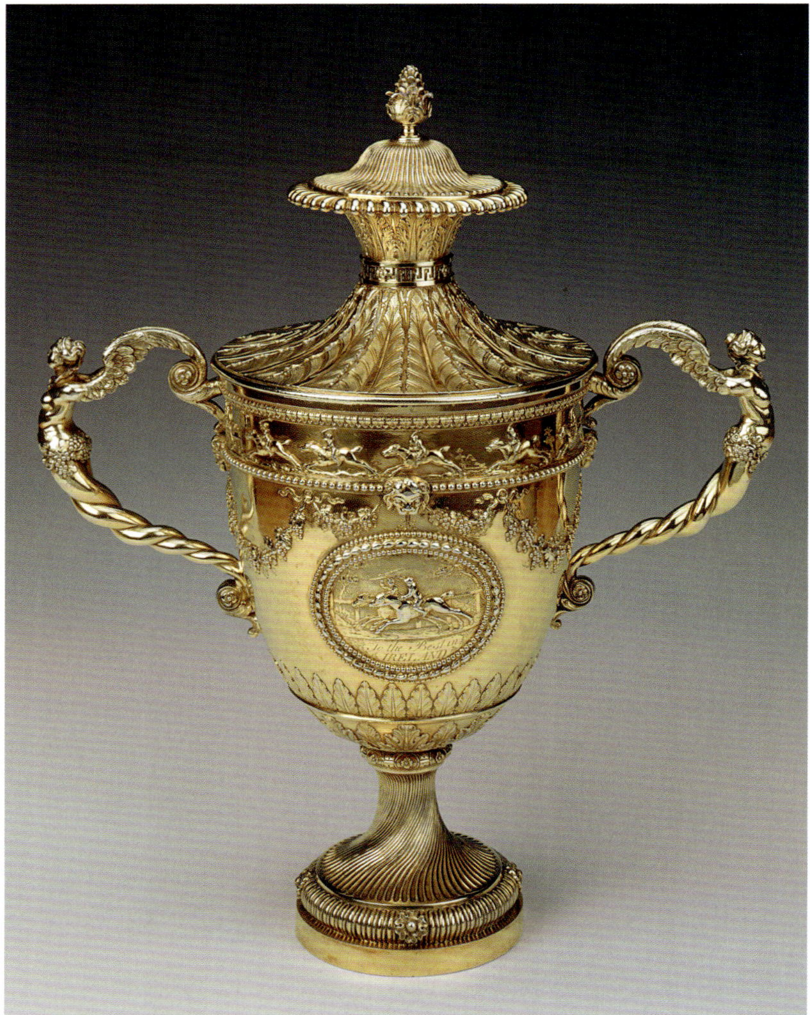

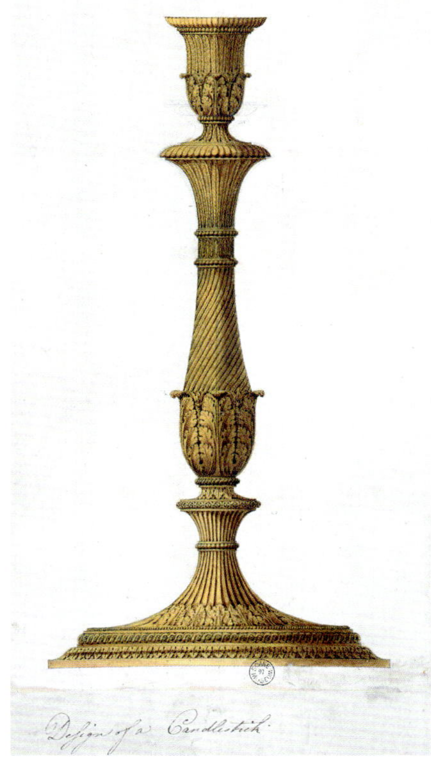

labelled at a later date as a "Terrine for Lord Bute", shows a naturalism grafted onto a baroque form that seems at first glance to have little to do with neo-classicism . But the Greek key border, the splayed fluting and anthemion denote a confident understanding of ancient ornament, albeit through the eyes of Piranesi, the friend Adam had made in Rome who dedicated one of his books to him. Yet none of the Bute designs appears to have been executed; in any event silversmiths would have baulked at having to raise such a massive elliptical bowl and then apply such seemingly flimsy rope twist handles to it.

Many of the drawings show a lack of understanding of the construction of silver objects; often, as in the case with some of Adam's designs for Sir Watkin Williams-Wynn, the end product has been significantly simplified for ease of manufacture and greater durability (figs. 39–40).

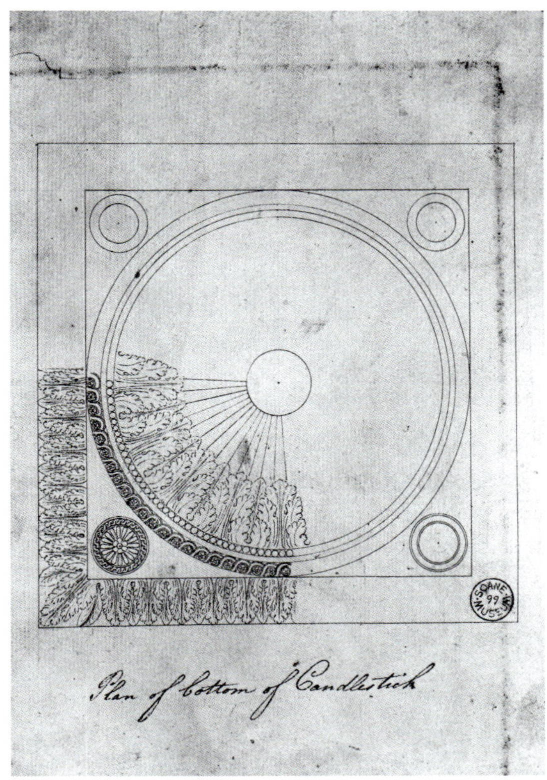

27
Plan of bottom of Candlestick,
**pen and wash, c. 1766, an Adam
office hand after Robert Adam
(1728–1792).** *Lent by the
Trustees of Sir John Soane's
Museum.*

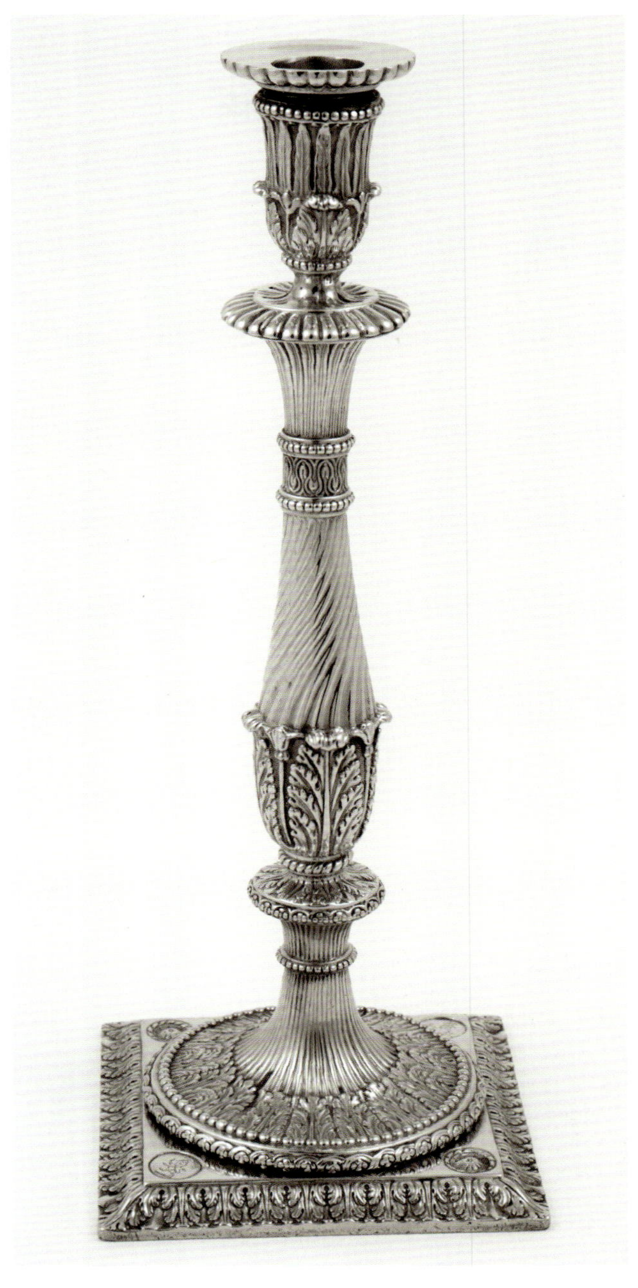

28
**Candlestick, silver, London,
1767–8, maker's mark of David
Whyte & William Holmes. One
of the earliest examples of
Adam's famous design, made
for an unknown client. John
Carter's workshop produced
further candlesticks to the same
design in the same year, but the
rosettes in each corner of the
base were omitted in order to
leave room for an engraved
crest (fig. 29).** *Lent by
Manchester City Galleries.*
Cat. no. 6

Often published and discussed, Adam's two designs for race cups (figs. 23–4),[3] show his genius at assimilating baroque features with seemingly classical forms and ancient ornament. The first design, supposedly rejected, for no silver versions appear to have survived, incorporates standing lions as handles, an allusion to the supporters of the Dundas arms and in fact taken from a Renaissance design for an ewer. The second, approved, design has winged caryatid handles which are a synthesis of various seventeenth-century handle designs.[4] The decoration, with bands of ornament swinging, swirling and marching across the surface, exemplifies Adam's *horror vacui*. A version of the second vase was made in silver-gilt as the 1764 Richmond Gold Cup by Smith & Sharp, presumably for a retailer as yet unidentified. Thomas Dundas, son of Sir Lawrence Dundas who was among Adam's earliest architectural patrons, was one of the stewards of the race. This, together with an undated bill from Adam for

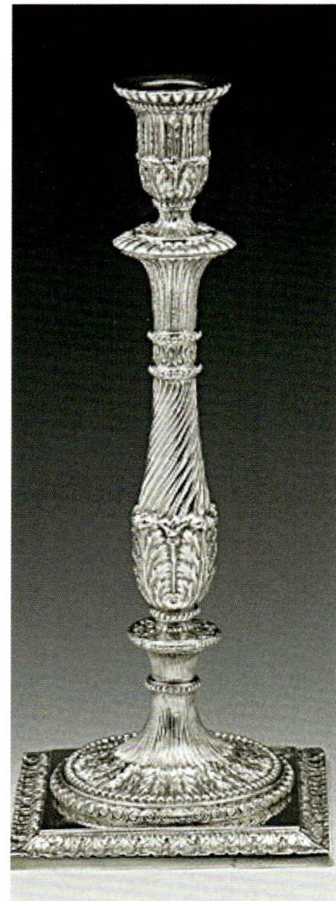

29
Candlestick, silver, London, 1767–8, maker's mark of John Carter II. One of a set of four engraved with the crest of **Philips of Picton Castle.** *Lent by Leeds Museums and Galleries (Temple Newsam House).*
Cat. no. 5

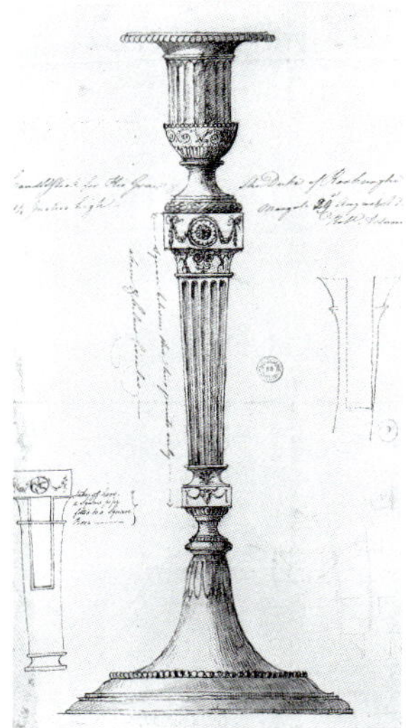

30
Robert Adam (1728–1792), Design for a candlestick for the Duke of Roxburgh, pen and pencil. The squareness of the stem and its vertical fluting are, unusually for Adam, French features, but the lightness of touch is typically his. *Lent by the Trustees of Sir John Soane's Museum.*

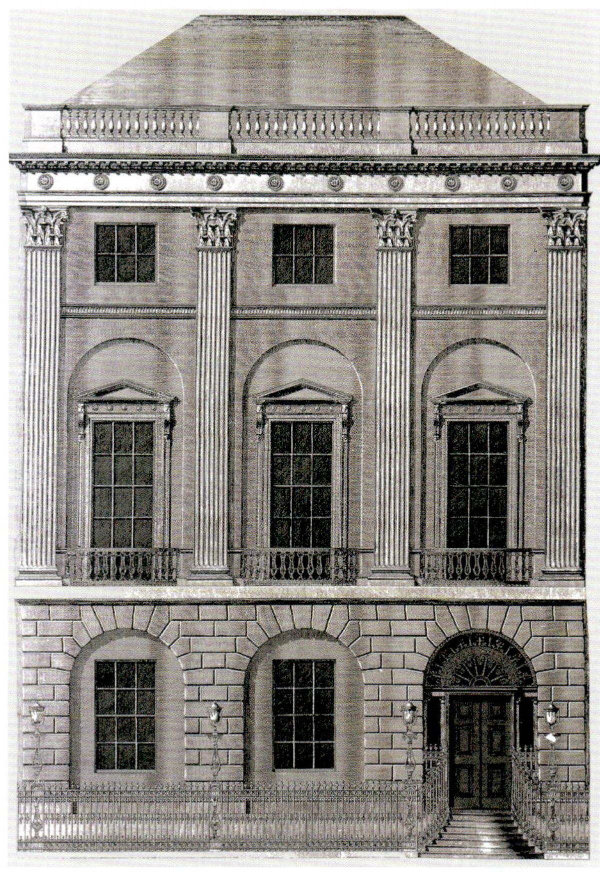

31
No. 20 St James's Square, engraving, after Robert Adam (1728–1792). The house was built for Sir Watkin Williams-Wynn between 1771 and 1774 by the Adam brothers.

"2 drawings" for Sir Lawrence and later inscriptions on the drawings themselves stating that they were done for Thomas, corroborate the identification of the patron.[5] But there is another version of the cup in silver-gilt, with the same maker's mark and dating from the same year (fig. 25). This cup was made for the Earl of Northumberland, another of Adam's significant patrons, to give as a race prize in Ireland, where he was Lord Lieutenant. Once they had made the Dundas cup, did Smith & Sharp make another to sell to another client, or to the same retailer, or was Adam involved with both cups? The cup went on to be reproduced, with small variations, for the next fifteen years.

Adam's designs for Sir Watkin William-Wynn are a rare survival.[6] They represent virtually all of a dinner service commissioned by the Welsh baronet for the house he was having built to Adam's designs at 20 St James's Square, London. The Adam partnership designed everything in the house down to the door handles, so it was only natural that the silver on Sir Watkin's table should also be from the same studio. In this the service is revolutionary, for the idea of a complete service in strictly matching style was unknown. It is true that William Kent's silver sometimes had a uniformity of concept, such as his work for George II, but the idea of a homogenous design on the dining table was new, and part of the move towards regarding the table top as a

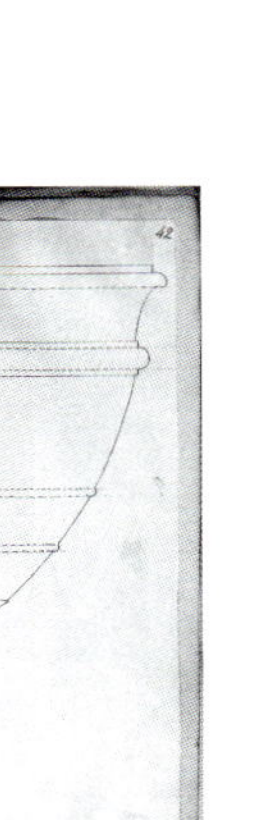

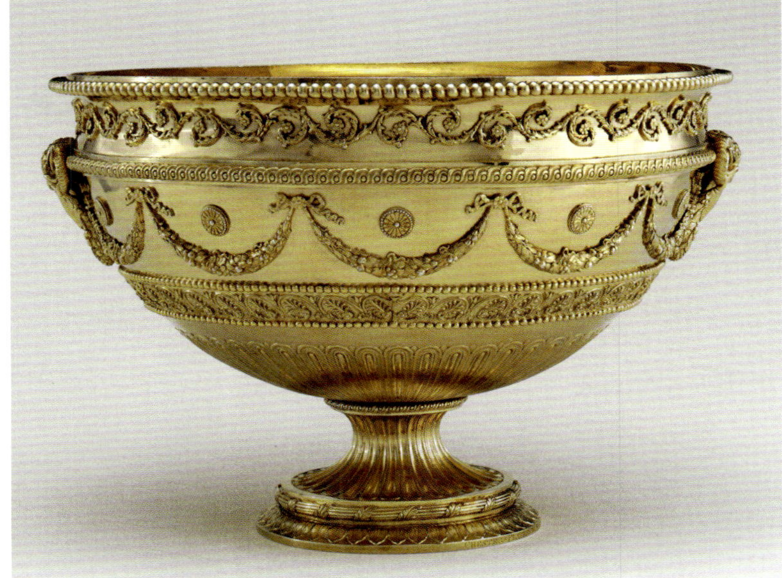

32
Punch Bowl for Sir Watkin Wynn, pen and pencil, Robert Adam (1728–1792). The first of a series of some twenty silver designs carried out by the Adam studio for Sir Watkin Williams-Wynn. *Lent by the Trustees of Sir John Soane's Museum.*

33
Punch-bowl, silver-gilt, London, 1771–2, maker's mark of Thomas Heming, designed by Robert Adam (1728–1792). Ordered to celebrate Sir Watkin Williams-Wynn's racehorse Fop, the bowl was invoiced to him on 21 September 1772 as "a Superbe punch Bowl, very highly finish'd in an Antique Taste". *Lent by the National Museum and Gallery of Wales, Cardiff.*
Cat. no. 11

landscape inhabited by silver sculpture forming its own decorative scheme. Changes in dining habits had required a host of new silver vessels such as tureens that cried out for some form of uniformity of design, and Adam's Williams-Wynn service is perhaps the earliest instance of this. Luckily, not only the drawings but also most of the service itself survives, although dispersed at auction in the 1940s, and it has been possible in this exhibition to bring much of it together to show with its drawings.

[1] Both of these features of course have no precedent in the ancient world: the two-handled vase derives from shouldered ewers of the Renaissance, made English by the addition of two loop handles in the seventeenth century. Michael Snodin has perceptively analyzed Adam's silver designs. See Snodin, "Adam" and Snodin, "Adam into Context".

[2] Udy, "Adam's Vase", p. 194.

[3] See, most recently, Clifford, "Richmond" and Snodin, "Adam".

[4] The lion handle is taken from an engraving for an ewer by Enea Vico of 1543, illustrated in Snodin, "Adam", fig. 33, p. 20; the winged handles are based on Jacques Stella's design for a vase of 1667 (Snodin, *op. cit.*, fig. 32, p. 20) combined with a design for an ewer by Jean Lepautre (Préaud, no. 1982).

[5] The Adam drawings were annotated in the early nineteenth century prior to be offered for sale. In many cases the patron or date may be wrong. For example, the Bute wine cistern, one of a group all with the same label, is clearly not a "terrine", but the fact that it was done for Bute can be confirmed by his arms in the centre. I am grateful to Stephen Astley for this information. Despite the bill for "2 drawings" the inscription on the two versions of the cup may be incorrect, too.

[6] The service has been extensively researched by Oliver Fairclough; see Fairclough, pp. 55–9.

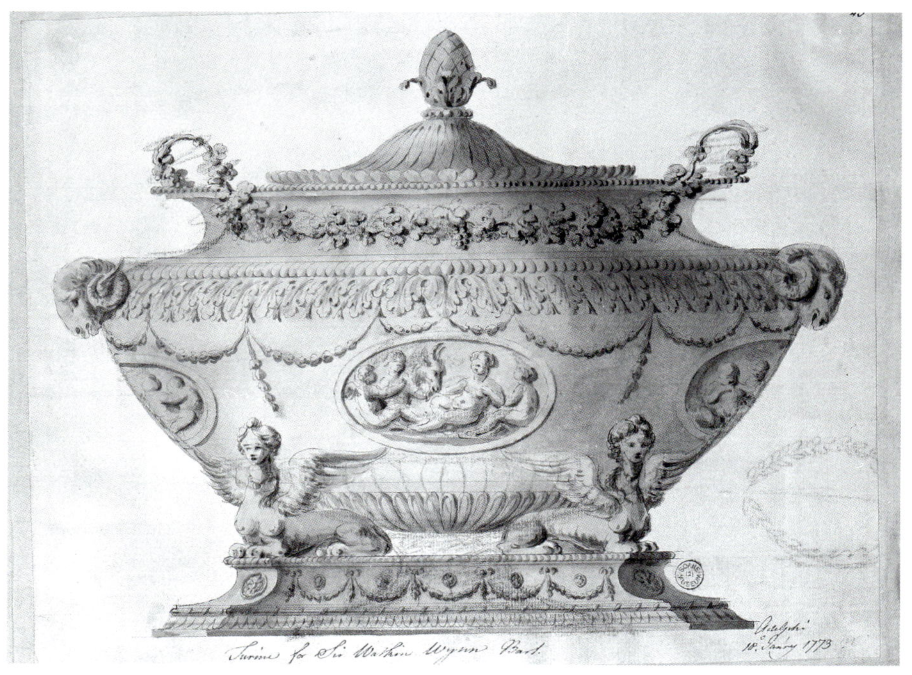

34

Terrine for Sir Watkin Wynn, Bart., Adelphi, 18th January 1773, pen, pencil and wash, Robert Adam (1728–1792). The drawing has pencil additions changing the complex sphinx supports into a single spool-form foot. *Lent by the Trustees of Sir John Soane's Museum.*

35

Soup tureen, cover and stand from the Williams-Wynn service, silver, London, 1774–5, maker's mark IC, probably for John Carter II, retailed by Joseph Creswell, designed by Robert Adam (1728–1792). Adam's original design for a monumental tureen raised on elaborate sphinx supports has been simplified. The stand is a later addition. In 1773, owing over £2,000 to Thomas Heming, Williams-Wynn placed his order for a dinner service with Joseph Creswell, a retailer in the Adelphi, the Adam brothers' fashionable terrace. *Lent by the National Museum and Gallery of Wales, Cardiff.*

Cat. no. 23

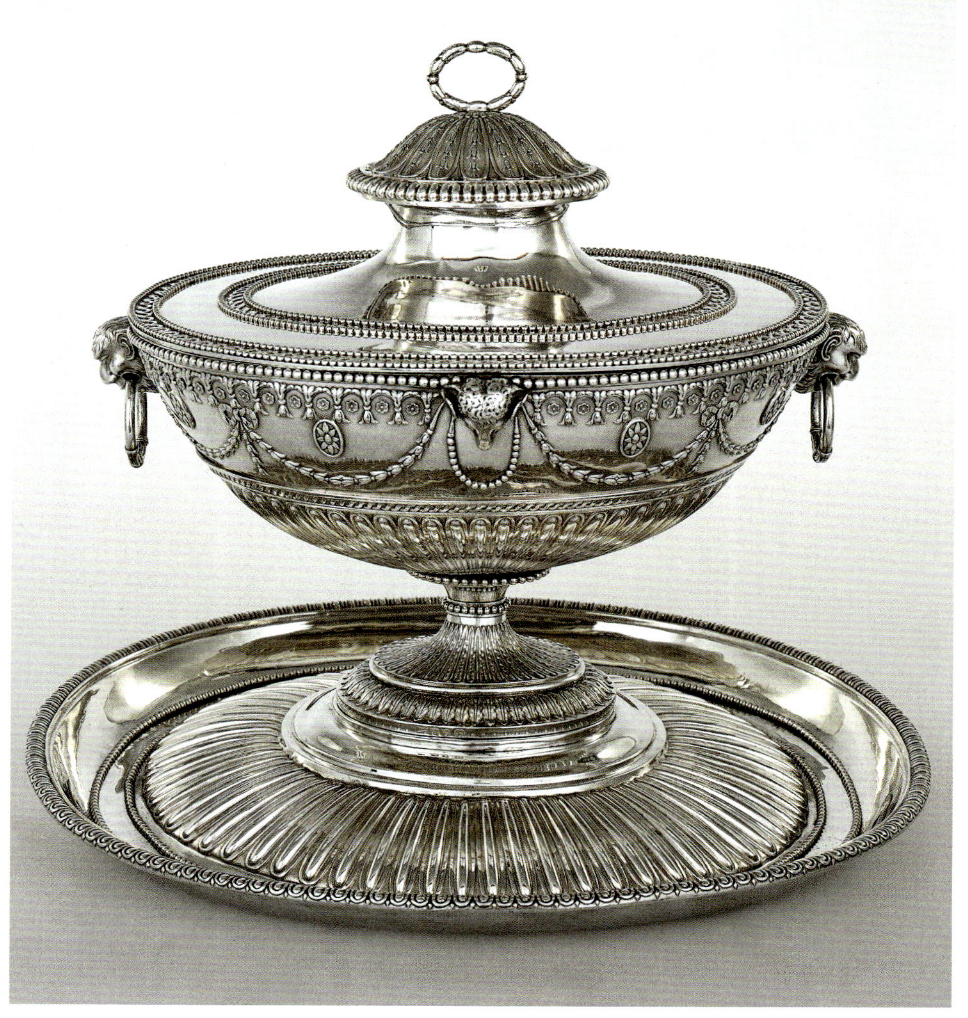

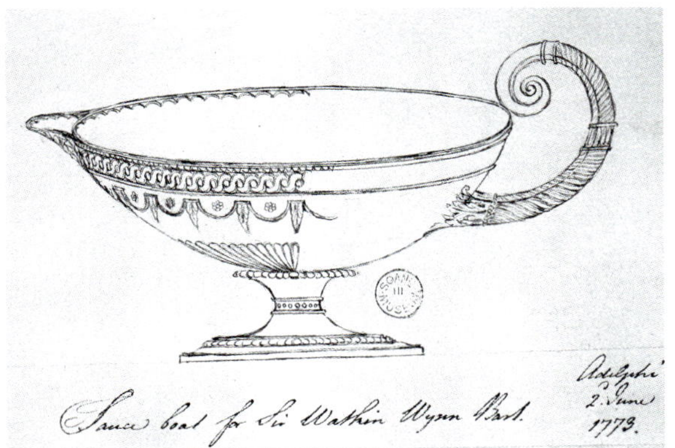

36
Sauce boat for Sir Watkin Wynn, Bart., Adelphi, 2 June 1773, pen, pencil and wash. **Robert Adam (1728–1792).** *Lent by the Trustees of Sir John Soane's Museum.*

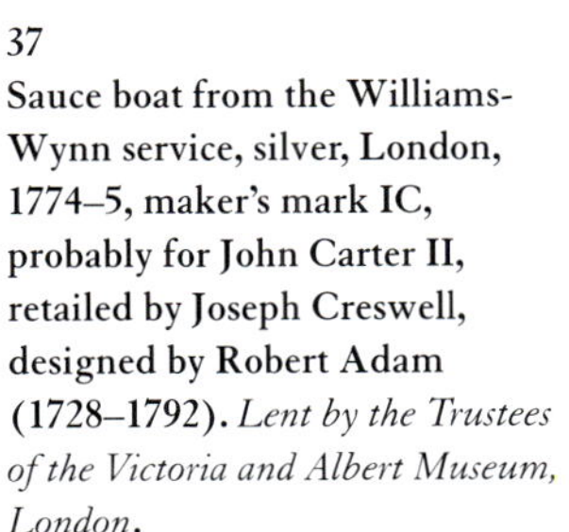

37
Sauce boat from the Williams-Wynn service, silver, London, 1774–5, maker's mark IC, probably for John Carter II, retailed by Joseph Creswell, designed by Robert Adam (1728–1792). *Lent by the Trustees of the Victoria and Albert Museum, London.*
Cat. no. 22

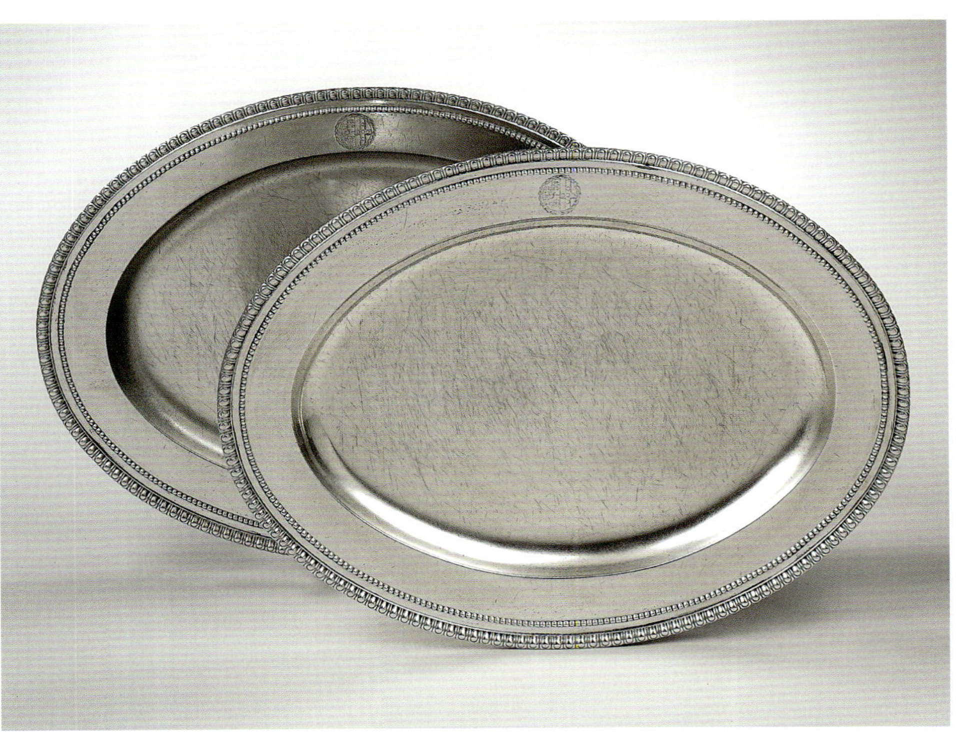

38
Two meat dishes from the Williams-Wynn service, silver, London, 1773–4, maker's mark IC, probably for John Carter II, retailed by Joseph Creswell, designed by Robert Adam (1728–1792). The maker's mark IC which appears on the Williams-Wynn service is similar to that attributed to John Carter II, specialist supplier of candlesticks and large-scale hollow ware. Another possible candidate for this mark, suggested by Oliver Fairclough, is the retailer Joseph Creswell himself. Unfortunately, the relevant volume of marks registered at Goldsmiths' Hall is missing. *Lent by a private collector.*
Cat. no. 18

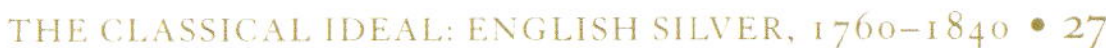

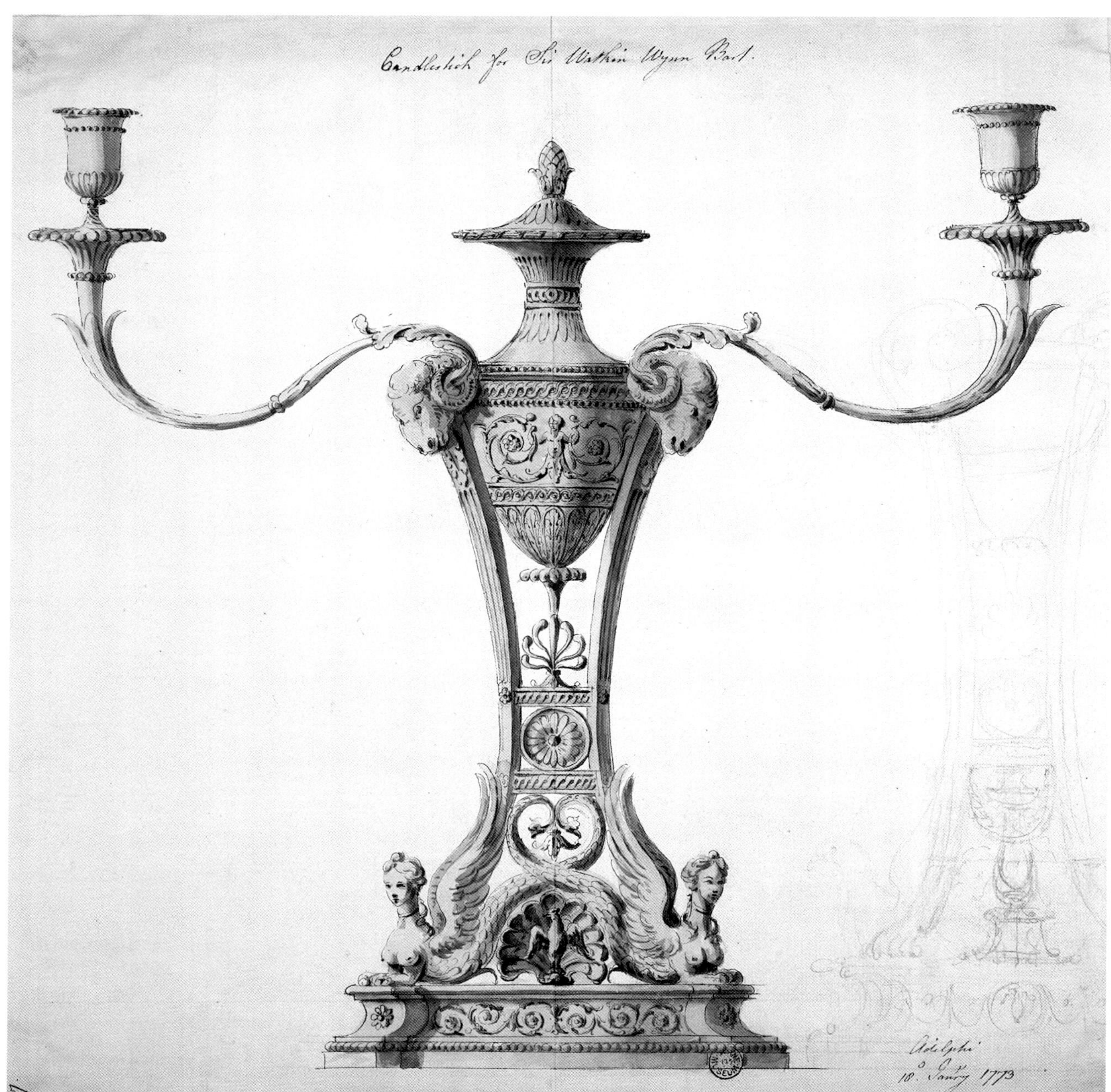

39
*Candlestick for Sir Watkin Wynn,
Bart., Adelphi, 18th January 1773*,
pen, pencil and wash, Robert
Adam (1728–1792). A sketch,
where the base has been
simplified by substituting slender
paw feet, has been added in
pencil. *Lent by the Trustees of Sir
John Soane's Museum.*

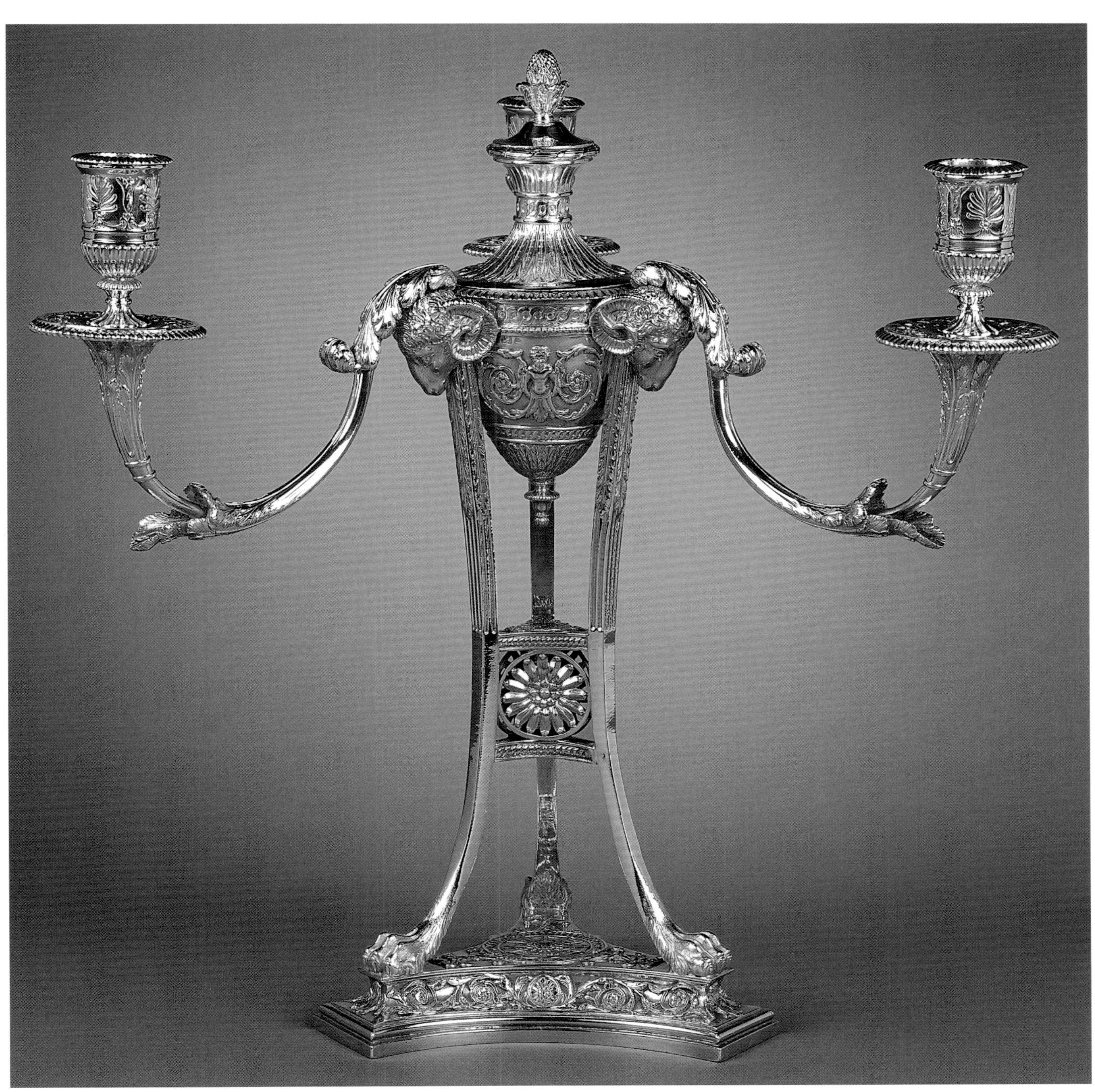

40
Three-light candelabrum from
the Williams-Wynn service,
silver, London, 1774–5, maker's
mark IC, probably for John
Carter II, retailed by Joseph
Creswell, designed by Robert
Adam (1728–1792). The simpler
design was probably substituted
on the recommendation of the
silversmith. *Lent by Lloyds
Corporation*.
Cat. no. 21

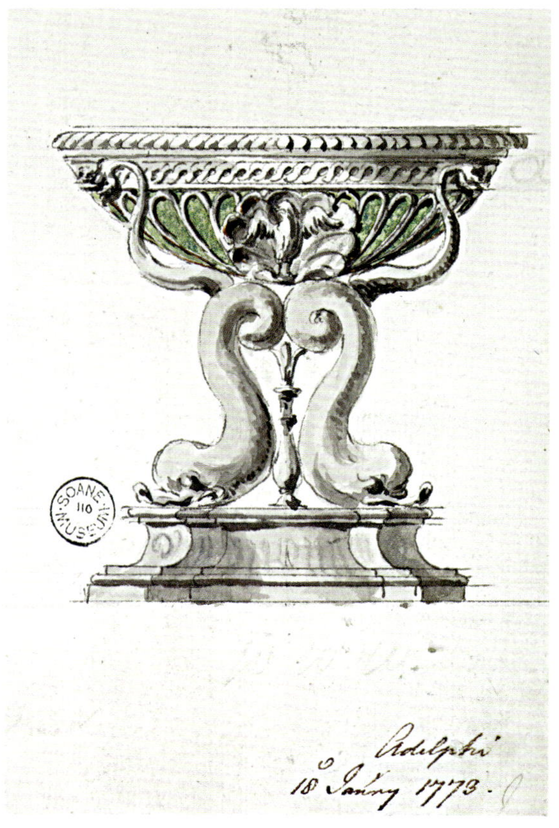

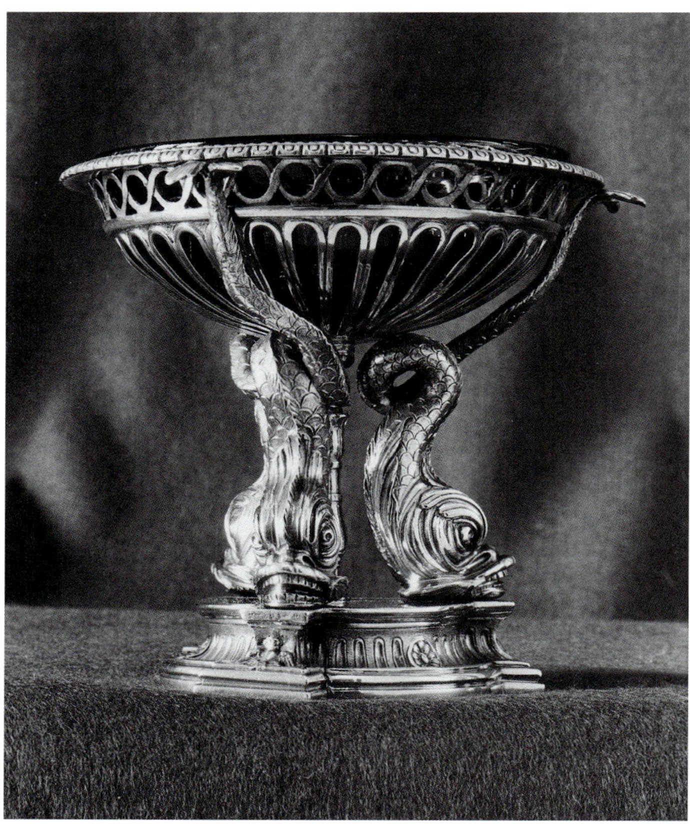

41
Design for a salt, *Adelphi, 18th
January 1773,* **pen and
watercolour, Robert Adam
(1728–1792). The supporting
dolphins and the tri-form
pedestal base are both baroque
features.** *Lent by the Trustees of Sir
John Soane's Museum.*

42
**Salt from the Williams-Wynn
service, silver, glass, London,
1774–5, maker's mark IC,
probably for John Carter II,
retailed by Joseph Creswell,
designed by Robert Adam
(1728–1792).** *Lent by
Nottingham Castle Museum and
Art Gallery.*
Cat. no. 16

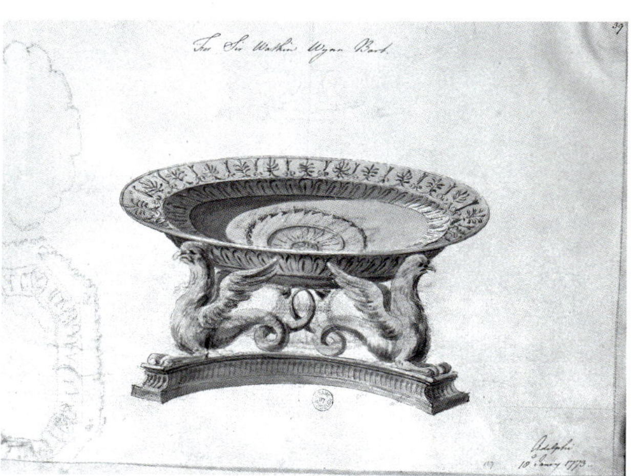

43
Design for a dish, *For Sir
Watkin Wynn, Bart., Adelphi,
18th January 1773,* **pen and
wash, Robert Adam
(1728–1792). One of several
designs presumably not
executed.** *Lent by the Trustees
of Sir John Soane's Museum.*

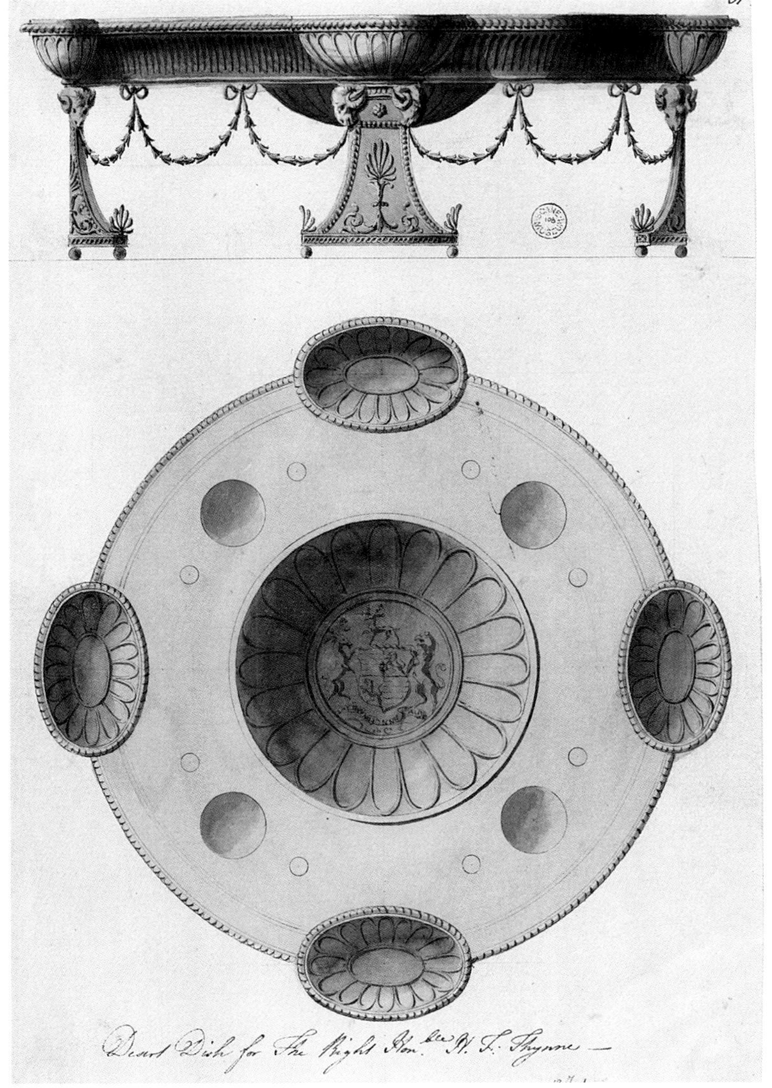

44

*Dessert Dish for the Right Hon[bl].
H.F. Thynne, 1773*, pen and
watercolour, Robert Adam
(1728–1792). One of three
versions for a dish for the centre
of a table for Henry Frederick
Thynne (1735–1826). Adam
undertook alterations and
improvements to his house in
Curzon Street in the early 1770s.
*Lent by the Trustees of Sir John
Soane's Museum.*

45

Design for an ornamental vase,
engraving, c. 1782,
Michelangelo Pergolesi (d.
1801). Pergolesi worked for the
Adam brothers, most notably
at Syon, and from 1777
onwards he published sheets of
decorative designs. His vessels,
such as this vase, tend to be
insubstantial and are clearly
intended as models for painted
decoration rather than
functional objects.

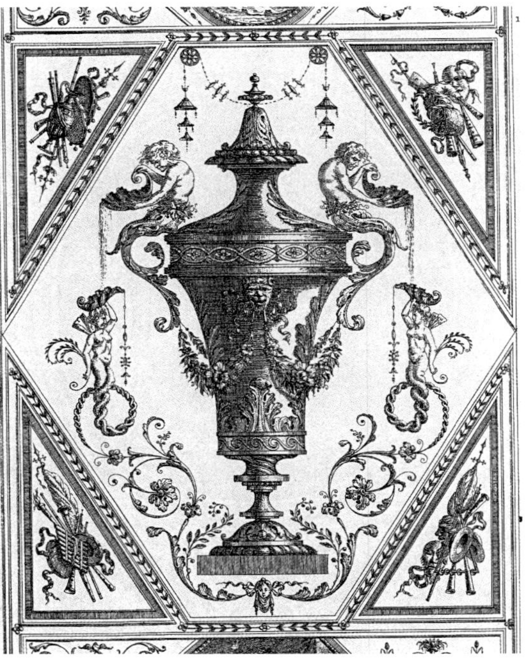

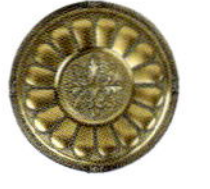

IV James Wyatt and the manufacturers

"I would have elegant simplicity the leading principle"

Matthew Boulton

A contemporary of Robert Adam, James Wyatt had a career as crowded with activity and as inspired as Adam's, but his approach to business could not have been more dissimilar, and he lacked Adam's eye for self-promotion. His drawings, even those done in the studio, are less polished and lack the detail found in Adam's drawings. Many, such as the ones in an album formerly belonging to the Vicomte de Noailles,[1] are unfinished sketches that seem to have been dashed off as his coach, hopelessly late, lurched towards a meeting with another disgruntled client. Part of the genius of his

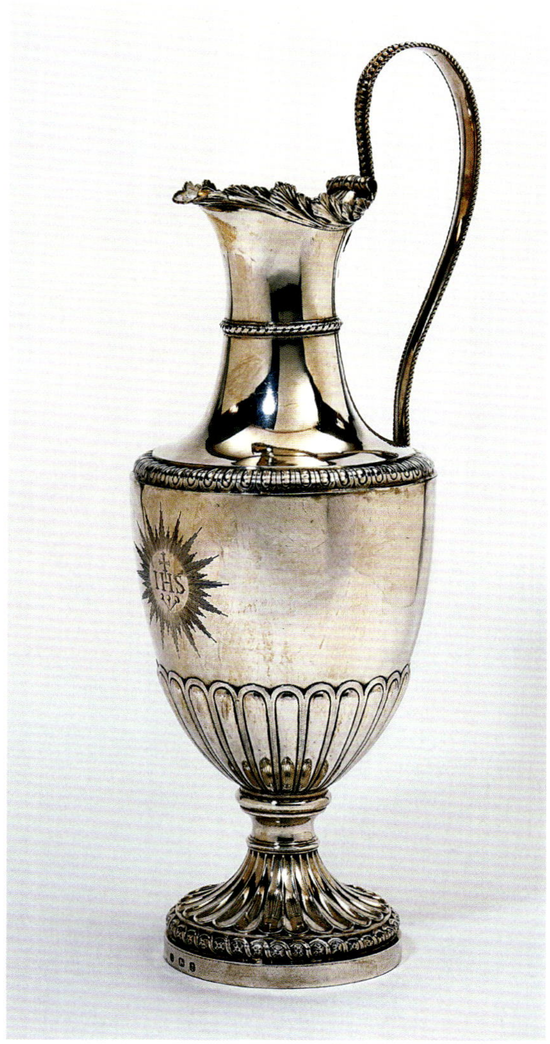

46
Communion flagon, silver, Birmingham, 1773–4, maker's mark of Matthew Boulton & John Fothergill. Both the elegant simplicity of this flagon's outline, and its expanses of reflective surfaces, are typical of James Wyatt's designs for metalwork. It was given to St Bartholomew's Church, Orford, by Lord Hertford, who stipulated that it should be "as light as the nature of the work would possibly admit". *Lent by St Bartholomew's Church, Orford, Suffolk.*
Cat. no. 12

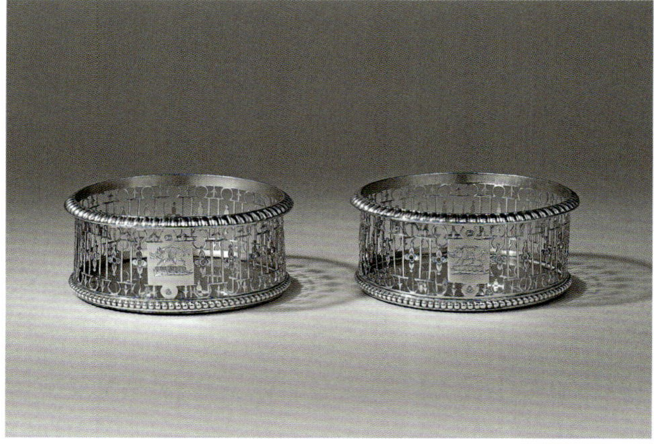

47
Pair of wine coasters, silver, wood, felt, Birmingham, 1773–4, maker's mark of Matthew Boulton & John Fothergill. Among the first objects hallmarked by the newly opened Birmingham Assay Office, these coasters were pierced by hand with a fret saw but in time piercing like this was being done by machine. *Lent by a private collector.*
Cat. no. 15

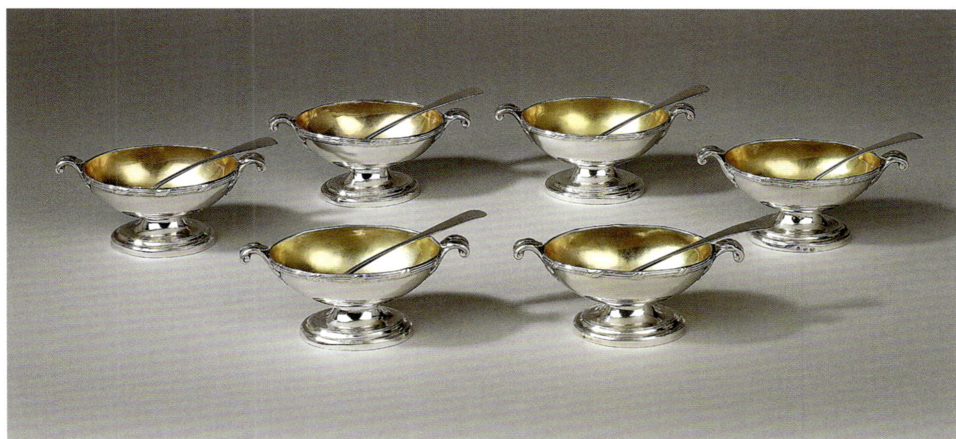

48
Six salts, silver, Birmingham, 1773–4, maker's mark of Matthew Boulton & John Fothergill. *Lent by a private collector*.
Cat. no. 13

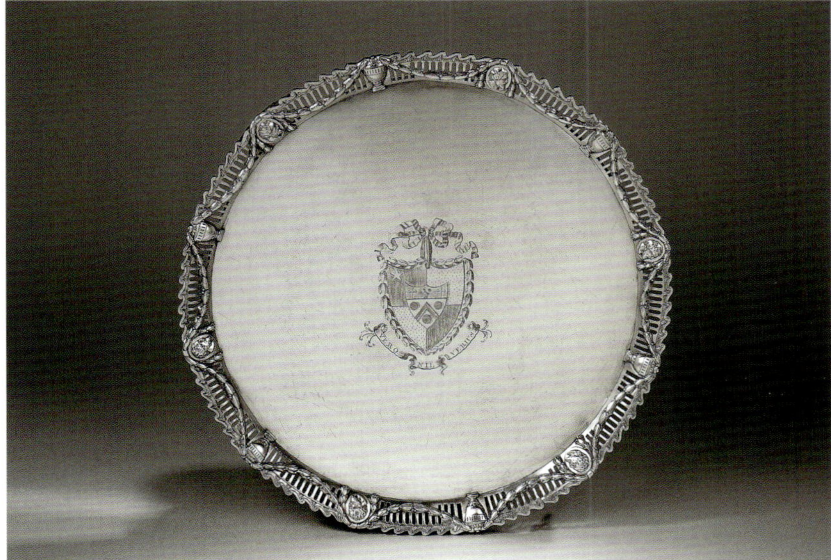

49
Salver, silver, London, 1773–4, maker's mark of John Carter II. Part of a group of plate ordered by Charles Vere which included tureens supplied by Boulton & Fothergill (fig. 50). The manufacture of heavy-gauge salvers such as this example, however, continued to be carried out by London workshops. *Lent by a private collector.*
Cat. no. 17

style doubtless stems from his spontaneous and more idiosyncratic approach. But while many of Wyatt's silver designs have an immediacy, they nevertheless share with the Adam drawings an assured knowledge of the classical vocabulary. Whereas the Adam drawings appear to have been executed for individual clients for whom his practice was carrying out architectural work, Wyatt was designing for manufacturers and suppliers as well as for private clients. With Adam's practice and likewise with that of Sir William Chambers, one senses that operations were carefully orchestrated, from designing the silver in consultation with the client to selecting the supplier for the silverware and placing the order on the client's behalf. On the other hand, Wyatt, with his chaotic finances, was clearly all too happy to supply generic designs for cash.

Although the Parker & Wakelin accounts in 1772 record, "Cash paid Mr Wyatt",

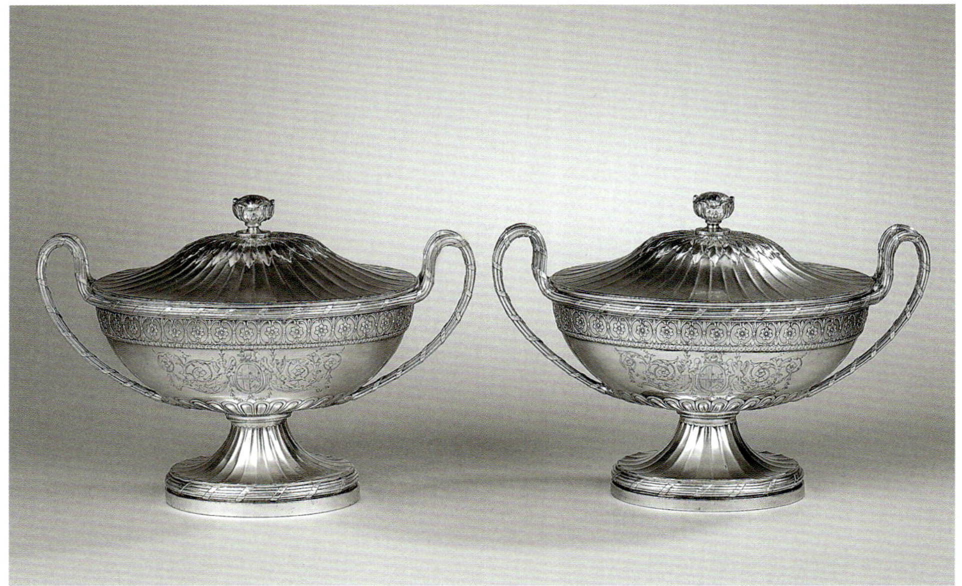

50
Pair of sauce tureens and covers, silver, Birmingham, 1773–4, maker's mark of Matthew Boulton & John Fothergill. Engraved with the arms of Charles Vere and his wife Martha Lucas, whom he married in 1771. The lightness of the design, due to the shallow fluting and swept handles, suggests James Wyatt as designer. *Lent by a private collector.*
Cat. no. 14

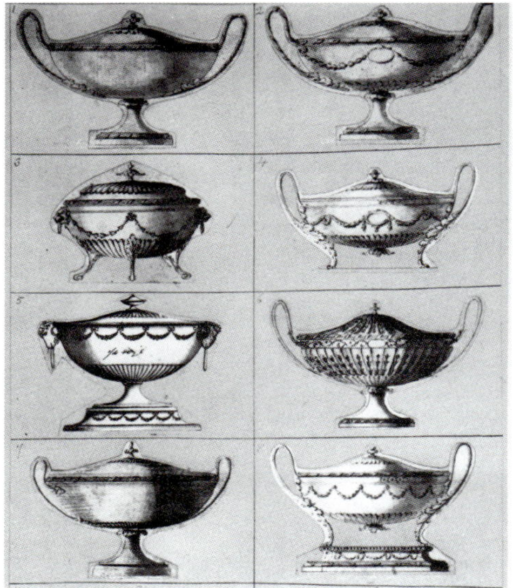

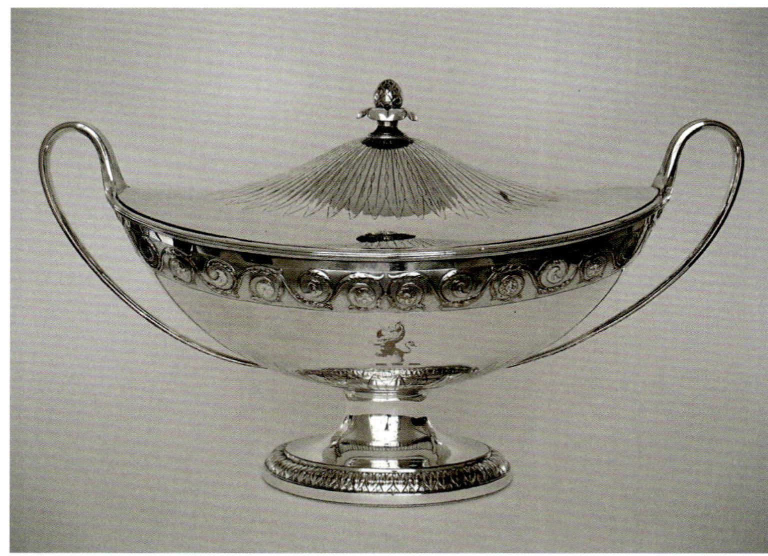

51
Soup tureens based on designs by James Wyatt (1746–1813), from Boulton & Fothergill Pattern Book no. 1. *Birmingham Archives and Heritage, MS 3782/21/2.*

53
Soup tureen, cover and stand, silver, Birmingham, 1777–8, maker's mark of Matthew Boulton & John Fothergill. The simple composition is an amalgam of decorative features, probably produced by Francis Eginton, Boulton's manager of silver production.
ADC Heritage.

52
Soup tureen, fused plate, c. 1775–80. The elliptical tureen on central foot with swept loop handles proved to be an enduring model for silver and silver-plate manufacturers during the last quarter of the eighteenth century. *Lent by Dr David Needham.*
Cat. no. 68

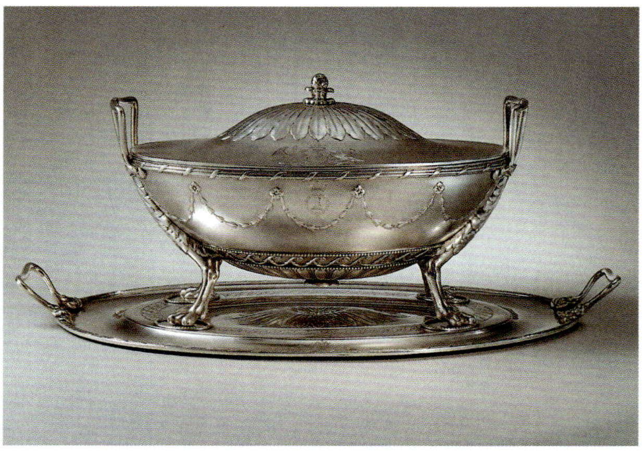

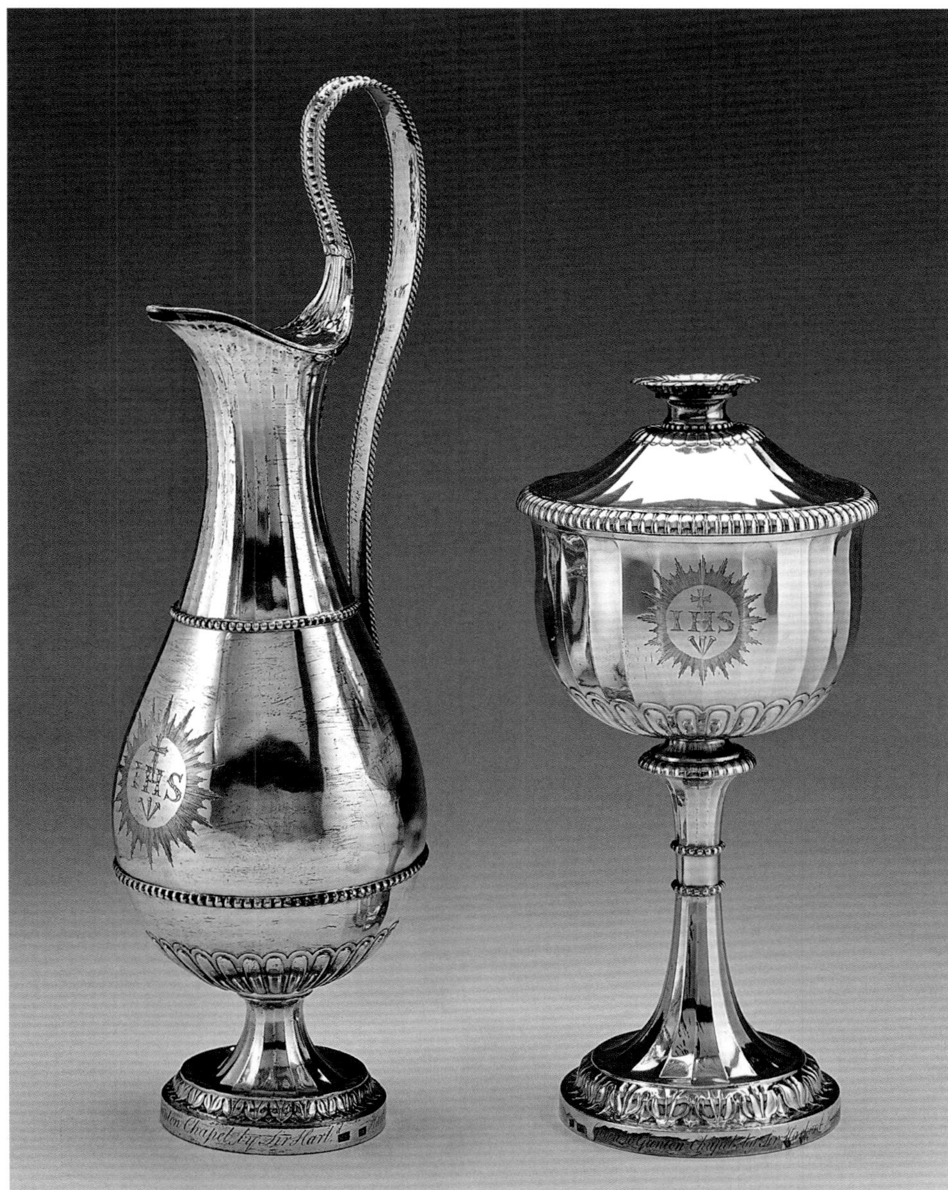

54
Communion cup, paten/cover
and flagon, silver, Birmingham,
1774–5, maker's mark of
Matthew Boulton & John
Fothergill. The contrasting
panels of plain and fluted silver
divided by delicate beading are
characteristic of James Wyatt's
plate designs. The set was given
to Gunton Church by Sir
Harbord Harbord, son of Sir
William Harbord for whom the
church had been designed by
Robert Adam in 1765–9. *Lent by
St Andrew's Church, Gunton,
Norfolk.*
Cat. no. 20

evidently for designs,[2] the firm with which Wyatt had a close relationship was that of
Boulton & Fothergill. His name figures frequently in their records; for example,
"Wyatt's pattern silver candlesticks" feature in the firm's Pattern Book 1. Other
members of the extended Wyatt clan were involved as building contractors for Boulton
or were employed by him in sales as well as in the manufacturing side at the Soho
Manufactory. Wyatt carried out design commissions for some of the firm's clients,[3]
though it was not always a smooth relationship and Wyatt clearly regarded himself as
his own man. When Sir Robert Rich returned a silver-gilt epergne to Boulton in 1776,
he wanted alterations and refused to pay for them, even though Wyatt's design had
been followed to the letter. Asked to arbitrate, Wyatt sided with Rich and Boulton was
forced to bear the cost.[4]

Matthew Boulton had decided to go into silver manufacturing, forming a
partnership with John Fothergill, who acted as general manager. In the late 1760s the

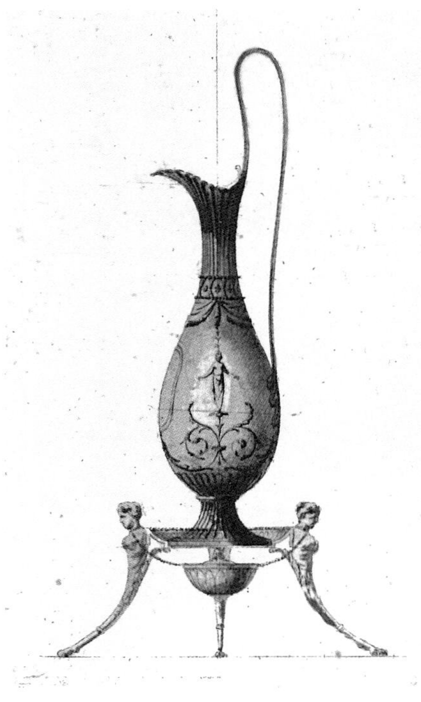

55
Design for a jug on stand, pencil and wash, James Wyatt (1746–1813). The areas of plain and fluted silver and the lightness of the proportions are now seen as Wyatt's trademark. A virtually identical jug on stand is in Boulton & Fothergill's *Pattern Book no. 1*. *V&A Images.*

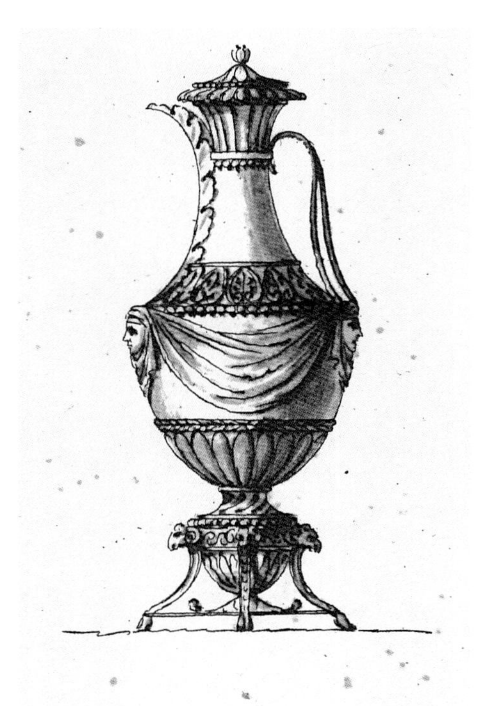

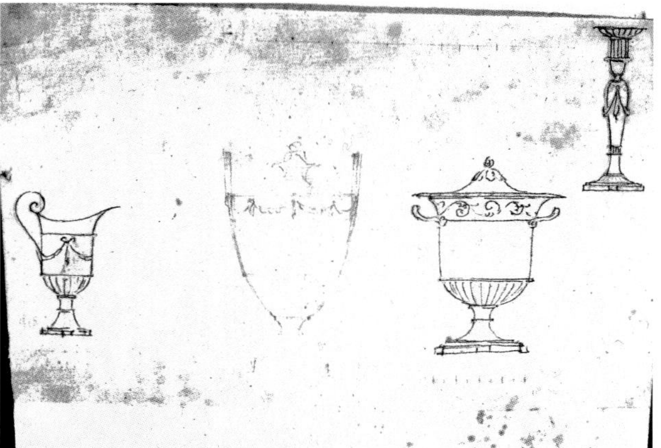

57
Designs for silverware, pencil, James Wyatt (1746–1813). The garlanded candlestick with fluted socket is characteristic of Wyatt. *V&A Images.*

58
Design for a jug on stand, pencil and wash, James Wyatt (1746–1813). The ponderous form of the jug is unusual in Wyatt's work. A similar jug, now in Birmingham Museum and Art Gallery, was produced by Boulton & Fothergill and hallmarked in Chester in 1769–70. *V&A Images.*

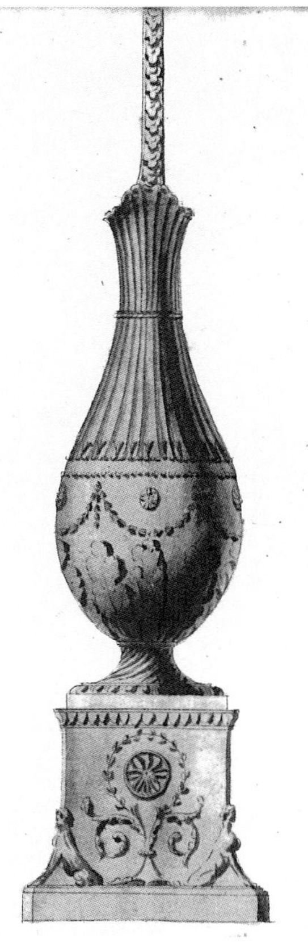

56
Design for a jug on pedestal, pencil and wash, James Wyatt (1746–1813). *V&A Images.*

firm experimented with the French "lyon faced" candlestick design (fig. 9). Their early efforts were hampered, however, by the lack of an assay office in Birmingham, forcing them to send their products to Chester for hallmarking. After much lobbying, in which Boulton and Fothergill spearheaded the negotiations, assay offices at Birmingham and Sheffield were established in 1773. At first they encountered customer resistance to work struck with the unfamiliar hallmarks, and indeed London retailers found that they had to overstrike London marks on the candlesticks they bought from Birmingham and Sheffield manufacturers.

In the early days decoration such as piercing on the sides of wine coasters was done by hand at the Soho Manufactory (fig. 47), in imitation of die-cut London examples.

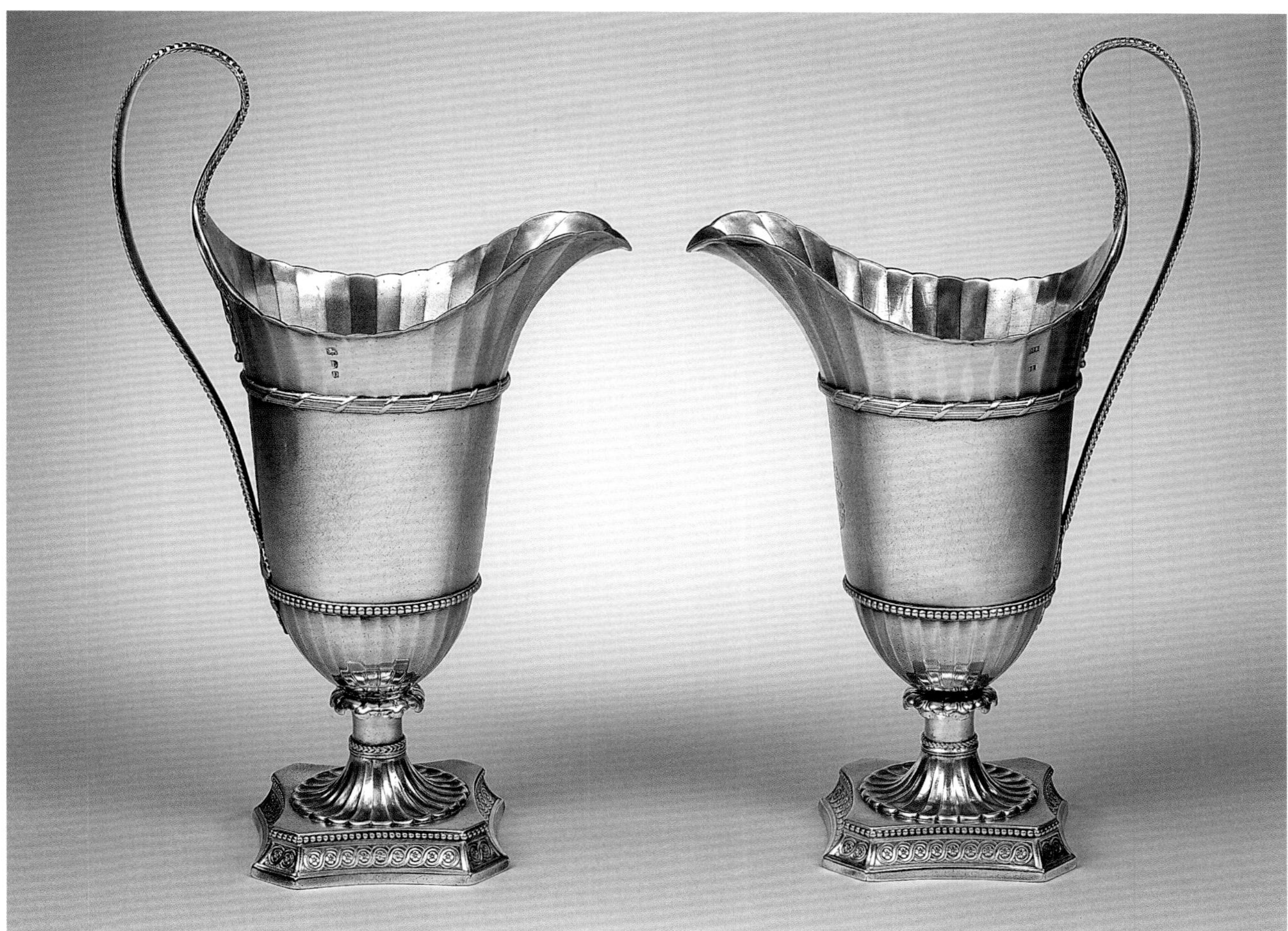

59
Pair of ewers, silver,
Birmingham, 1776–7, maker's
mark of Matthew Boulton &
John Fothergill. Several versions
of this design, probably by James
Wyatt, are known. *Lent by Leeds
Museums and Galleries (Temple
Newsam House, acquired in 2010
in honour of the late Robert
Rowe).*
Cat. no. 28

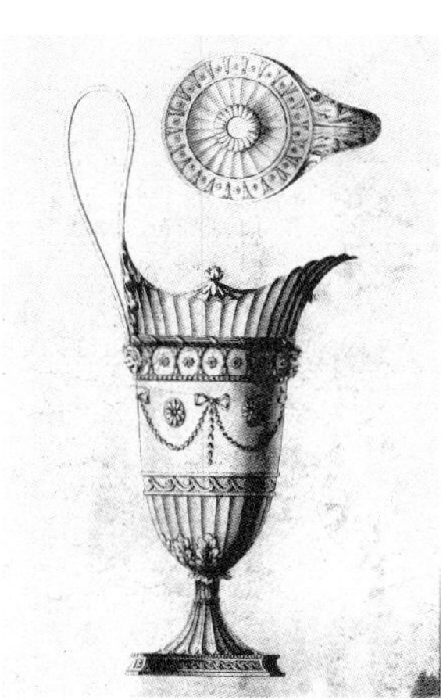

60
Pattern for a jug after James
Wyatt (1746–1813), engraving
pasted in one of the Boulton &
Fothergill pattern books. The
bands of pateræ and Vitruvian
scrolls against fluting are
repeated on the sauce tureens
(fig. 50).

Soon Boulton's technological expertise had taken over and components as well as decoration could be carried out by machine. The use of technology to produce useful yet beautiful things was embraced by manufacturers as diverse as François-Thomas Germain, Hester Bateman and Matthew Boulton and seen as part and parcel of the growth of their industry. Only with the publication of Ruskin's writings in the nineteenth century were the machine and art deemed to be incompatible.

Boulton & Fothergill thought that they could compete with the London retailers by going directly to clients and offering them good design without the high London mark-ups. Boulton realized that the profit margins of the market leaders such as Parker & Wakelin were impressive: their mark-up on Chambers's service for the Duke of Marlborough was some fifty per cent. They were able to secure some aristocratic

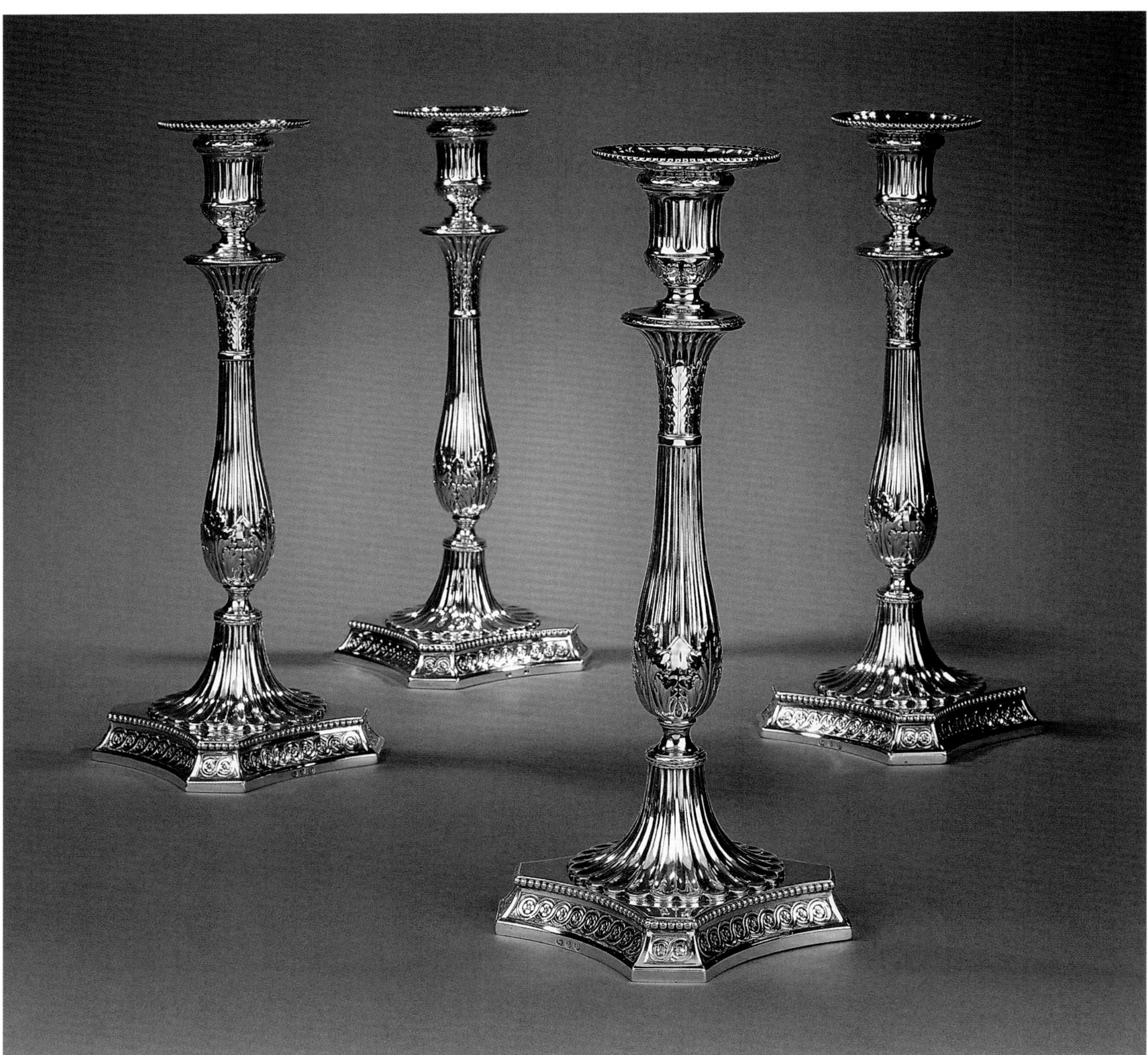

61
Four candlesticks, silver, Birmingham, 1776–7, maker's mark of Matthew Boulton & John Fothergill. Based on a design by Wyatt, these candlesticks proved to be one of Boulton & Fothergill's most successful productions. Examples exist in fused plate as well as in silver (fig. 63). *Lent by an American charitable trust.* Cat. no. 27

patronage, such as that of Mrs Elizabeth Montagu,[5] Lord Hertford (fig. 46) and Sir Harbord Harbord (fig. 54), sometimes by quoting ridiculously low prices to secure the business. However, relying on agents and lacking impressive shop premises in the capital made the development of this side of their business difficult for them and in the end they made virtually no money from it. Their biggest challenge was combining the time-consuming business of providing clients with the attention to detail and level of service usually provided by fashionable shops in the capital with manufacturing and supplying at low cost. Many of Boulton & Fothergill's clients, such as Lord Hertford, were lured to the firm with the prospect of low prices but at the same time they expected the latest design.

In this last regard, Boulton found a way to offer them what they wanted. A man of boundless energy, he put together an impressive library on ancient art and tirelessly sought out new models in London and Paris. But his relationship with James Wyatt was the saving grace. Wyatt's distinctive brand of elegant classicism, where the tension

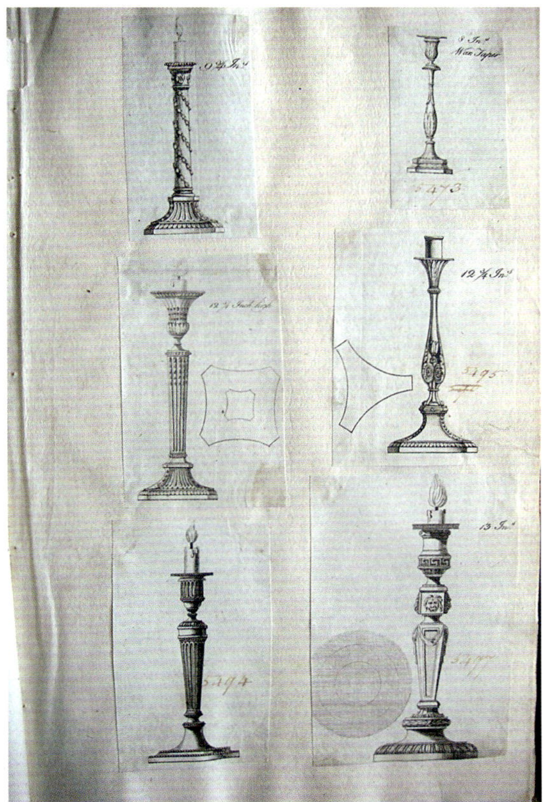

62
Designs for candlesticks, from a Sheffield Plate trade catalogue, c. 1775. Versions of Wyatt's designs for candlesticks sit next to the ubiquitous "Lyon faced" French candlestick that Boulton popularized in England. *Lent by Dr David Needham.*

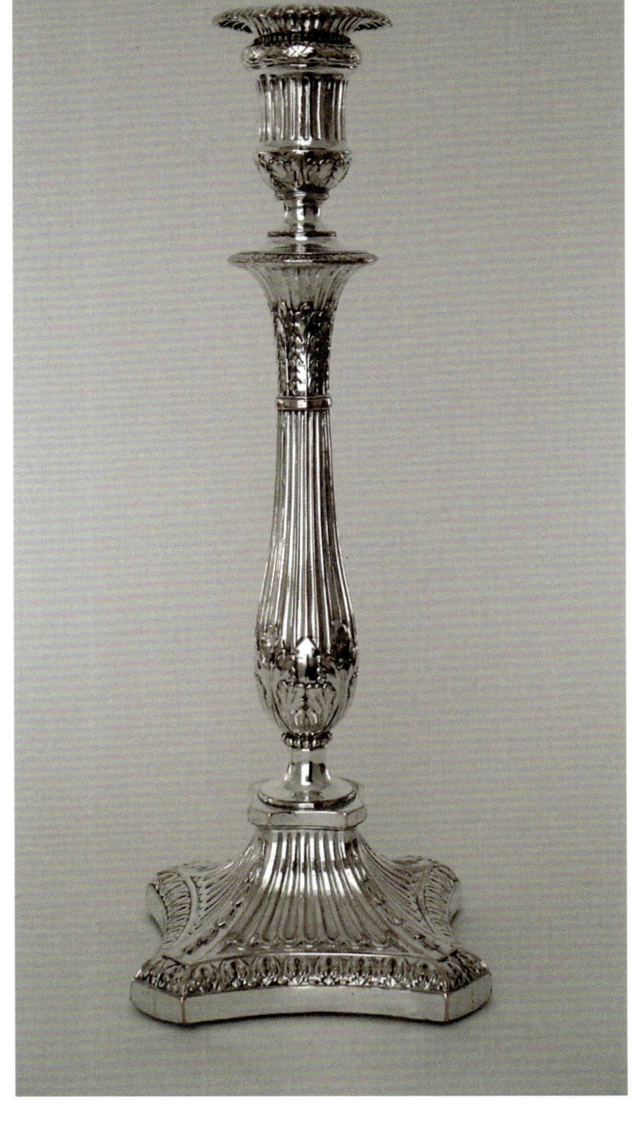

63
Candlestick, fused plate, c. 1775. *Lent by Dr David Needham.*
Cat. no. 67

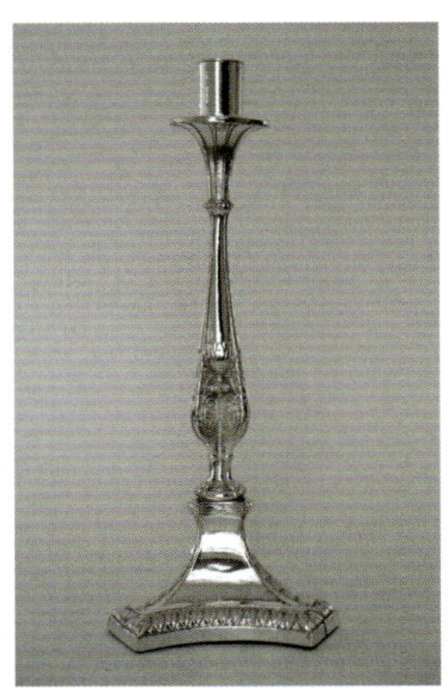

64
Candlestick, fused plate, c. 1775. *Lent by Dr David Needham.*
Cat. no. 66

between polished and fluted surfaces and intricate bands of ornament was exploited to the full, adapted well to Boulton's increasingly mechanized methods of manufacture. Boat-shaped tureens with bands of varying ornament and swept loop handles could be produced in endless variations in both silver and Sheffield Plate (figs. 50–3). This element of 'mix and match' in the firm's tureen and candlestick designs became a characteristic feature not only of their silver output, but also of the growing range of Sheffield Plate. Most of these hybrid designs, such as the soup tureen in fig. 53, were probably produced by Boulton's own employees such as Francis Eginton.

The designs directly attributable to Wyatt show how well he understood the classical repertory. His trademark slender jug form (figs. 54–6), with or without his characteristic splayed tripod stand, remains one of the icons of English neo-classicism.[6] Even his weightier design for a jug (fig. 58) was ultimately produced by the firm as an object of assured delicacy[7] and makes it easy to understand Horace Walpole's assertion about Wyatt that he used the antique with more taste than Adam.

Unfortunately, as Wyatt's architectural practice grew and he turned more to ancient

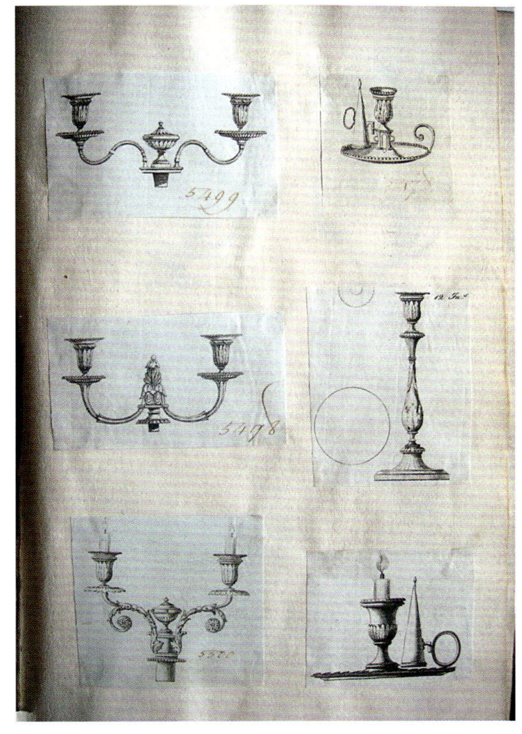

65
Designs for candlesticks and candelabra branches, from a Sheffield Plate trade catalogue, c. 1775.
Lent by Dr David Needham.

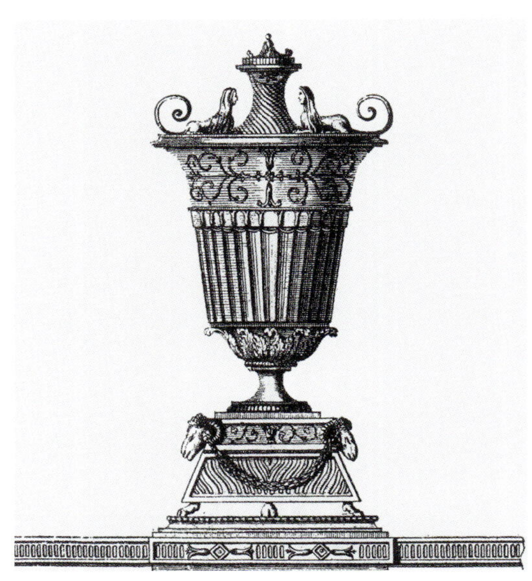

66
Decorative urn, engraving from *The Builder's Magazine, or Monthly Companion*, **London, 1774. Based on designs published in Robert and James Adam's** *The Works in Architecture* **the year before, this urn shows how design was rapidly disseminated to a wider audience of craftsmen and builders.**

Greece for his inspiration, he seems to have had no more time, or patience, for designing silver. For Boulton & Fothergill, producing bespoke silverware of sophisticated neo-classical design was barely practical for a factory that was becoming increasingly mechanized. The whims of individual clients could not be catered for, and at the cutting edge of taste, styles often moved far too fast for mechanization to respond. Like any business, the Soho Manufactory, and its competitors in London such as the Bateman factory,[8] had to grow, and to do so had to increase its consumer base. Inevitably, new custom was to come not from the aristocracy but from the burgeoning middle classes who wanted simple, practical design at reasonable cost, whether it was in silver or Sheffield Plate. Plain silver had never been out of fashion but Boulton's well-proportioned wares, with plain surfaces that were easy to keep clean and lent themselves well to mass production, were to be his most enduring legacy to the silver trade.

[1] Drawings from the album were first published in the 1940s (see Dale, pp. 526–9, and *Country Life*, CIV, no. 2685 (2 July 1948), pp. 24–5; see also Fergusson, pp. 751–5 and Cornforth, pp. 71–3. It was said to have been purchased in an auction in Paris in 1947; it is no longer in Noailles's library at the Villa Noailles in Hyères.

[2] Clayton, p. 44.

[3] Mason, p. 40.

[4] Quickenden, "Epergne", p. 416.

[5] Quickenden, "Montagu".

[6] Examples are in the Metropolitan Museum of Art, New York, and the Nelson-Atkins Museum, Kansas City.

[7] Boulton & Fothergill's silver example is in the Birmingham Museum and Art Gallery.

[8] A study of the Bateman factory in London, as significant as the Soho Manufactory in the development of the low-priced silverware market, is sorely needed.

V The Holkham Service

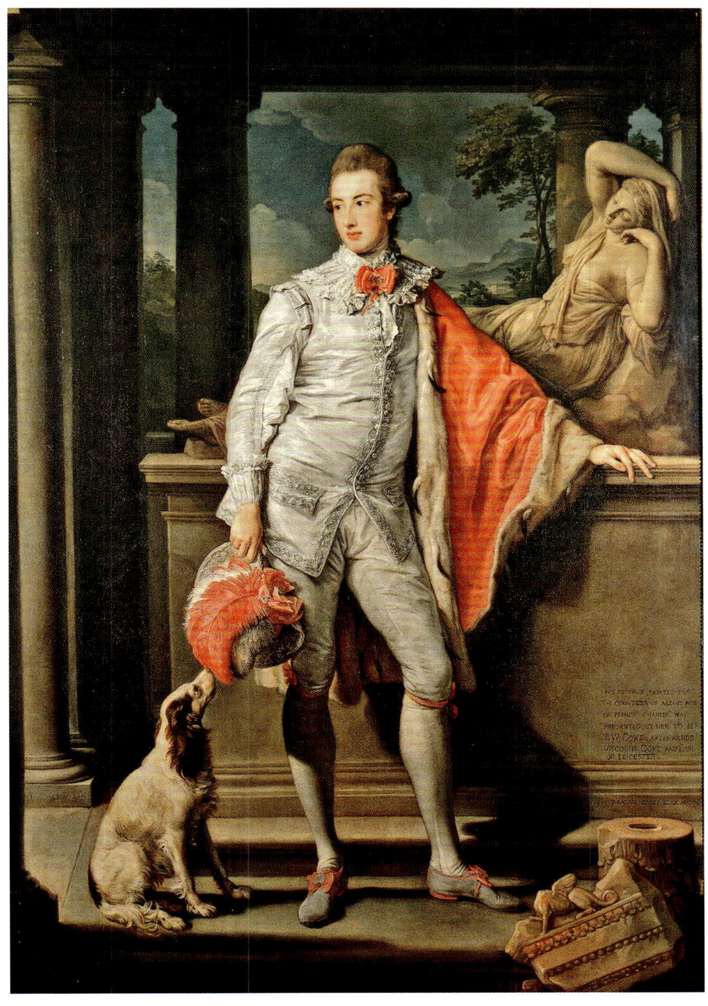

67
Thomas William Coke (1754–1842), oil on canvas, Pompeo Batoni (1708–1787). Coke, known as 'Le bel anglais' during his Grand Tour, inherited the Holkham estate in 1775. He immediately commissioned an extensive dinner service in the neo-classical style. *Viscount Coke and the Trustees of the Holkham Estate.*

One of the most impressive neo-classical silver services to survive almost intact, the Holkham Service remains in the house for which it was purchased, but has not been published. Unlike the Williams-Wynn service, however, no bills or other documentation for it appear to exist in the Holkham archives. Ironically, a record of the purchase of another extensive service, commissioned some fifty-five years earlier from Paul de Lamerie by Thomas Coke, the builder of the house, does survive.[1] This service was probably melted down to pay for the new one purchased in 1776–7.

Coke had begun the building of Holkham Hall in 1734 in the austere Palladian style of Colen Campbell. Recent research has shown that although Coke employed Campbell and others the overall concept was his own. William Kent was employed to carry out the rich interior decoration, which included an alabaster entrance hall, an apsed sculpture gallery and a library the ceiling of which was based on Roman prototypes. The house, its park and furnishings were conceived as a temple of the arts and together they form one

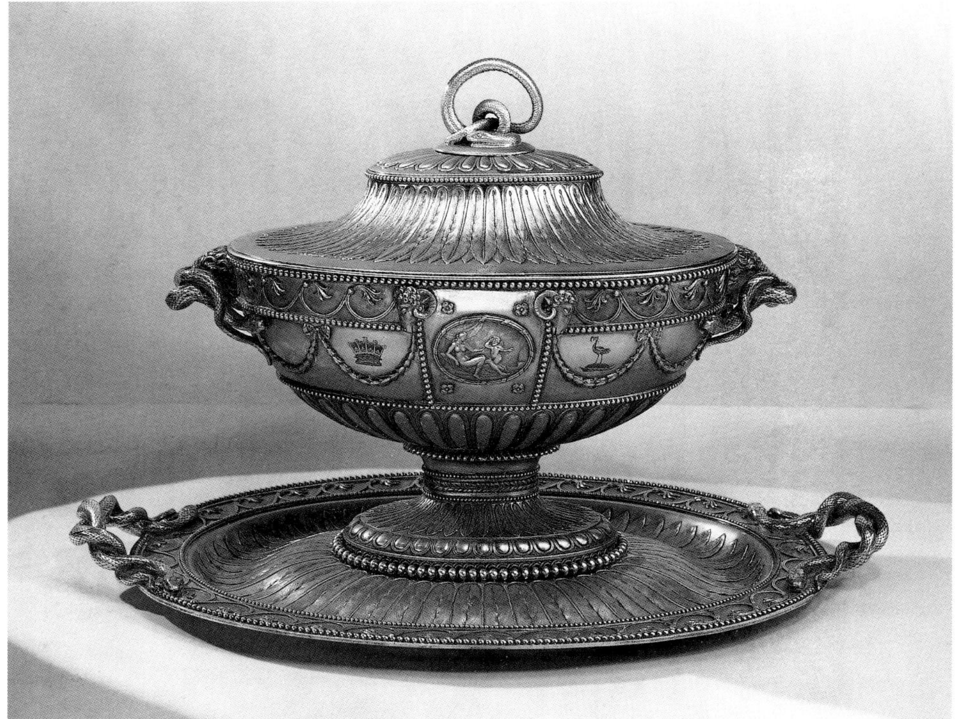

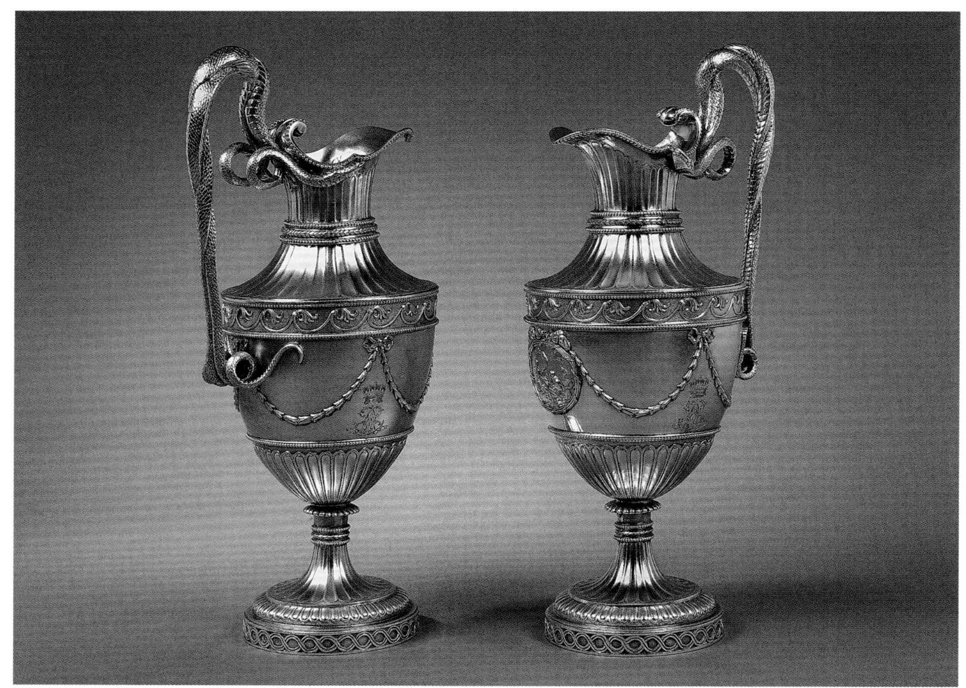

of the most complete Whig "power houses" in England.

Thomas Coke's dinner service, purchased from de Lamerie between 1718 and 1720, comprised 60 plates and 21 dishes as well as an "Epargne or Saveall", salts, baskets, cruet frames and salvers. The relatively low cost of the fashioning of the plates and dishes, at five pence per ounce, suggests they were plain with merely a moulded rim. The idea of all the pieces of a dinner service having an integrated design, or even being in a style that matched the rooms in which they were to be used, was to come later. Indeed, it was

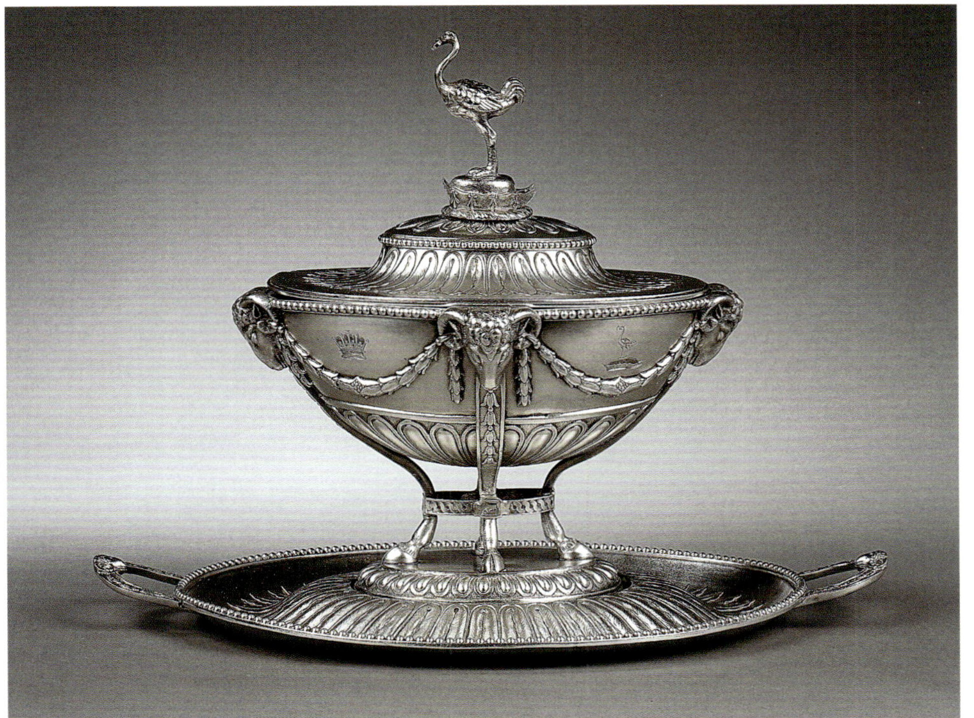

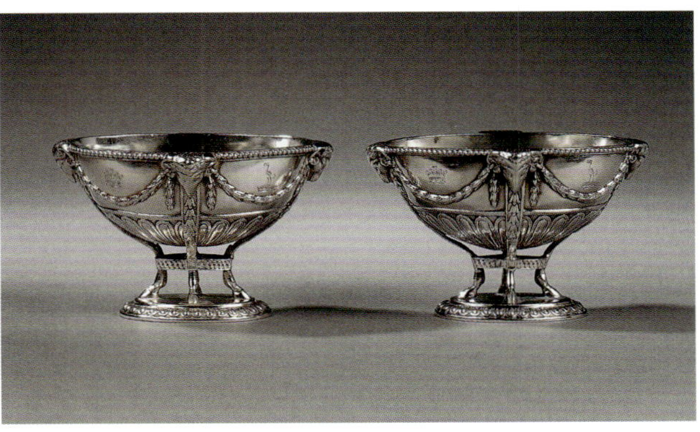

William Kent who was among the first artists to supply designs for silver, but he is not known to have supplied silver designs to Coke.

After Coke's death in 1759, it was left to his widow to carry out the remaining work which went on for almost another ten years. On her death in 1775, Holkham was inherited by Thomas William Coke (1754–1842), the grandson of Thomas Coke's sister. Recently returned from an extensive Grand Tour during which he had been painted with characteristic richness by Pompeo Batoni, the young Coke, who was to become known as "Coke of Norfolk" and equally famous for his improvements to the estate and for his liberal Whig politics, immersed himself in his inheritance. Holkham and its contents remained virtually intact during his lifetime, but one of the few acquisitions he did make was a new dinner service in the "antique" or neo-classical style. In response to new fashions of the table top, it comprised four elliptical soup tureens, four circular *pots à oille*, twelve sauce boats and twenty-four salts, as well as ewers, candlesticks, covered cups and sets of condiment vases. A variety of maker's marks appear on the components

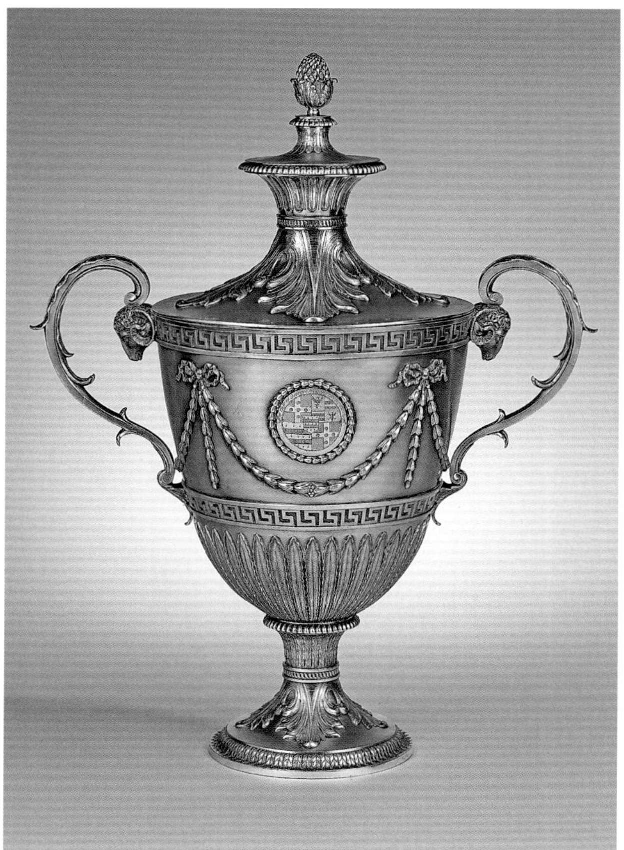

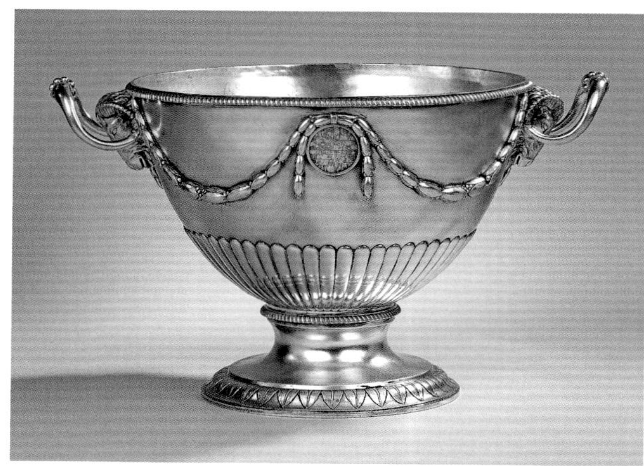

reflecting use of specialist outworkers by a retailer. The Hennell workshop supplied sauce tureens and salts, the partnership of Daniel Smith and Robert Sharp the soup tureens, William Holmes large ewers and covered cups, John Carter II candlesticks and James Young condiment vases. The hallmarks date from 1776 to 1778.

The service has a confident cohesiveness of design that suggests one individual was responsible for its conception. Seventeenth-century baroque features, such as applied medallions and vigorously modelled entwined snakes as handles, are revived here and are destined to become stock features on the silver of the following decades. Yet it is not so easy to ascribe the service's design to an individual artist. The distinctive Virtruvian scrolls with variegated ends are repeated on later Smith and Sharp work such as the ewer and basin of 1783–4 (fig. 86). The horizontal partitioning and continuous patterns of palmettes and beading have some similarities with Adam's William-Wynn designs. But the snake handles are much more boldly modelled than Adam's snakes on his vase for General Lascelles of 1764,[2] and the bands of ornament on the Holkham Service have a solidity that is lacking on most of the silver designs from the Adam workshop.

Another candidate is James Wyatt. There is a connection with the Wyatts and Holkham, where James's brother Samuel worked extensively for Thomas William Coke, but the first mention of Samuel in the Holkham archives is in 1780.[3] James

Wyatt's use of contrasting areas of plain silver and shallow fluting can be seen in the pair of ewers (fig. 69), but the overall solidity of all the Holkham pieces is in contrast to Wyatt's delicate forms.

The lack of any bills or correspondence relating to the service makes it likewise impossible to identify the retailer. Parker & Wakelin are known to have used Smith & Sharp but no mention of the service appears in their surviving ledgers. Another, and perhaps more likely, retailer is the firm of Pickett & Rundell who, from signatures on a number of their surviving works, we know utilized not only Smith & Sharp but also William Holmes and the Hennell workshop. Pickett & Rundell, at the sign of the Golden Salmon in Ludgate Hill, could trace their origins back to the 1720s. In 1769 Alderman Pickett had entered into a partnership with Philip Rundell, his shopman. The firm, later known as Rundell &s Bridge, went on to be the leading retailer of the Regency period, specializing in silver, jewellery and other luxury goods.[4]

Shortly after it was made, the Holkham Service appears to have been used as security for a mortgage,[5] as it was the subject of several squibs published in 1780 by Coke's disgruntled former employee, Richard Gardiner, who used it as part of a political campaign against him during the election of that year. One of them reads:

LINES
Written on a Window, near a Banker's –
Shop in Norwich

O! May the orange-colour'd fool I hate,
Affect to live in grandeur and in state,
While banker's clerks bestride his mortgag'd plate
Lumbering the shop. Imprison'd in a chest,
To all who enter, a true standing jest.[6]

Coke was finally persuaded to accept the re-created title of Earl of Leicester given to his ancestor in 1837. Heraldic finials in the form of the Coke crest of an ostrich, as well as engraved interlaced Ls and coronets, were added to service by Thomas William Coke's son after he inherited Holkham in 1843.

The Holkham Service made a bold statement on Thomas William Coke's dining table, elegantly reflecting his ancestor's quest to create a temple of the arts. But it went further than that: as Coke presided over banquets given for his political allies, and dinners for his tenants as well as agricultural writers during one of his celebrated "Sheep Shearings" (forerunners of the agricultural show), the service's bold classicism reinforced his social prestige and political importance. It was a forerunner of the imperial style of the early years of the nineteenth century.

[1] Mortlock, pp. 552–8.
[2] Snodin, "Adam", p. 22, fig. 36.
[3] Wade Martins, p. 49.
[4] Hartop, *Rundell*, pp. 23–4.
[5] Coke used mortgages and the sale of property in other parts of the country to fund the purchase of land contiguous with his own in Norfolk. By the 1820s the Holkham estate in Norfolk comprised some 25,000 acres; see Parker, pp. 83–8.
[6] From the *Morning Herald* of Saturday, 25 November 1780, in *Memoirs of the Life and Writing (Prose and Verse) of R-ch—D G-RD-N-R, Esq. Alias Dick Merry – Fellow…* London & Norwich, 1782 (British Library 1202.g.6.G.14798); see also Stirling, pp. 118–24.

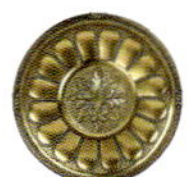

VI The dissemination of design: how the trade worked

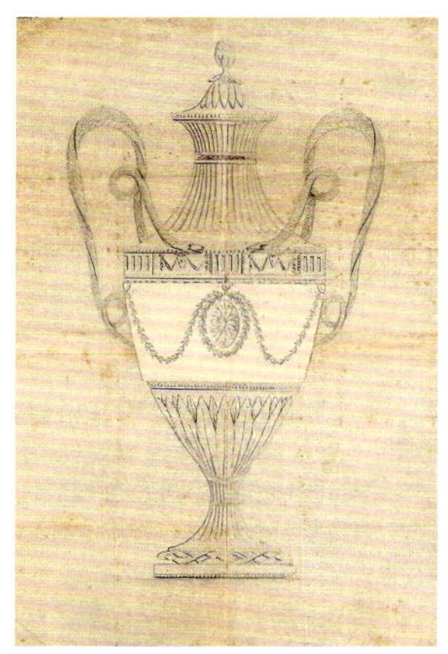

74
Drawing of a condiment vase,
c. 1777. One of two drawings
sent by Pickett & Rundell, the
London retailers, to Herman &
Joseph Berens, silver retailers in
the Netherlands, for their client
to consider. *The archives of
Kasteel Duivenvoorde.*

The Holkham Service's consistency of design is such that it was almost certainly the outcome of a collaboration between one designer and one supplier. Only a major retailer had the resources to fulfil such a large commission and no single workshop could supply all the objects required in the time available. But where did the designs come from, and what was the relationship between supplier and customer? The trade had been gradually changing during the eighteenth century: with the development of the paper economy the business of banking became separated from silversmithing, and with the growth of the consumer base the supplier increasingly took the lead in the adoption of new styles and designs. The age when the supply of silverware in Britain was fundamentally a financial transaction was over.

One of the biggest problems facing a supplier was piracy of designs. Craftsmen saw nothing wrong in copying objects which were regarded as "neat" or "elegant". The practice of inscribing finished silverware with the name of the retailer and so in a sense claiming ownership of the design began at this time, and Pickett & Rundell were among the first. The natural outcome of this was a proprietary feeling towards designs; they became assets to be bought and sold. But the idea of a particular artist being linked to a particular design was still in its infancy; François Gravelot and William Kent were among the first artists to be recognized as designers of silver in London, but, as we have seen, it was Robert Adam who elevated the designer to celebrity status. With the Holkham Service we have no way of knowing if Thomas William Coke was involved

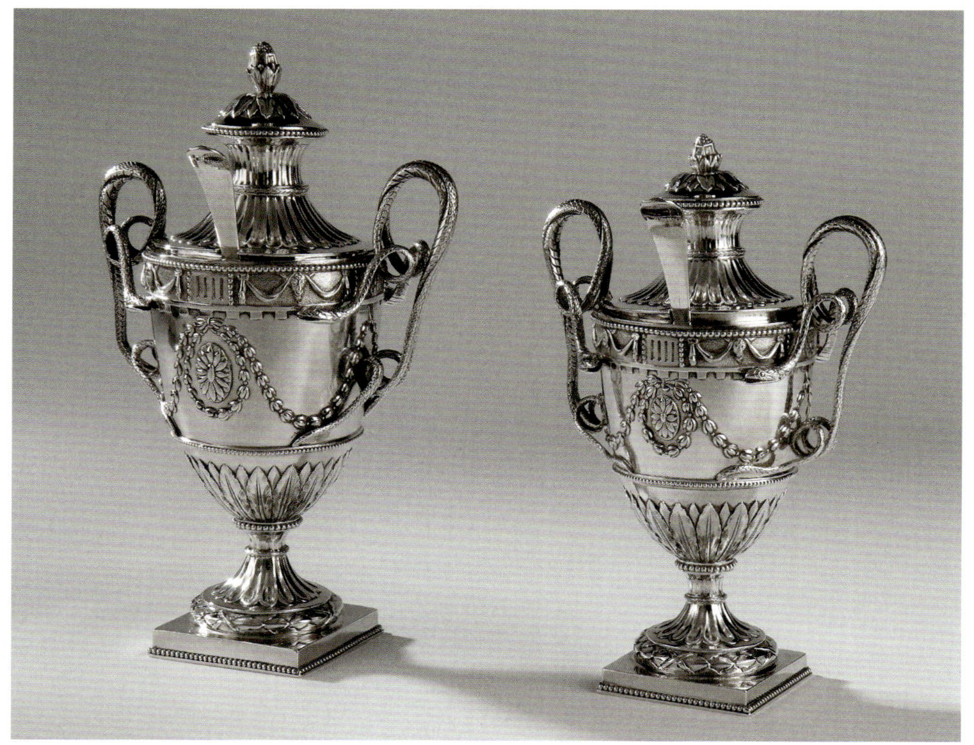

75
Two condiment vases (from a
set of four), silver, London,
1777–8, maker's mark of James
Young. The order for vases to
the design submitted (fig. 74)
was placed by the retailers
Herman & Joseph Berens on
behalf of Nicolas Steengracht
van Oosterland of Middelburg,
Zeeland, who had married that
year. The order was filled by
Pickett & Rundell in London
with silver from James Young's
workshop. The vases are
identical to six examples in the
Holkham Service, suggesting
that Pickett & Rundell may
have supplied that service too.
Kasteel Duivenvoorde.

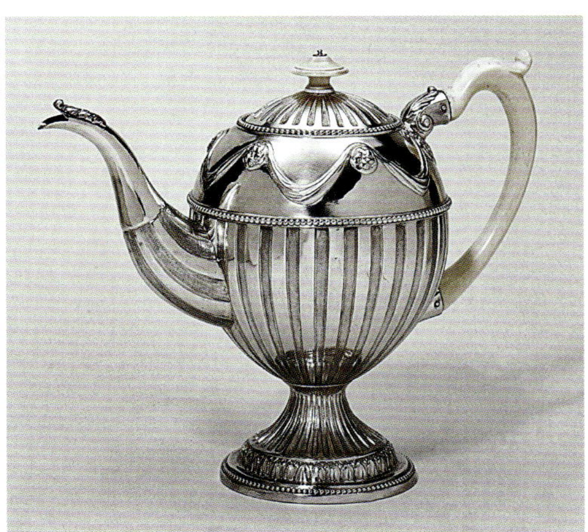

76
Teapot, silver, ivory, London, 1774–5, maker's mark of James Young & Orlando Jackson. Part of an impressive tea service made for the actor David Garrick, this teapot has alternating vertical bands of matt and polished silver. *Lent by the Trustees of the Victoria and Albert Museum, London.*
Cat. no. 26

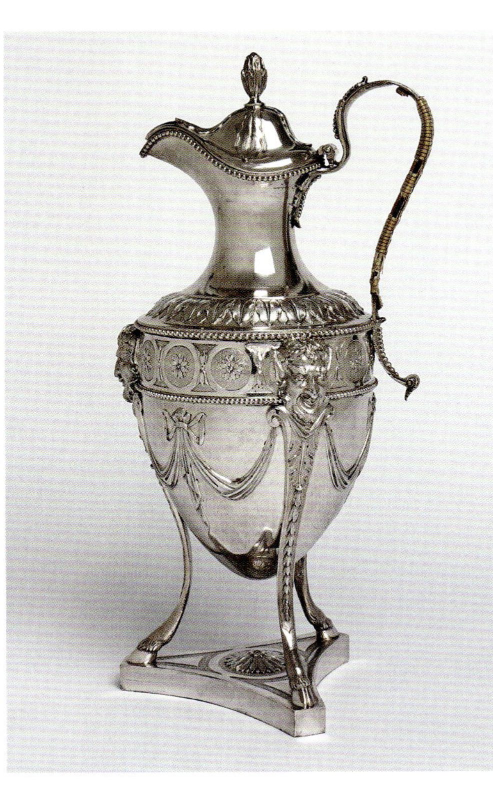

77
Jug, silver, London, 1777–8, maker's mark of Henry Greenway. The tripod legs of this jug are surmounted by satyr masks. *Lent by the Trustees of the Victoria and Albert Museum.*
Cat. no. 34

78
Jug, silver and raffia, London, 1774–5, maker's mark of John Denziloe. A simplified, cheaper and more durable version of **fig. 77**. *Lent by a private collector.*
Cat. no. 24

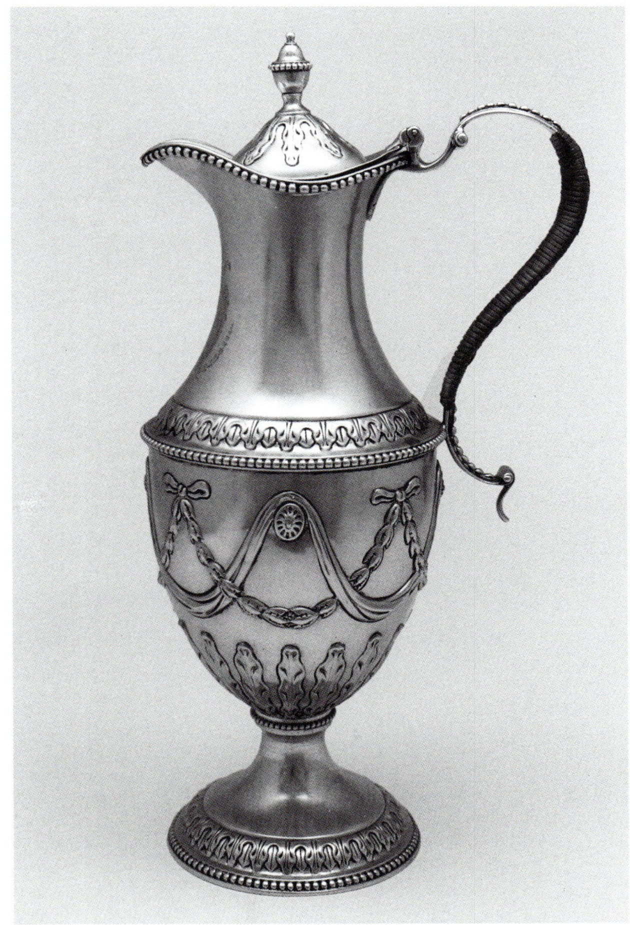

in the design process, or if it was supplied from stock items. Objects identical to those in the Holkham Service and with the same date letters are known to have been supplied to other customers, but were these supplied to the same retailer, or did the manufacturer, having received the design from a retailer, continue to use it for other customers?

One insight into what the process might have been can be obtained from a group of silver supplied to a Dutch client through a Dutch retailer, by Pickett & Rundell in

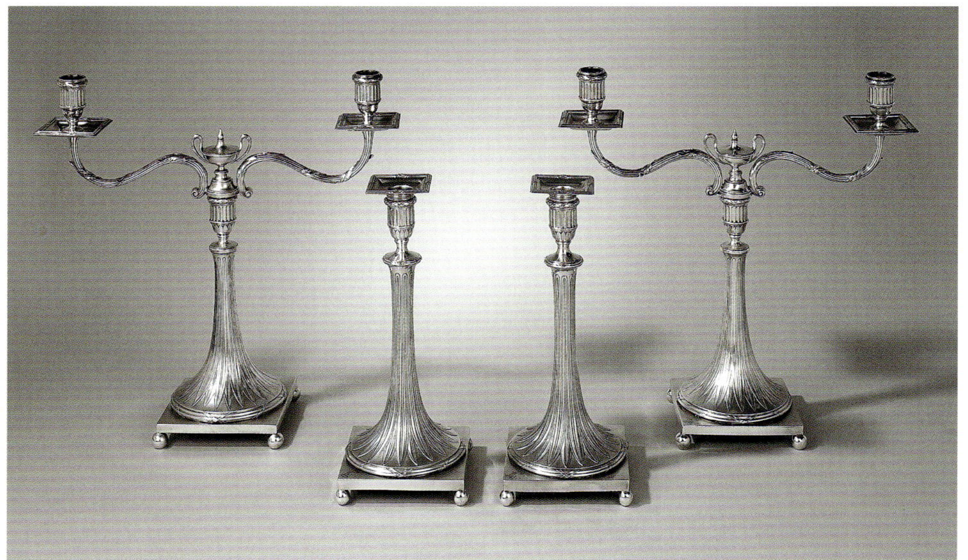

79
Pair of two-light candelabra and pair of candlesticks, silver, London, 1777–8, maker's mark of John Wakelin & William Tayler. The square raised platform bases and cylindrical sockets are neo-classical features but the curving fluted stems introduce a decidedly baroque feel to these candlesticks. *Lent by the Alan and Simone Hartman Collection.*
Cat. no. 35

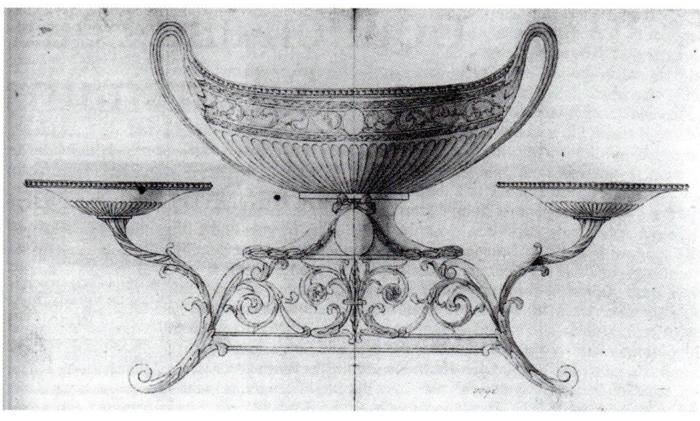

80
Design for an epergne, pen, pencil and wash, c. 1780, anonymous. Drawings such as this one raise the question whether they were working drawings given to the silversmith, or ones intended to be shown to the client, or if they were records of what had been made and sold. *V&A Images.*

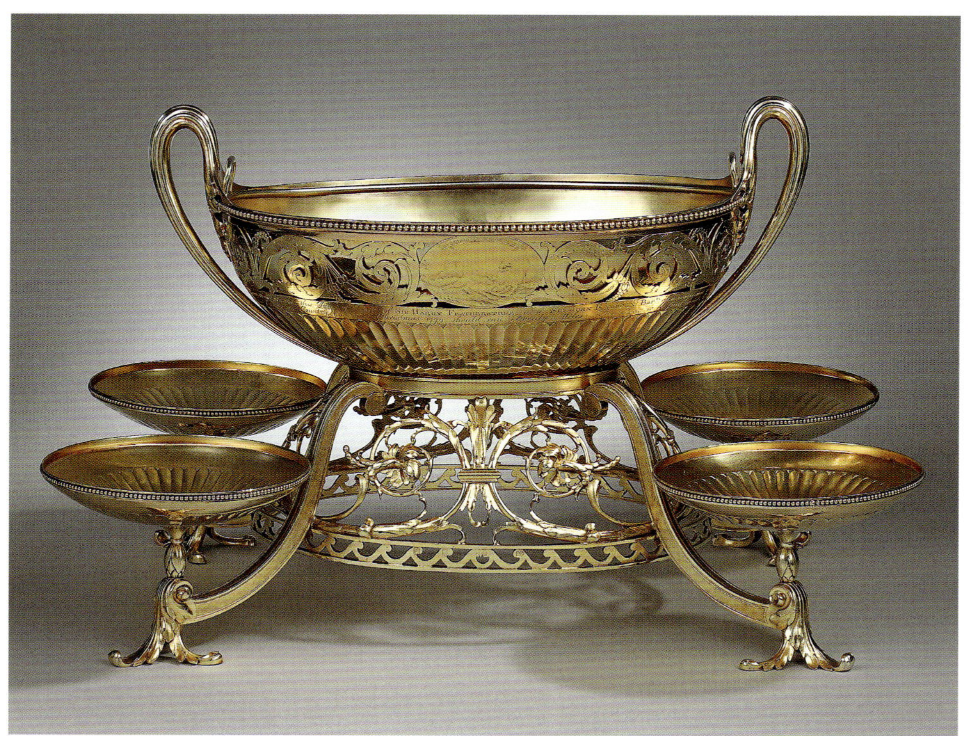

81
Epergne, silver-gilt, London, 1782–3, maker's mark of John Wakelin & William Tayler. Colonel Thornton received this epergne from Sir Harry Featherstone and Sir John Ramsden as a result of a bet over the distance of a fox-hunting run. *Lent by an American private collector.*
Cat. no. 37

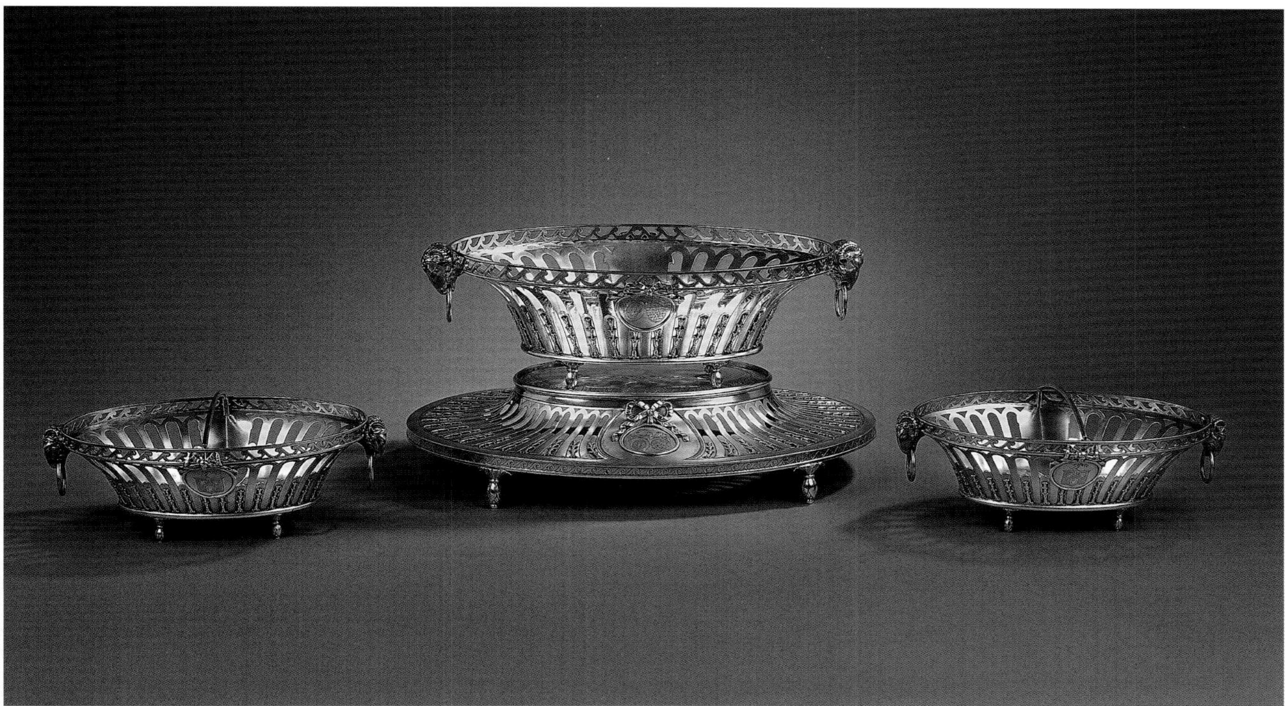

82
Centrepiece and pair of fruit dishes, silver, glass, London, 1789–90, maker's mark of John Wakelin & William Tayler and 1793–4, maker's mark of John Wakelin & Robert Garrard I. These restrained baskets were a popular model in the 1780s and 90s. *Lent by a private collector.* Cat. no. 47

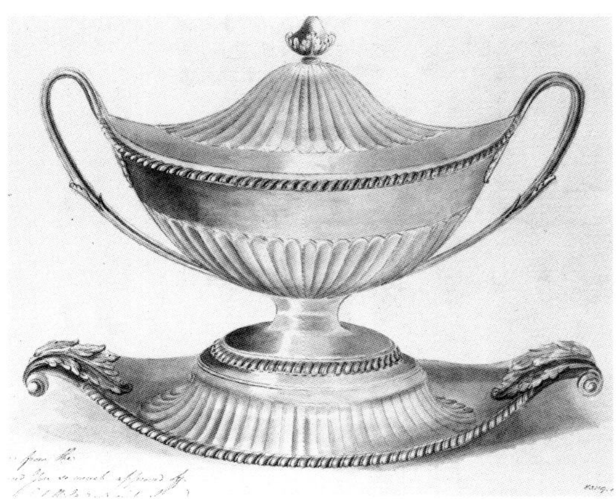

83
Drawing of a soup tureen, cover and stand, pen and wash, c. 1790, anonymous. Inscribed: "… made from the Sauce Tureen and Stand You so much approved of when in London". *V&A Images*.

1777–8 (figs. 74–5). Drawings were sent out from London for vases for sugar and pepper of virtually identical form to those in the Holkham Service. Minor changes were suggested, presumably by the client, and then the finished articles, made in the James Young workshop (as the Holkham condiment vases had been), were sent to Holland.

Other designs with more popular appeal may have been made as stock items and offered to clients off the shelf, such as the jug in fig. 78, while the teapot from David Garrick's service, fig. 76, and the Henry Greenway jug, fig. 77, were probably special commissions involving discussion with the client of the overall design. In 1774 Thomas Scrope of Coleby wrote to Sir William Chambers: "I wish you would also put together for me (for I cannot Draw) an idea I have for an Epergne; the part to hold the lemons to be a cornucopia, the frame a tripod, the things for pickles, Pateræ, light and elegant and truly Antique". Presumably, once the design had been drawn, the order would be placed with a supplier by the client, or possibly by the designer.[1]

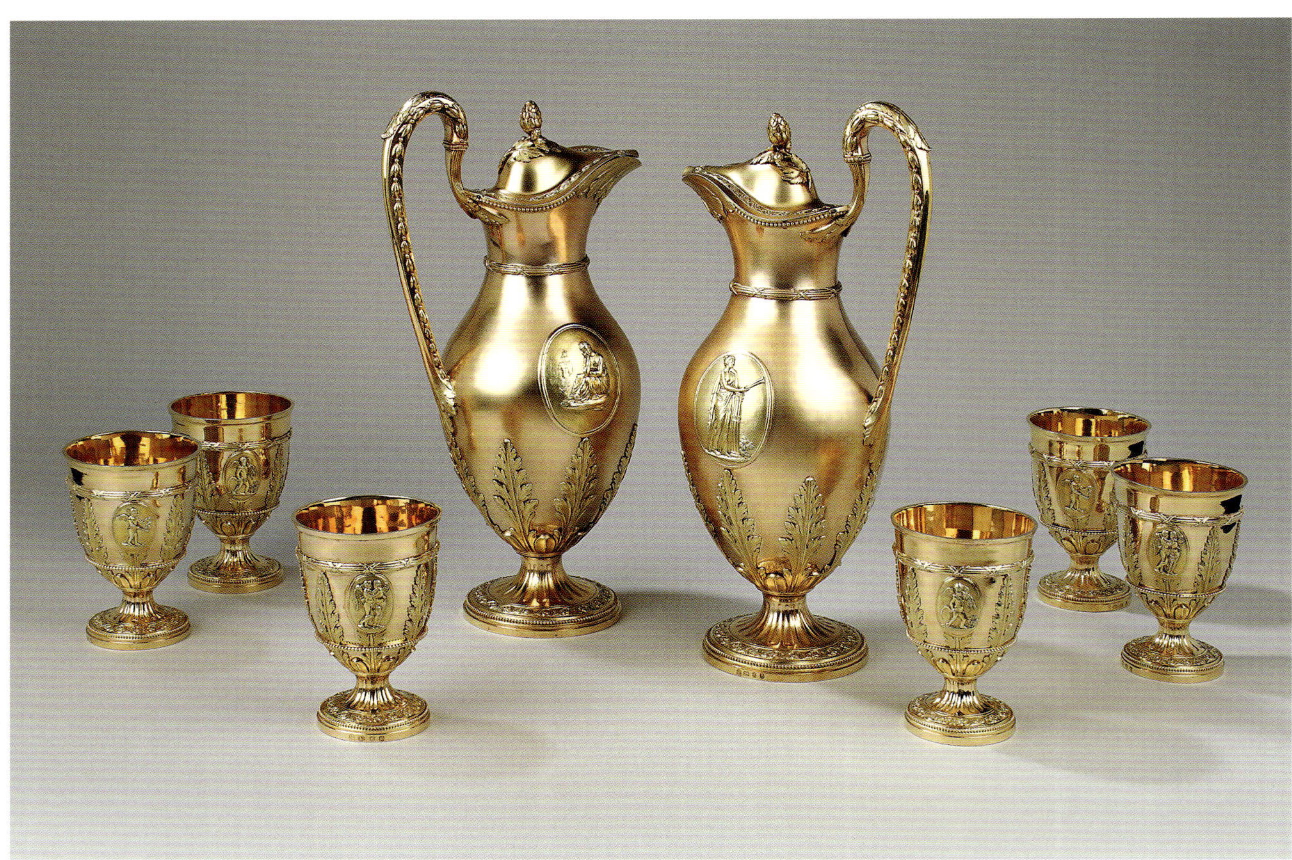

84
Pair of ewers and six goblets, silver-gilt, London, 1780–1, maker's mark of Andrew Fogelberg & Stephen Gilbert. Medallioned bas-reliefs depicting classical figures or scenes were a speciality of the Fogelberg & Gilbert workshop; they are often based on paste examples sold by James Tassie. *Lent by a private collector.* Cat. no. 36

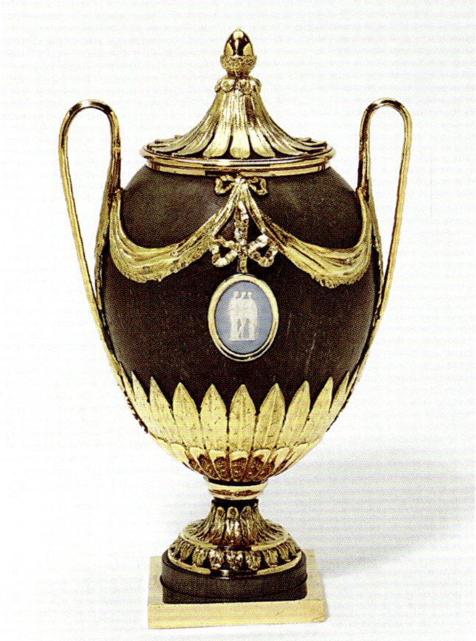

85
Vase and cover, silver-gilt, coconut, wood, c. 1785, the plaque by Josiah Wedgwood and Son. The vase was given by Lord Frederick Campbell to Assheton, Viscount Curzon (1733–1800), whose brother Nathaniel Curzon employed Robert Adam to create stunning interiors in the new neo-classical style at Kedleston. *Lent by the Trustees of the Victoria and Albert Museum.* Cat. no. 40

The role of the drawings themselves is also worthy of scrutiny. Well-finished drawings such as that for the epergne in fig. 80 raise the question as to whether they are working drawings for the silversmith, designs submitted to a client for approval, or record drawings of pieces that had been made. Drawings sent to clients probably seldom came back, and it is unlikely that working drawings would have withstood life on the workbench. Only the largest retailers could afford to have finished silverware to show clients: John Wyatt, one of Matthew Boulton's agents in London in the 1770s,

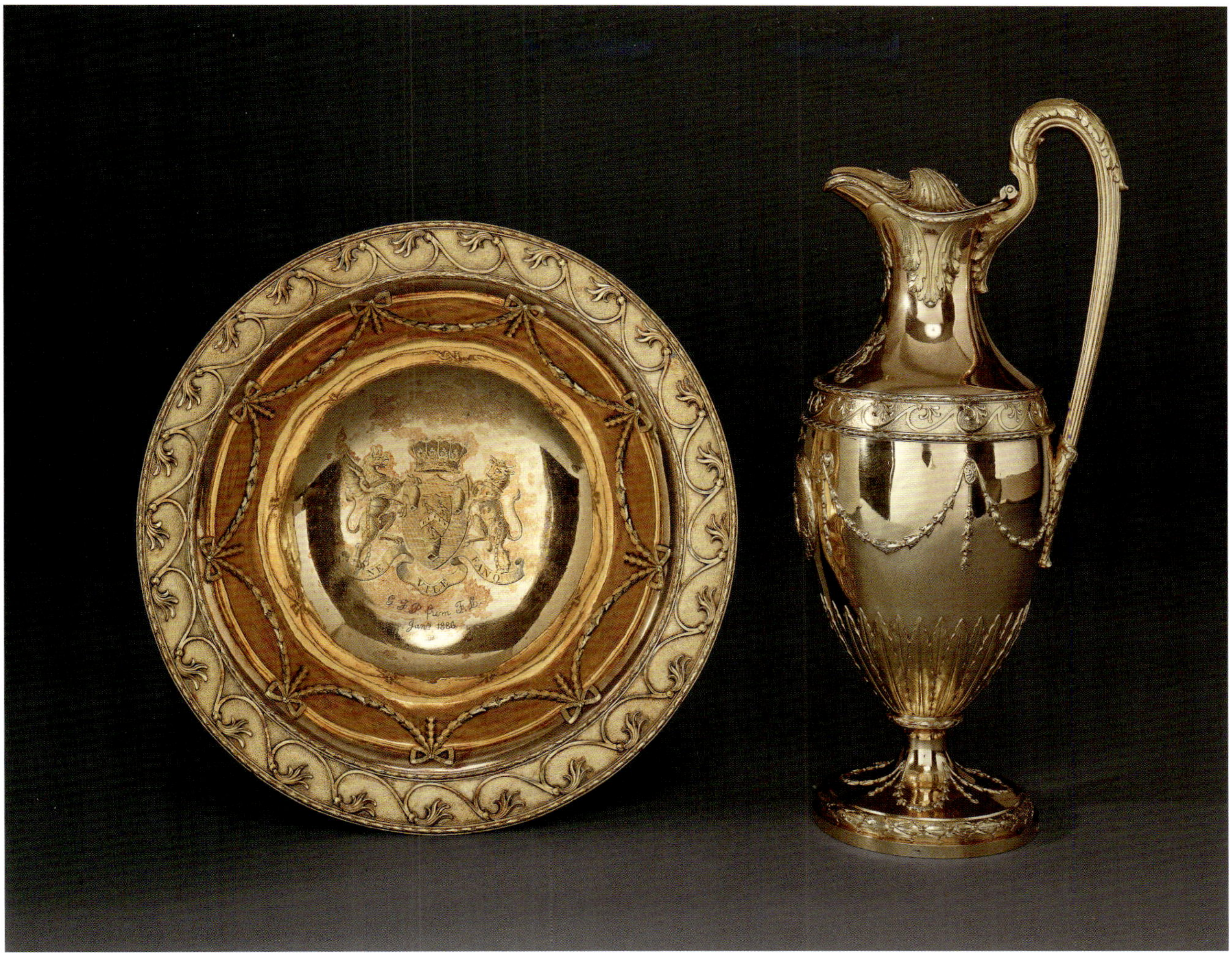

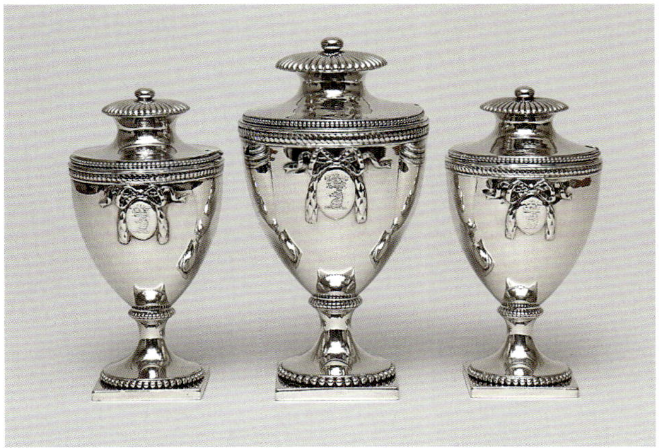

86
Ewer and basin, silver-gilt,
London, 1783–4, maker's
mark of Daniel Smith &
Robert Sharp. Part of an
extensive toilet service
commissioned for Sarah
Anne, daughter and heiress of
Sir Robert Child, the banker,
who eloped with John Fane,
10th Earl of Westmorland to
Gretna Green in 1782. *Lent by
the National Trust, Osterley
House, the Jersey Collection.*
Cat. no. 39

87
Three condiment vases, silver,
London, 1783–4, maker's mark
of Daniel Smith & Robert
Sharp. Made for Edwin
Lascelles, 1st and last Baron of
Harewood (1712–1795), these
comparatively plain vases have
covers inspired by Vien's book
of vases published in 1760.
*Lent by the Earl and Countess of
Harewood and the Trustees of
the Harewood House Trust.*
Cat. no. 38

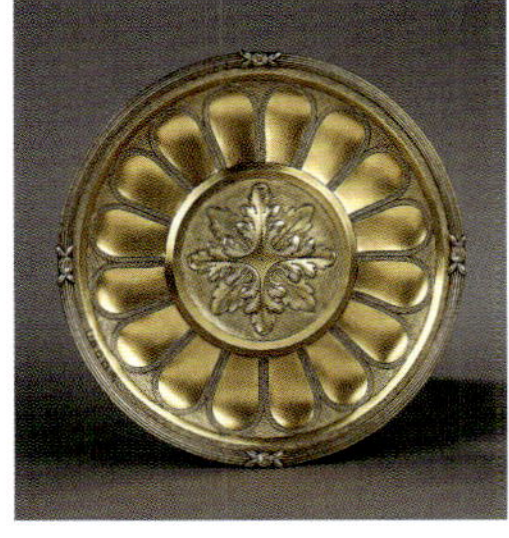

88
Dish, silver-gilt, London,
1787–8, maker's mark of
William Pitts. *Lent by Timothy
Schroder, Esq.*
Cat. no. 45

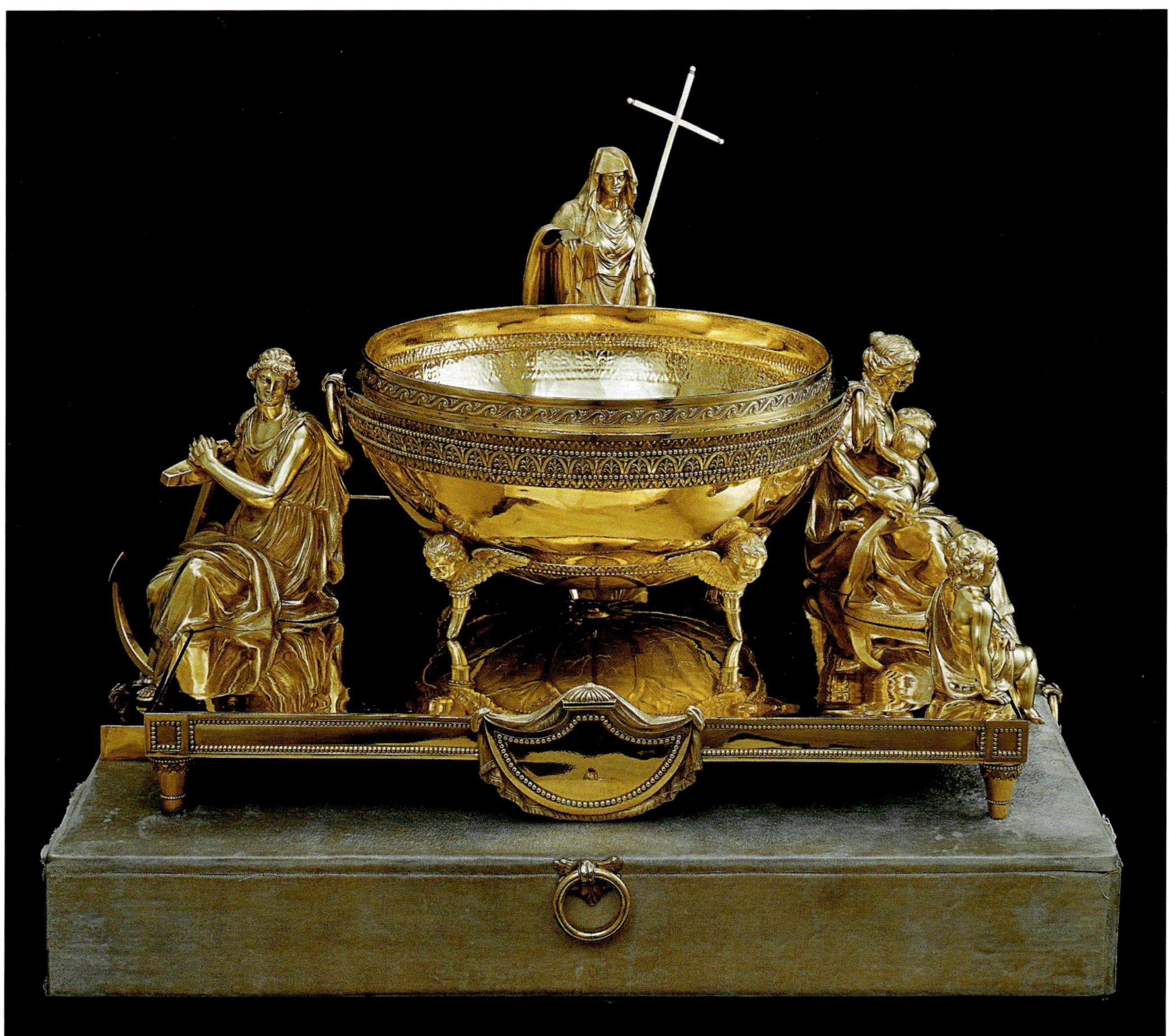

complained that he lacked shop premises, and was obliged to visit potential customers and show them drawings.[2]

Fogelberg & Gilbert, the firm that succeeded Ansill & Gilbert, manufacturers who supplied Parker & Wakelin, specialized in elegant forms with applied medallions. These, often copying ancient or Renaissance cameos, were based on paste examples sold by James Tassie. Others were designed for Tassie by the sculptor John Flaxman. The client could probably be offered a range of subjects and chose what he liked. When Colonel Bulwer visited Rundell & Bridge in 1796, he ordered a cup and cover weighing 86 ounces at a cost of £46 15s and was charged an extra 25s for the medallion.[3]

Because familiarity with the classical vocabulary was universal, artists of widely diverse specializations could express themselves in the classical idiom. It is perhaps not so difficult, therefore, to believe the landscape gardener Humphry Repton's bold claim that he designed the Portland Font in 1797 (fig. 89). "One of the most sumptuous presents of gold plate that was ever executed in this country", as Repton described it, the font was commissioned by the 4th Duke of Portland to commemorate the birth of

89
The Portland Font, gold, London, 1797–8, maker's mark of Paul Storr. Designed by Humphry Repton (1752–1818) for the 4th Duke of Portland, the font is without parallel in English decorative arts. Although Repton claimed that he also designed neo-classical silver for the duke, this appears to be the only object in precious metal designed by him. *Lent by the Trustees of the British Museum.*
Cat. no. 51

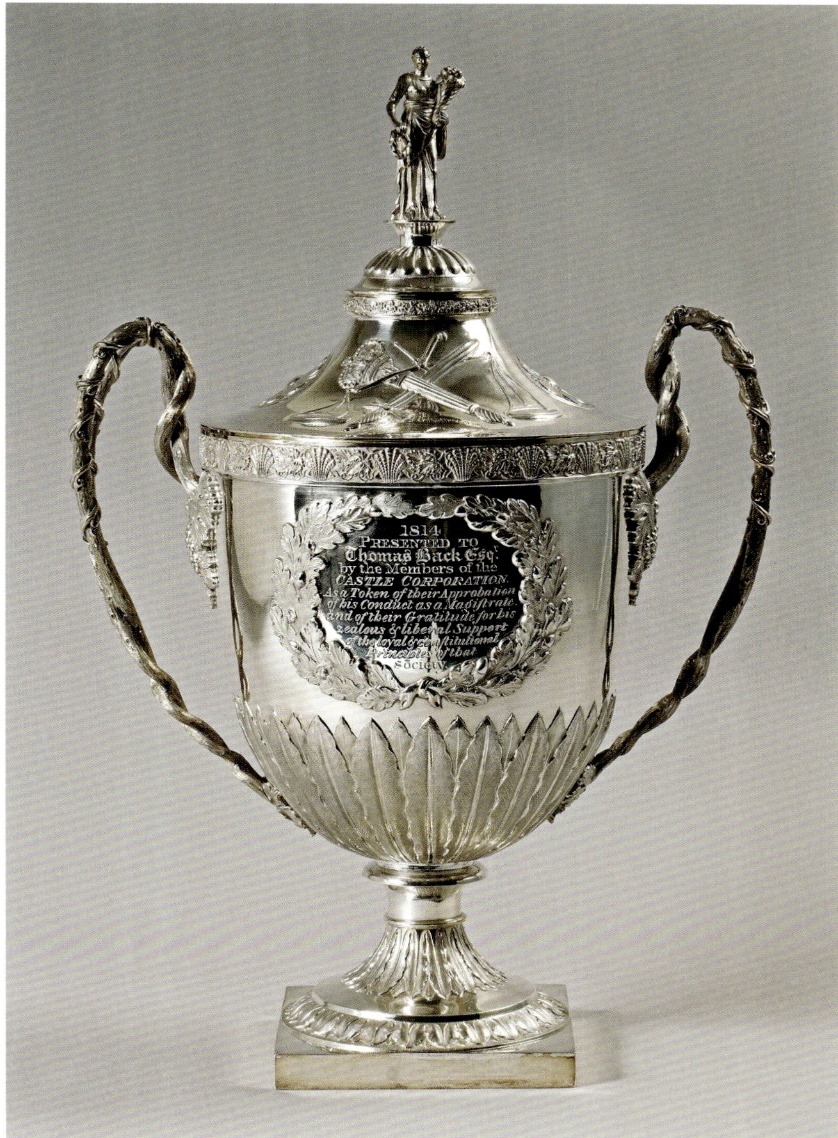

90
The Castle Corporation Vase,
silver, London, 1814–5, maker's
mark of Thomas Wallis &
Jonathan Hayne. The vase was
designed by James Bennett, a
Norwich clock and watch maker
who was a member of the
society. Drawings and
documents show how the design
of the cup and its iconography
were debated and modified by
the committee of the society.
The classical visual vocabulary
provided a *lingua franca* for all
those conversant with the art of
the ancient world. *Lent by
Norwich Castle Museum and Art
Gallery.*
Cat. no. 58

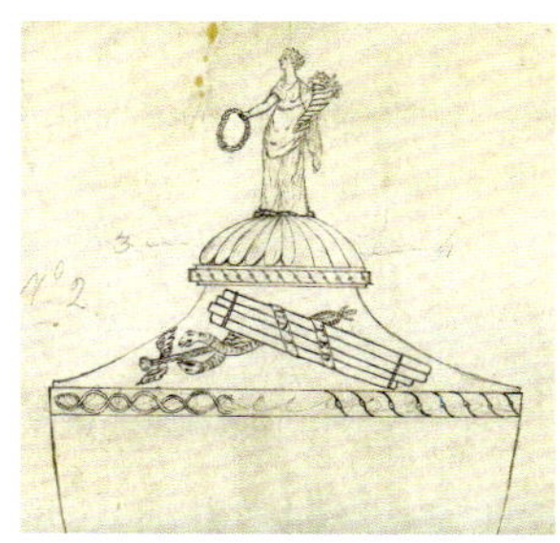

91
Drawing of the cover of the
Castle Corporation Vase, pen
and pencil, c. 1814, James
Bennett (d. 1845). *Norwich
Castle Museum and Art
Gallery.*

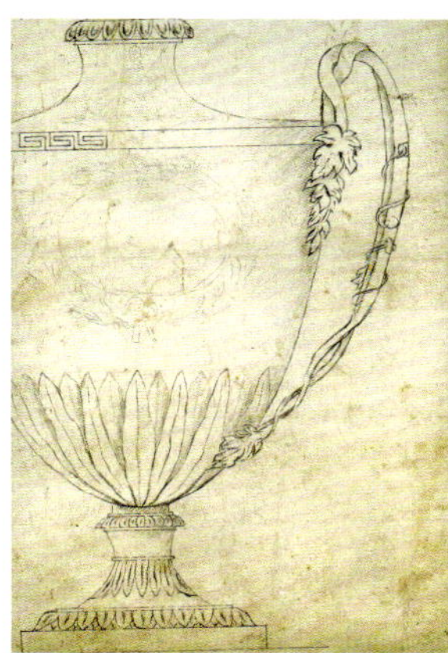

92
Drawing of the body of the
Castle Corporation Vase, pen
and pencil, c. 1814, James Bennett
(d. 1845). *Norwich Castle
Museum and Art Gallery.*

his son's first child. According to Repton, Portland was "a nobleman to whom I am more deeply indebted than to any in my list of professional patrons".[4] Repton carried out extensive work for the duke at his various seats. No doubt Repton's particular brand of suave and familiar salesmanship contributed to this most unlikely choice of designer. Repton is not known to have designed any other works in precious metal and the extent of his authorship must be questioned. Unfortunately, no correspondence or bills appear to survive which might shed light on how the commission went from design to finished object: the font was made in the workshop of Paul Storr, who at the time was supplying different retailers.[5] If Repton (or indeed his architect son John Adey Repton, then working in John Nash's office) conceived the overall design, the figures of Faith, Hope and Charity are clearly the work of a modeller of stature. The shallow bowl on its three splayed supports has some similarities with the silver designs attributed to Jean-Jacques Boileau (*fl.* c. 1787–1851), a French decorative painter who came to England to work for the Prince of Wales at Carlton House. An album of drawings for silverware attributed to him is in the Victoria and Albert Museum.[6] The

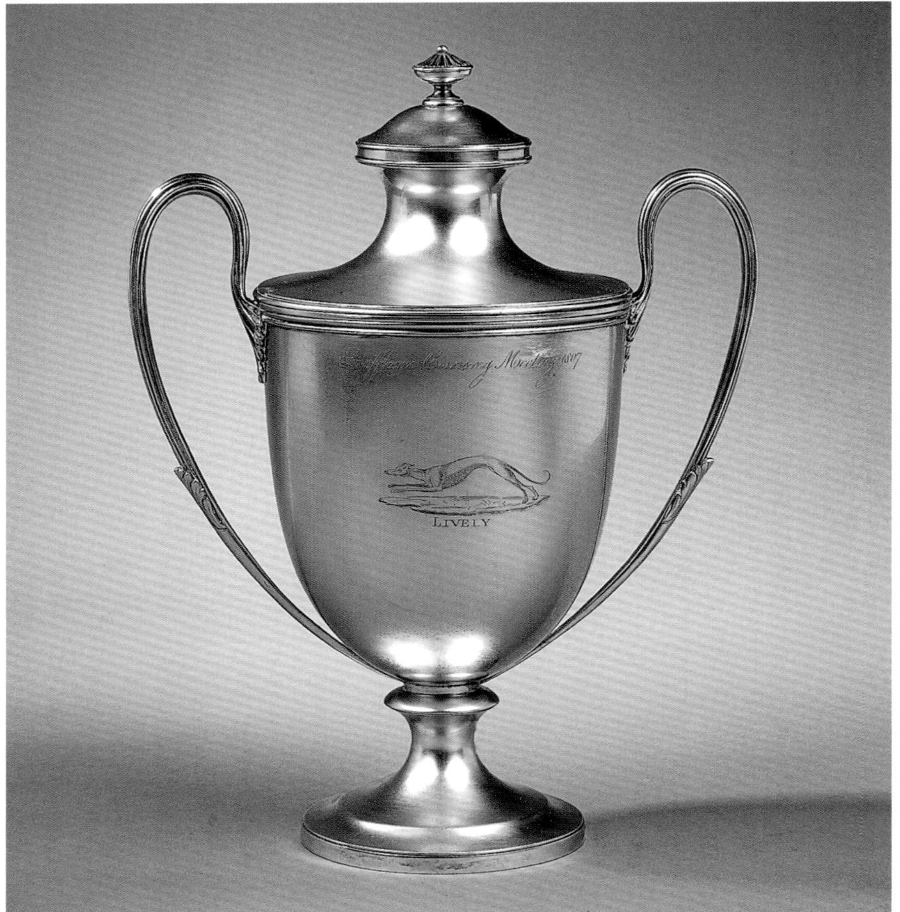

93
The Swaffham Cup of 1807,
silver, London, 1806–7, maker's
mark of John Emes. A high
quality object of austere design,
this cup and cover, given as a
prize for hare coursing, illustrate
the popularity of simple neo-
classical forms and decoration
throughout the period 1770–1840.
Lent by a private collector.
Cat. no. 53

sculptor John Flaxman's name was traditionally associated with the font; he had
returned from Italy in 1794 and the figures show a familiarity with Italian baroque
sculpture. Another candidate for modeller, suggested by Charles Truman in 1985, is
Joseph Nollekens, who is known to have corresponded with the 3rd Duke of Portland
some years before.

We should not think, however, that it was only artists who spoke the *lingua franca* of
classicism. Documents and drawings that have survived with the Castle Corporation
Vase (figs. 90–2), commissioned in 1814 by a Norwich political club, show how
members of the club's committee debated not only which classical symbols to include in
the decoration but also the design of the cup itself. The approved design was the work
of a member of the committee, James Bennett, a local clock and watch maker whose
drawings show a competent working knowledge of the classical vocabulary.

[1] Harris and Snodin, p. 155.
[2] Quickenden, "Chippendall", p. 52.
[3] Norfolk Record Office, Bulwer Papers. John Flaxman had been employed by Wedgwood from about 1775
onwards, and in 1783 supplied designs for a medallion to Wakelin & Tayler. Garrard supplied a "Flaxman
coffee pot" in 1797. We know this to have been globular with applied classical medallions as it was
reproduced during the nineteenth century.
[4] Gore and Carter, p. 29. Repton's claim appears in his *Observations on the theory and practice of landscape
gardening* (London, 1805), p. 165; the font was first recognized as Repton's design by Kedrun Laurie after
its sale at Christie's in 1985.
[5] I am grateful to David Adlam and Rachel Elwes for their advice.
[6] Snodin, "Boileau".

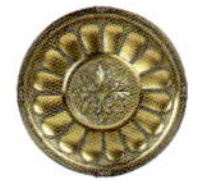

VII Unearthing design: the emergence of archaeology

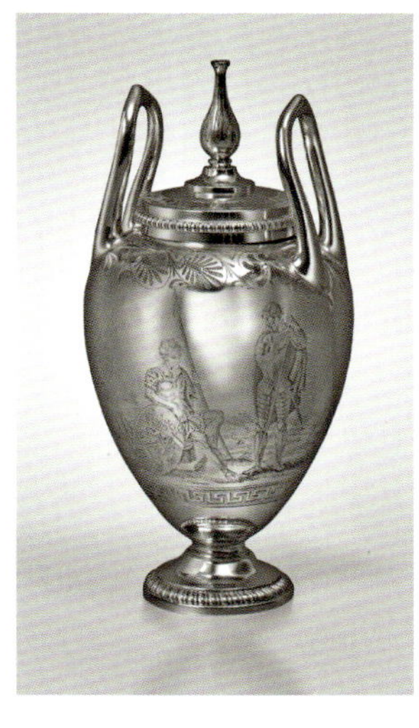

94
Condiment vase, silver, London, 1771–2, maker's mark of Louisa Courtauld & George Cowles. One of a set of three made for Charles Birch of Woodford, Essex, it is conceived as a *lebes gamikos*, or marriage bowl, copying examples illustrated in d'Hancarville's catalogue of Sir William Hamilton's collection of ancient vases. However, the engraved decoration appears to depict scenes from ancient British history. Sir Nathaniel Curzon of Kedleston had an identical set of three vases made in the same workshop in the same year, but with engraved scenes from Greek mythology. *Lent by the Azko Nobel Corporation Collection, on loan to the Courtauld Institute of Art.* Cat. no. 10

Ancient architecture provided not only one of the essential elements of neo-classicism, the column, but also a rich variety of examples of surface ornament. Other basic forms, such as the vase and the baluster, came, by way of the Renaissance and baroque designers, from ancient sculpture. But there were few everyday vessels to copy, except those published as plates in catalogues of antiquities such as that of the de Wilde collection in Holland, which appeared in the 1680s. Some ancient domestic articles were to be found in the crowded plates of Barnard de Montfaucon's *Antiquité expliquée*, a compendium of ancient works of art – real, fake and misidentified – first published at the beginning of the eighteenth century.

The dearth of surviving examples of ancient metalwork meant that ceramics provided most of the models from the ancient world that could be produced in silver. The *kylix* and the *krater*, as depicted in d'Hancarville's catalogue of Sir William Hamilton's collection of ancient vases, published in 1766, were not, however, popular as a model for drinking vessels in eighteenth-century Europe. Rather, they were reserved for ornamental vases or, in the case of the *krater*, for wine coolers. The *lebes gamikos*, or marriage bowl (fig. 94), enjoyed a brief vogue as the model for condiment vases in the 1760s and 70s, but the vase on foot (fig. 87) was ultimately to be the most enduring design for domestic items.

The discovery and excavation of Herculaneum, and the subsequent publication of *Le Antichità de Ercolano Esposte* over a period of some forty-six years from 1755 onwards, made available a wealth of new examples which could be used as models for decorative arts. But the function was often changed. The candlestick, that essential feature of every room in the eighteenth century, had been made in the form of an architectural column since the seventeenth century (fig. 3), but a purely archaeological example to use as a model was non-existent for the simple reason that the ancient world did not use candles. However, slender stands for oil lamps, tall enough to cast the light from the lamp upwards and across a room, were excavated at Herculaneum. Their publication in volume 8 of *Le Antichità* provided the model for a set of four candlesticks made for William Beckford in 1787–8 (figs. 95–8).[1] At the time Beckford was enlarging his father's Palladian house in Wiltshire, Fonthill Splendens, and purchasing elegant silver and gold objects in the neo-classical style. Later, even when the Gothic style had succeeded in dominating his life, he appears to have retained his love of neo-classical silver.

Illustrated books of archaeological discoveries became more and more common during the final decades of the eighteenth century. Some, like Giovanni Battista Piranesi's *Vasi, Candelabri, Cippi, Sacrofagi, Tripodi, Lucerne ed ornamenti antichi*, which appeared in 1778, offered meticulously detailed etchings of recently discovered, and often extensively restored, objects. In addition to a group of famous monumental vases, the book included prints of smaller Roman marble urns which provided the models for silver-gilt sugar vases retailed by Rundell, Bridge & Rundell from 1805 onwards; their original use as cinerary urns does not seem to have disturbed the sensibilities of Regency hostesses.

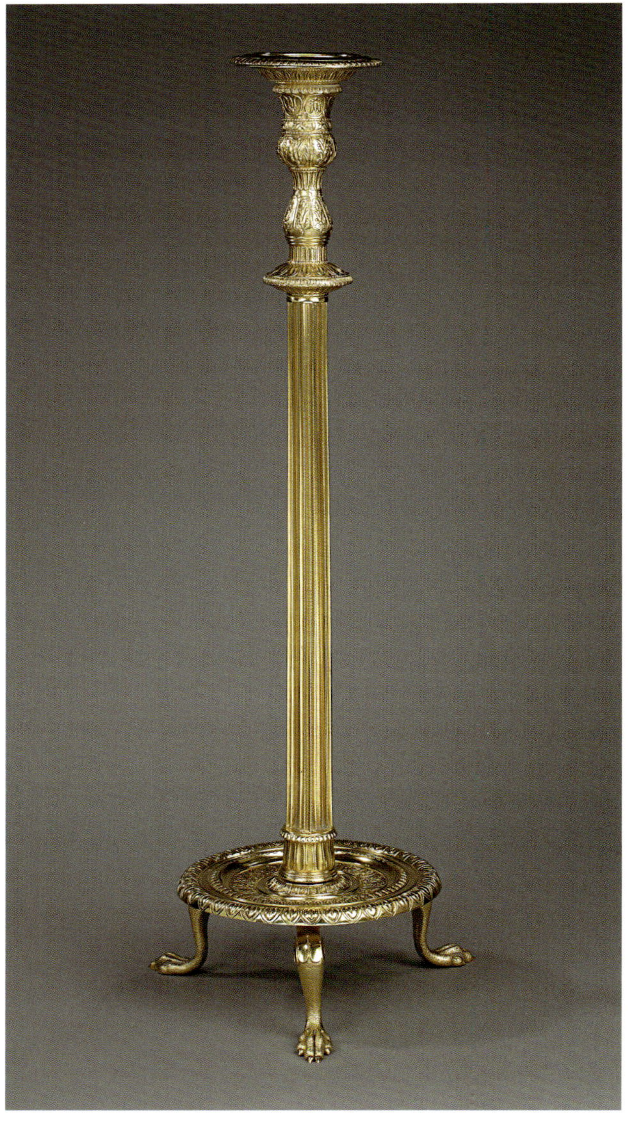

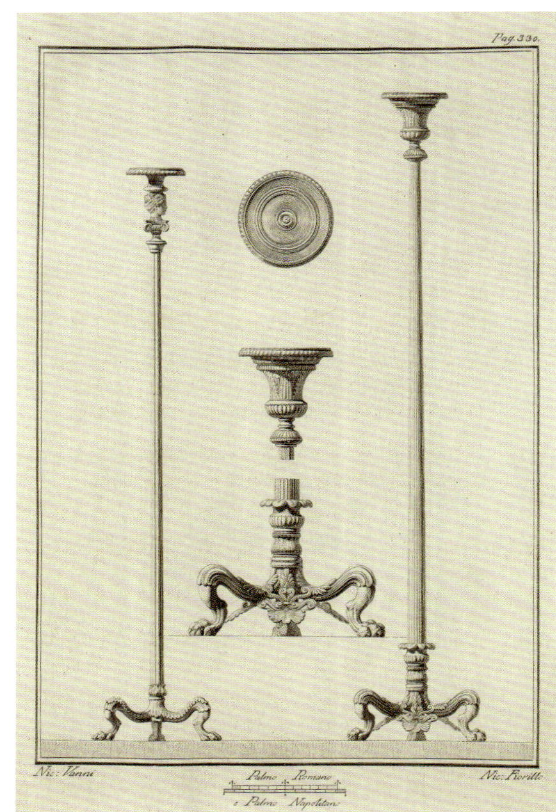

95
Candlestick, silver-gilt, London, 1787–8, maker's mark of Charles Aldrich. One of a set of four made for the collector and aesthete William Beckford (1760–1844), this candlestick is modelled on Roman lamp stands excavated at Herculaneum and illustrated in *Le Antichità de Ercolano Esposte*, vol. 8, published in 1782. As direct copies of ancient objects, they represent the purest form of classicism. *Lent by the Trustees of the Victoria and Albert Museum.* Cat. no. 44

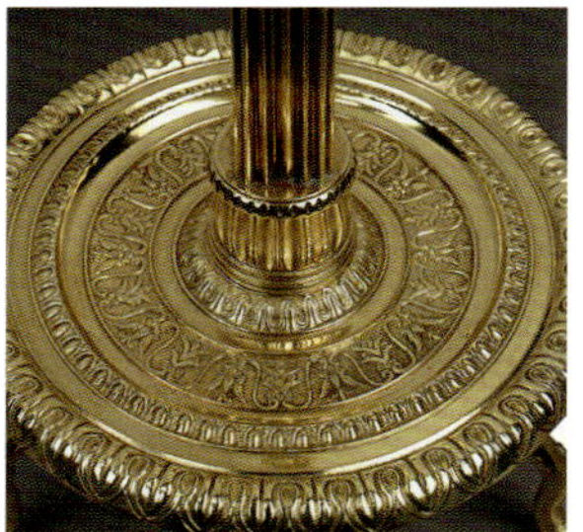

97
Detail of the base of fig. 95

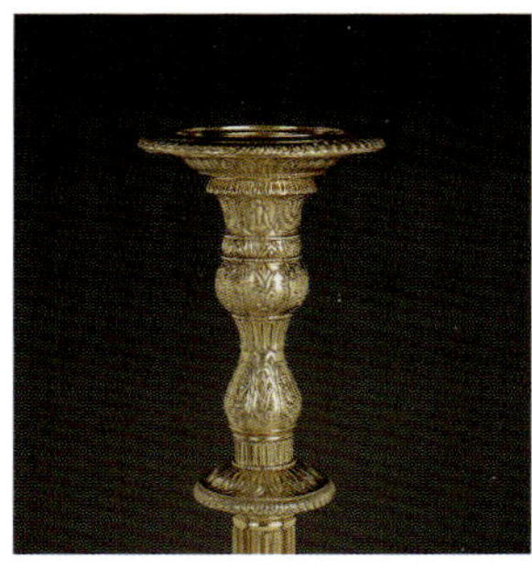

98
Detail of the nozzle of fig. 95

96
Design for a pair of Roman lamp stands, page 330 from *Le Antichità de Ercolano Esposte*, vol. 8, Naples, 1782. The Neopolitans jealously guarded the excavations at Herculaneum and forbad foreigners from entering the site, but this series of folios of engravings of excavated sculpture, vases and other objects was published during the 1770s and 80s. The prints provided an unprecedented opportunity for artists and craftsmen to copy ancient household objects. *The Syndics of Cambridge University Library*.

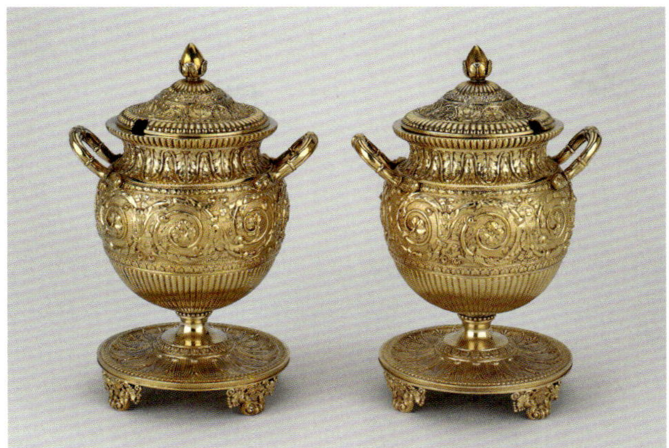

99

Pair of sugar vases, silver-gilt, London, 1814–5, maker's mark of Paul Storr for Rundell, Bridge & Rundell. A Roman marble funerary urn, formerly in the Lansdowne Collection, provided the model for these elegant sugar vases. Examples of the same form were also produced by Rundell & Bridge's other suppliers, Scott & Smith, as early as 1805. *Lent by the Alan and Simone Hartman Collection.*
Cat. no. 59

Silver versions of the Warwick Vase, the gigantic sculpture that was discovered at Hadrian's Villa in the 1760s, appeared from 1800 onwards. For the Royal Goldsmiths, Rundell, Bridge & Rundell, it proved to be one of their most enduring models. Piranesi's views of the original were used to make the early versions produced in their Dean Street workshop[2] but the Earl of Lonsdale's request for a life-size original in silver presented the firm with the opportunity to produce moulds which could be used to make silver reductions by casting rather than raising. Lonsdale's silver version was

100

Warwick Vase on stand, silver-gilt, London, 1814–5, maker's mark of Paul Storr for Rundell, Bridge & Rundell. According to Vivant Denon, "had the Emperor Buonaparte been successful in conquering England … the first note in his pocket-book was to possess himself of the marble vase at Warwick". Piranesi's etchings of the celebrated vase excavated in the grounds of Hadrian's villa enabled silversmiths to make reduced copies for use as presentation vases or wine coolers, but by 1814 cast reductions made from wax models of the vase itself were being produced by the firm. *Lent by the Trustees of the Rosalinde and Arthur Gilbert Collection on loan to the Victoria and Albert Museum.*
Cat. no. 60

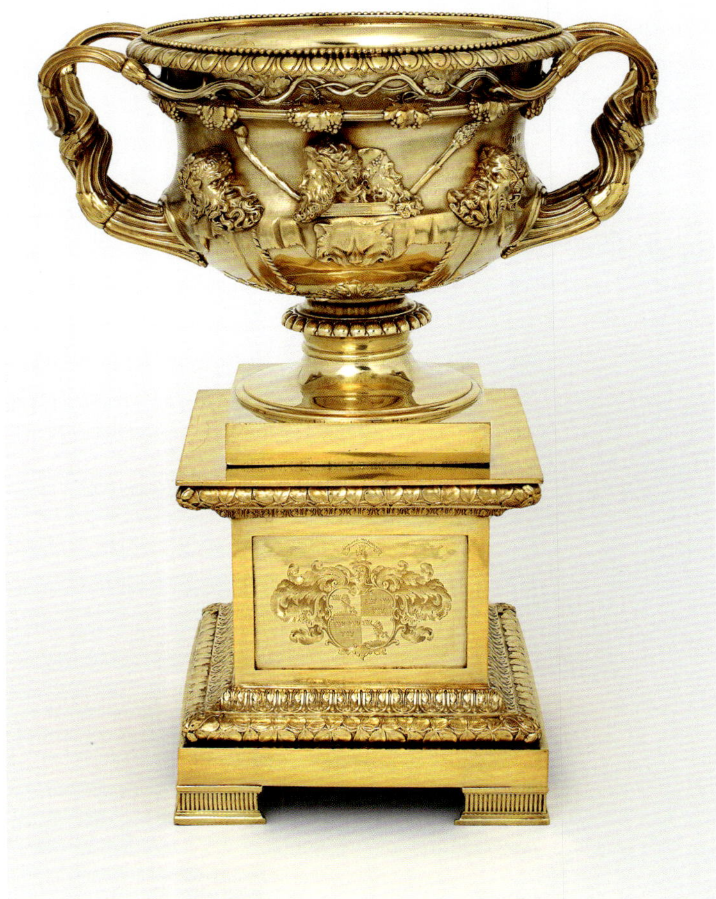

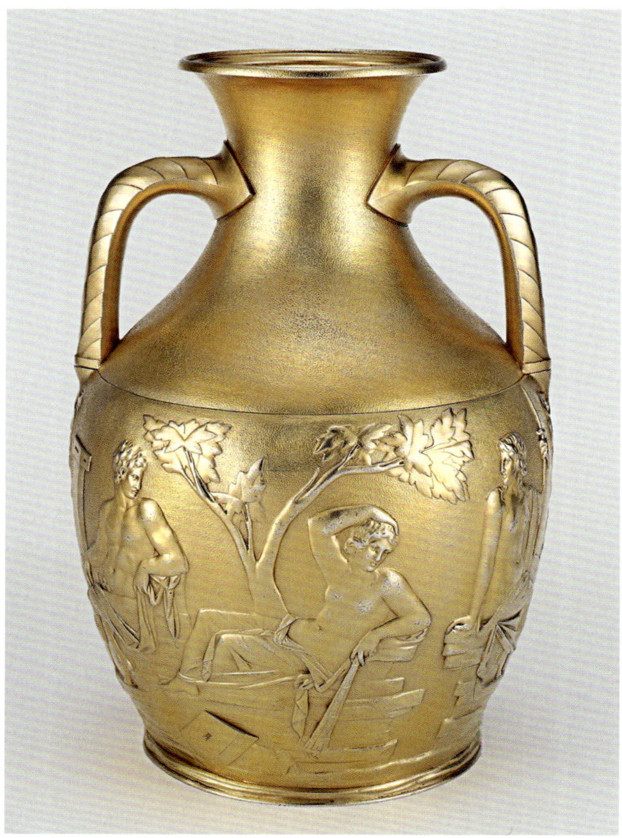

101
Portland Vase wine cooler, silver-gilt, London, 1823–4, maker's mark of Philip Rundell for Rundell, Bridge & Rundell. The Portland Vase, the celebrated Roman glass vase in the British Museum, was copied by Rundell's for use as a wine cooler. *Lent by Koopman Rare Art.*
Cat. no. 62

never produced, but the firm did produce life-size bronze casts of the vase. One stands in front of the Senate House in Cambridge while another, sold to George IV, is in the park at Windsor Castle.[3]

Virtually all of the great vases depicted by Piranesi were ultimately produced in silver as presentation pieces or wine coolers. The Buckingham Vase proved to be less popular than the Warwick Vase. Like most of the others it had come to England after its discovery. Piranesi's views provided the inspiration for several versions including a set of six made for the owner, the Marquess of Buckingham, in 1814, one presented to Sir Henry Russell in 1822[4] and another, which most faithfully reproduces the decoration on the original, used as the Doncaster Cup in 1828 (fig. 102).

Engravings of the Portland Vase had appeared as early as the 1760s but it was its presence in the British Museum, and the numerous ceramic versions of it made by Josiah Wedgwood, that had made this Roman cameo glass vase famous in England. A few exact-size copies were made by Rundell's in the 1820s, possibly using Wedgwood's moulds; the shoulder is removable to enable them to be used as wine coolers (fig. 101).

[1] The candlesticks were produced in the workshop of Charles Aldrich, a relatively little known silversmith who produced mostly small-scale works of high finish. A pen-and-wash drawing of a similar candlestick, possibly done to show the client (probably Beckford), is part of a group drawings, evidently from a major London retailer of the 1780s and 90s, in the Victoria and Albert Museum (M.8668.3). The identity of the retailer is unknown.
[2] The firm's silver workshop was at the time managed by Paul Storr, whose signature appeared on prints from Piranesi's *Vasi* which remained in his workshop premises through various changes of ownership until destroyed in an air raid in the 1940s (Grimwade, p. 672).
[3] Hartop, *Rundell*, p. 118.
[4] *Antiquity Unveiled: Masterworks, 1760–1840* (Koopman Rare Art, London, 2010), no. 34.

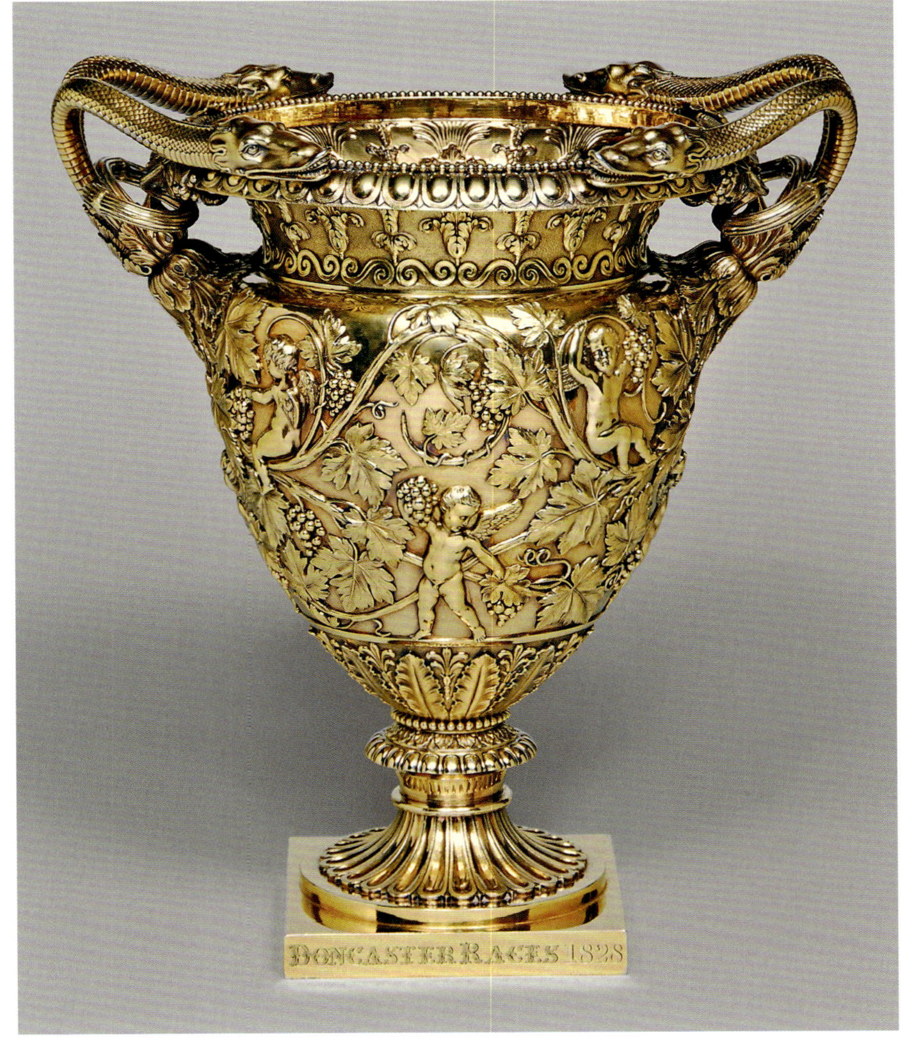

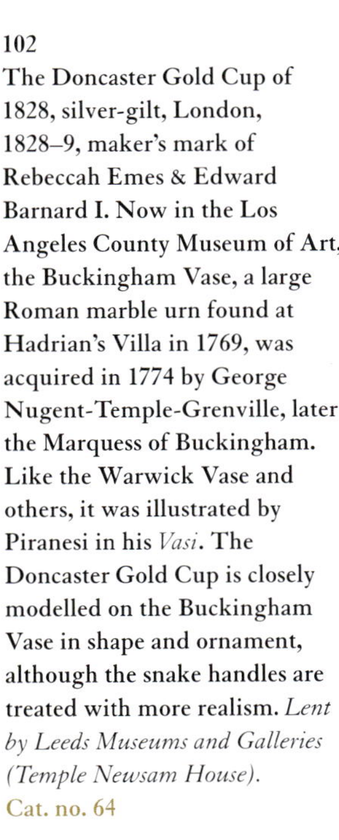

102

The Doncaster Gold Cup of 1828, silver-gilt, London, 1828–9, maker's mark of Rebeccah Emes & Edward Barnard I. Now in the Los Angeles County Museum of Art, the Buckingham Vase, a large Roman marble urn found at Hadrian's Villa in 1769, was acquired in 1774 by George Nugent-Temple-Grenville, later the Marquess of Buckingham. Like the Warwick Vase and others, it was illustrated by Piranesi in his *Vasi*. The Doncaster Gold Cup is closely modelled on the Buckingham Vase in shape and ornament, although the snake handles are treated with more realism. *Lent by Leeds Museums and Galleries (Temple Newsam House).*
Cat. no. 64

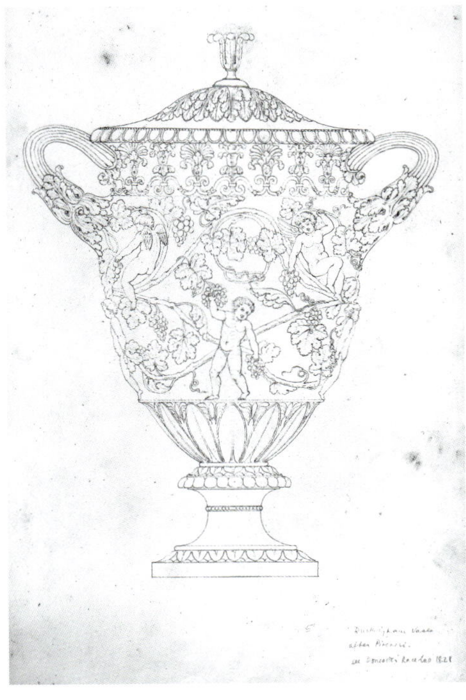

103

Drawing for a cup and cover, pencil and ink, c. 1814, anonymous. Part of a group of drawings from Rundell's, this adapts Piranesi's etching with a more practical form of handle for the vase to be used as a wine cooler. *V&A Images.*

VIII The imperial style

We live in an age obsessed with nomenclature; as we pigeonhole past fashions of style into a sequence of periods we run the danger of imagining some form of progression that may not be there. While "neo-classical" is an epithet that aptly describes the return to the antique, its succeeding tag, "Regency", offers us no such help. Among the adjectives that spring to mind when looking at silver of the first four decades of the nineteenth century are *heavy*, *massive* and *gilt*. But in the decorative arts there is no fault line dividing the eighteenth from the nineteenth century, and for craftsmen, designers and patrons no one dislodged the idea that the antique was the ideal. Yet just as in the 1750s and 60s there had been a groundswell of ideas of which a new style in art was just a small part, so, at the beginning of the new century, war in Europe helped galvanize and crystallize changing attitudes to what had gone before in the arts. In an age when the decorative arts expressed the attitudes of a nation, the rise of Napoleon saw a corresponding rise in British *amour propre* that expressed itself in a reaction against what were seen as the "sippets of embroidery" of the previous generation. The Palladian idea of creating a temple of the arts through which to return to a pastoral artistic ideal, discernible in Adam's arrangement of the dining-room apse at Kedleston (fig. 21), had been a dominant theme throughout the whole of the eighteenth century.

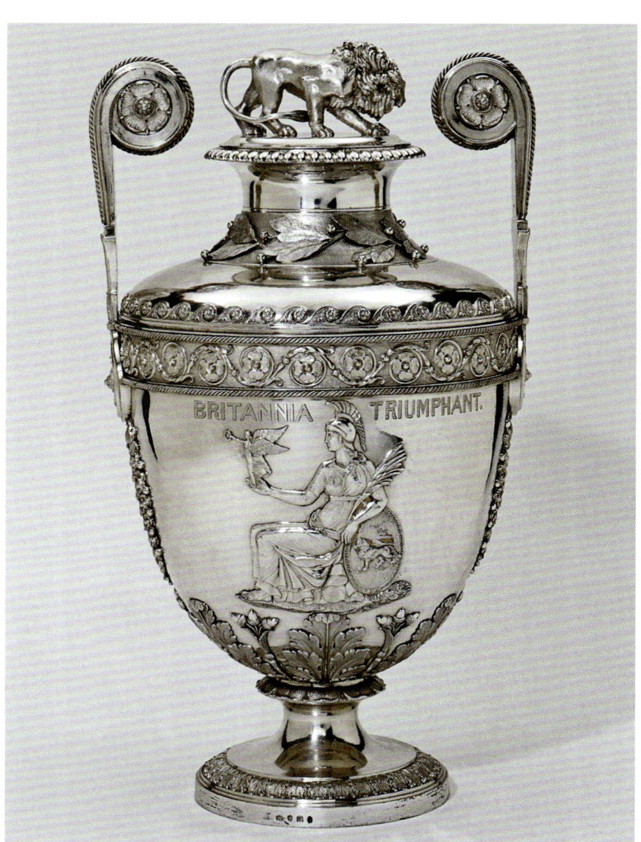

104
Trafalgar Vase, silver, London, 1805–6, maker's mark of Digby Scott & Benjamin Smith for Rundell, Bridge & Rundell. The competition for the design of a vase to be presented to eminent British officers during the Napoleonic Wars was won by John Shaw (*fl.* 1799–1851), an artist and architect. The sober form of the vase, modelled on a *krater*, did much to promote the new, "massive" style of plate.
Lent by the Trustees of the Victoria and Albert Museum.
Cat. no. 52

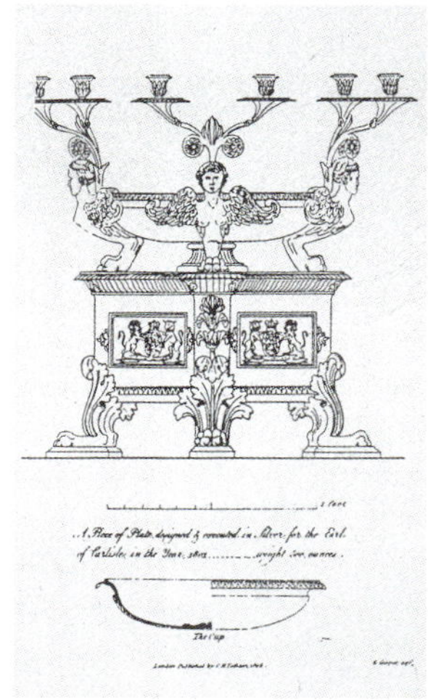

105

Design for a centrepiece, Charles Heathcote Tatham (1772–1842), engraving from *Designs for Ornamental Plate*, 1806. Tatham had declared that "Massiveness" was "the principal characteristic of good Plate".

106

Centrepiece, silver-gilt, glass, London, 1806–7, maker's mark of Philip Cornman for Rundell, Bridge & Rundell. Tatham based his models on ancient prototypes drawn at first hand in Italy. Grafted on to the Roman tripod form of this centrepiece are Egyptian features. *Lent by a private collector, courtesy of Philip Hewat-Jaboor*.

Cat. no. 54

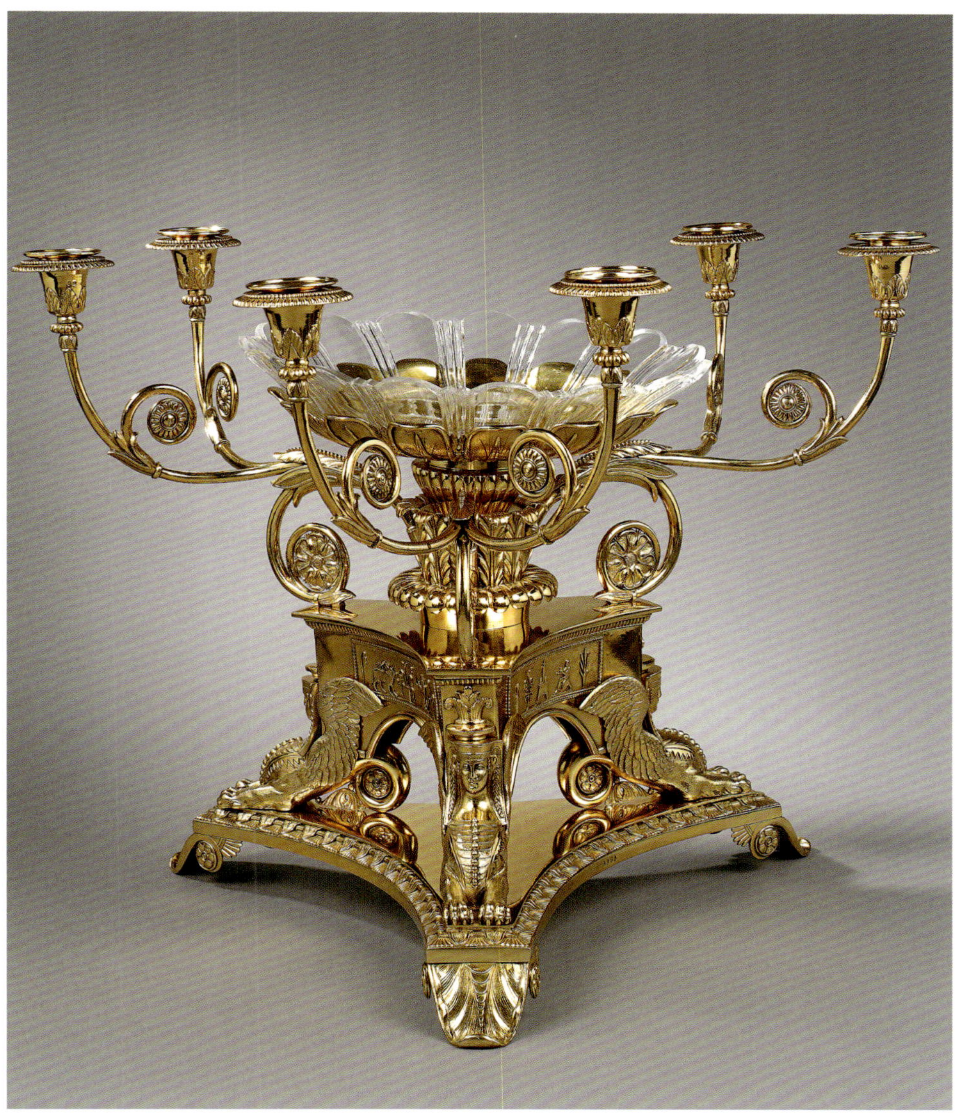

Now it was yielding to new aspirations. The decorative arts of the beginning of the nineteenth century were confident, triumphant and often militaristic. To this was added the somewhat incongruous new goal of comfort (a theme seldom addressed in the previous century), caused in part by burgeoning prosperity and a corresponding broadening of the consumer base. Instead of a return to Arcady, the decorative arts stated a prosperous, well-appointed, imperial Britain modelled on imperial Rome.

We would be mistaken, however, to dub this new style the bastard child of neo-classicism, in the same way as Hugh Honour described the Empire style. It is still neo-classicism, working within the framework of the classical rules and using the classical vocabulary, although the range of ornament continues to increase with the growth in

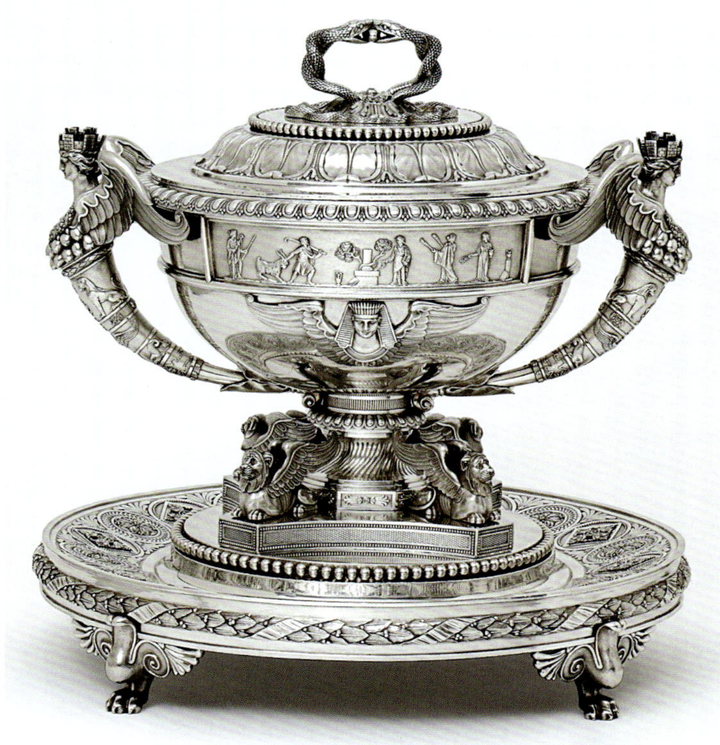

107
Soup tureen, cover and stand,
silver, London, 1806–7, maker's
mark of Digby Scott &
Benjamin Smith for Rundell,
Bridge & Rundell. Piranesi had
been largely responsible for
Égyptiennerie, which was, as
Hugh Honour observed, to
neo-classicism what *Chinoiserie*
had been to the rococo style. It
was, however, the publication
of Denon's views of Egyptian
monuments in 1802 that
provided designers such as
Jean-Jacques Boileau with the
style's vocabulary of ornament.
*Lent by the Rosalinde and Arthur
Gilbert Collection on loan to the
Victoria and Albert Museum.*
Cat. no. 55

illustrated reference books, and men such as Thomas Hope look further back to Greece, and to Egypt, for new forms and motifs.

In silver, new fortunes made from the Napoleonic wars, and the fashion for presenting military heroes with monumental vases (fig. 104) and dinner services, brought about a tremendous expansion of the trade. The architect Charles Heathcote Tatham, in an oft-quoted statement, railed against "light and insignificant forms", declaring that "massiveness" was "the principal characteristic of good Plate" (figs. 105–6).[1] All of this required large numbers of specialist craftsmen and a high degree of mechanization, as well as almost endless resources. The result was the emergence of a handful of major retailers who dominated the artistic as well as the business side. Rundell, Bridge & Rundell[2] towered above their rivals, Jefferys & Jones,[3] Garrard & Co.,[4] and Green, Ward & Green.[5]

Besides unlimited financial resources Rundell's needed access to the best craftsmen and designers in order to supply their clients with silver, ormolu, jewellery and decorations. About 1802, they cleverly solved the problem of piracy of designs by establishing their own workshop headed by Digby Scott & Benjamin Smith II in Greenwich. Smith was a silversmith who had worked for Matthew Boulton in Birmingham; Scott's role seems to have been as head designer. The Greenwich workshop apparently continued until about 1814, but in 1807 Paul Storr, who had already been working for the Rundell's, joined the firm and ran another workshop for them in Dean Street, Soho. Storr left the firm in 1819 but the firm's workshop continued there until the 1830s. The capital investment must have been considerable, for silversmithing in the new imperial style required more than mechanization, it

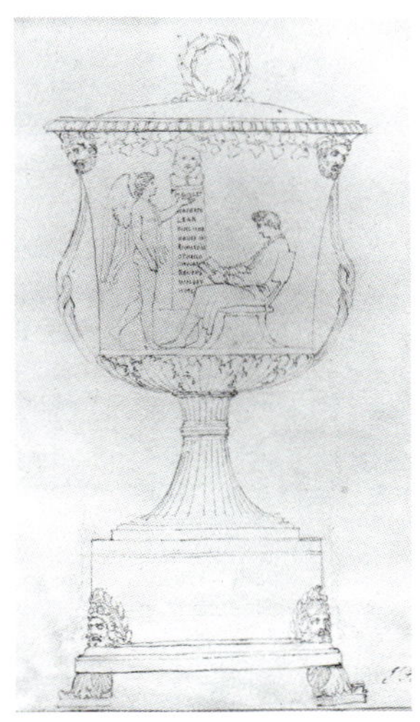

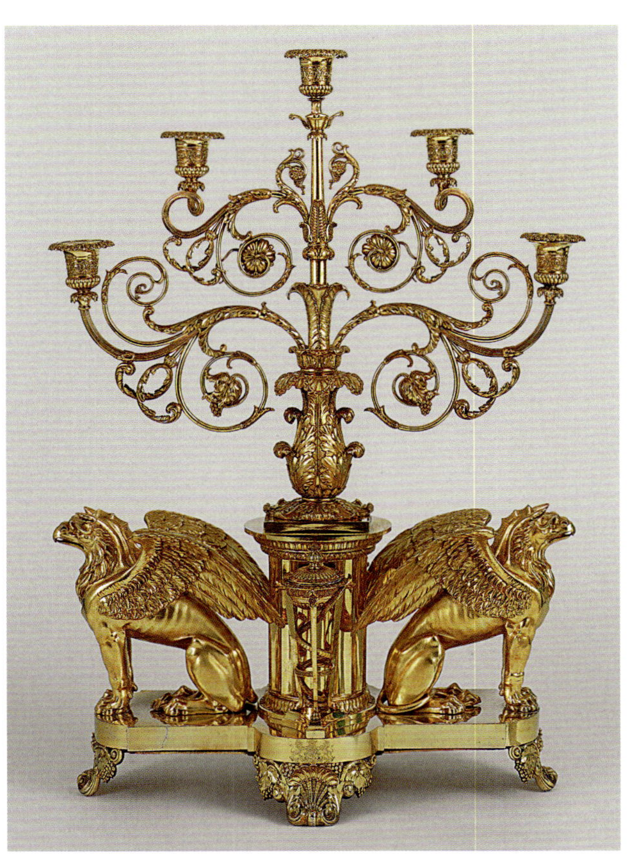

108
Drawing of the Kemble Cup, pen and pencil, c. 1817, after John Flaxman (1755–1826), from an album of drawings compiled by John Gawler Bridge. Flaxman designed the cup, presented to the actor John Kemble in 1817, and also modelled the plaques applied to each side. Flaxman supplied designs to Rundell's from about 1805 onwards. The present whereabouts of the cup are unknown but plaster casts of the two plaques are in Sir John Soane's Museum. *The Metropolitan Museum of Art, New York*.

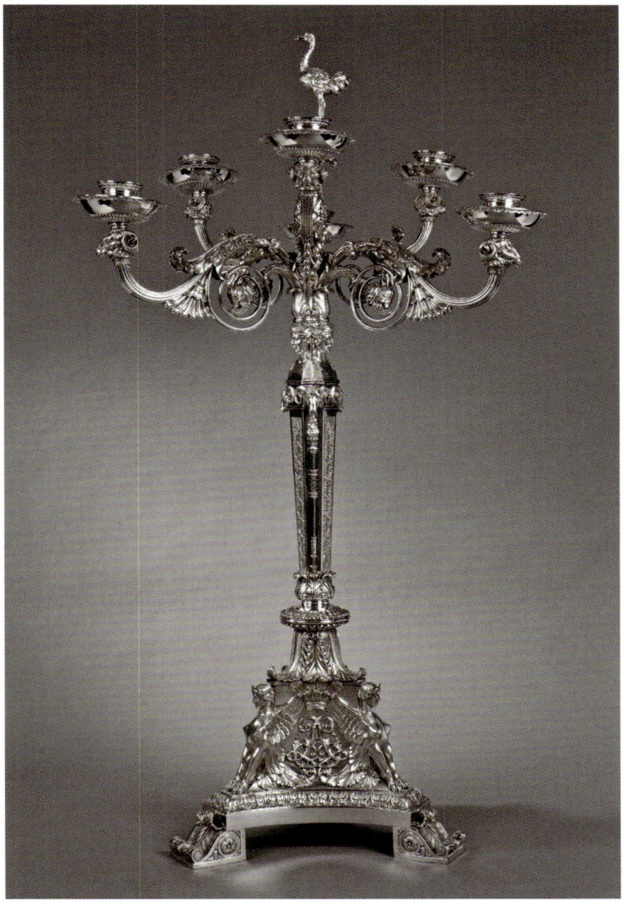

109
Six-light candelabrum, silver, London, 1811–2, maker's mark of Paul Storr for Rundell, Bridge & Rundell. One of a set made as additions to the Holkham Service, this candelabrum shows how the classical vocabulary had dramatically increased in the intervening thirty-five years. *Lent by Viscount Coke and the Trustees of the Holkham Estate.* Cat. no. 56

110
Five-light candelabrum, silver-gilt, London, c. 1812–1820, maker's mark of Paul Storr for Rundell, Bridge & Rundell. This candelabrum is one of pair which appears to have started life as a "superb Ornamental piece of Plate to receive a Dish or Basket for the Sideboard, or Centre of the Table, composed of four Griffins winged on a richly chased Base with Lamp in Centre". The centrepiece was subsequently made into two candelabra. Griffins appear as early as 1759 in James "Athenian" Stuart's drawings, but the ones used on this candelabrum appear to derive from Charles Heathcote Tatham's engraving of an "Antique fragment of a table foot" in the Vatican, published in 1799. *Lent by Her Majesty The Queen.* Cat. no. 57

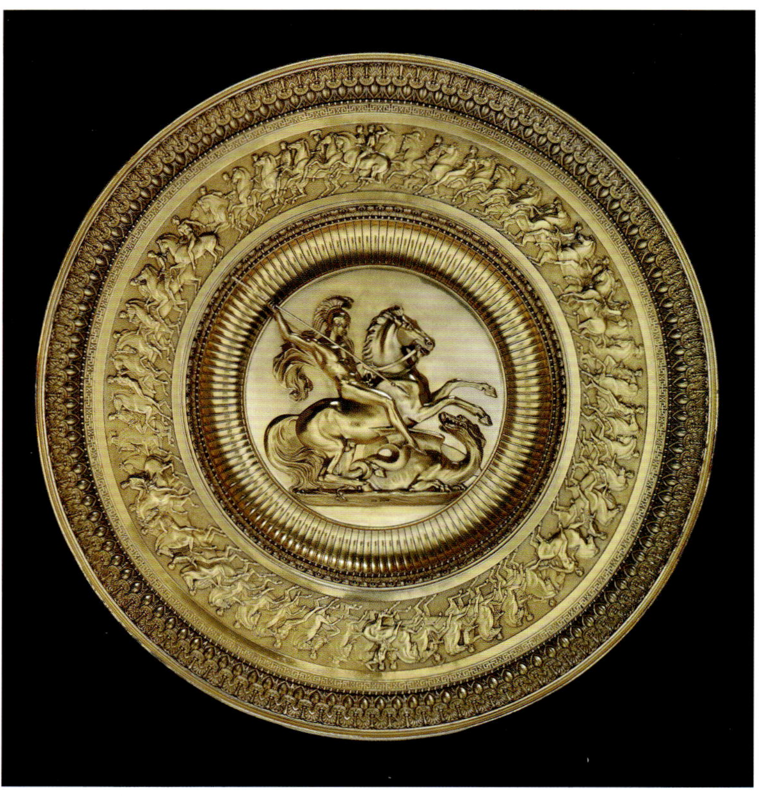

111
Sideboard dish, silver-gilt, London,
1822–3, maker's mark of Philip
Rundell for Rundell, Bridge &
Rundell, from a design by
Benedetto Pistrucci (1784–1855),
an Italian cameo carver who arrived
in 1815. His St George is clearly
influenced by the Elgin Marbles,
while the border directly copies the
frieze. *Lent by the Trustees of the
Victoria and Albert Museum*.
Cat. no. 61

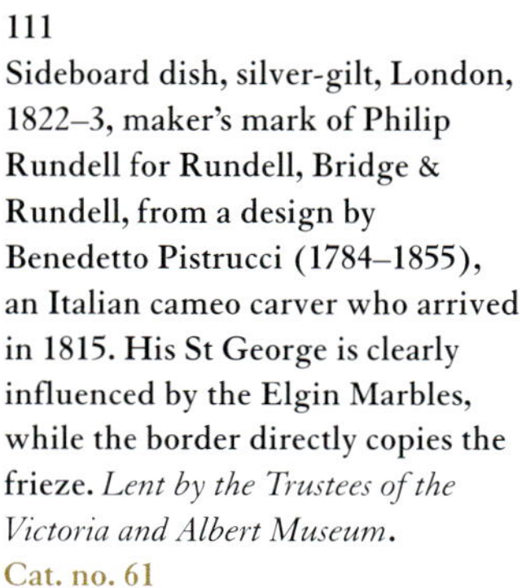

112
Four-light candelabrum, silver-
gilt, London, 1829–30, maker's
mark of John Bridge for
Rundell, Bridge & Rundell. One
of a set of sixteen which were
copied from ormolu examples
purchased by the Prince Regent
in 1811 which in turn were
copies of examples belonging to
the Marquess of Hertford.
Hertford's candelabra were
probably French. They show
the emergence of a picturesque
element in French neo-
classicism at the end of the
eighteenth century. *Lent by Her
Majesty The Queen*.
Cat. no. 63

needed ambitious casting facilities as well. In addition to their two workshops,
Rundell's also bought in silver from specialist outworkers such as the Pitts family and
Philip Cornman.

Rundell's investment in design was no less impressive. The firm could call on a
stable of accomplished artists such as Jean-Jacques Boileau (fig. 107) and John Flaxman
(fig. 108) to provide designs as needed, which were then translated into working
drawings. In time Edward Hodges Baily came to head their design studio. Later, John
Gawler Bridge, another partner in the firm and himself an accomplished artist, would
direct the design side of the business. Modelling was carried out by artists under the
direction of the sculptor Willliam Theed.

Boileau can be credited with silver in the Egyptian style produced by both of
Rundell's workshops during the first decade of the century. Many of the motifs come
from the etchings of Piranesi, but it was the appearance of Vivant Denon's book of
Egyptian scenes published in 1802 that gave the style an impetus. Tatham, in his

designs for tripod centrepieces (figs. 105–6) often mixed Roman features, such as heavy acanthus leaves, with Egyptian decoration.

The greatest boost to the spread of the imperial style, and to Rundell's dominance, was given by the Prince Regent. He was by far the firm's biggest client, spending over £250,000 with them over a ten-year period. Curiously, Rundell's took the lead in promoting new designs rather than the prince. Often the firm produced a new design and sold the first examples they made to other clients before the prince commissioned his own version.

The griffin candelabrum (fig. 110), one of a pair, shows how effective the theatricality as well as the monumentality of the imperial style could be. Alongside this florid, almost baroque, grandeur can be set far more archaeologically pure works such as the dish (fig. 111) with a central plaque designed by Benedetto Pistrucci. Although the imperial style retained its supremacy until well into the 1820s, the naturalism of the rococo was revived as early as 1804 in a pair of soup tureens sold by Garrard's. Led by the Prince Regent, the antiquarian movement inspired copies and adaptations from all centuries. Gothic cups and Caroline dishes as well as extravagant rococo works all competed with copies of the Portland and Buckingham Vases. The rules which had underpinned the classical movement in the previous century were increasingly ignored, leaving it to be a romantic evocation just like all the other revived styles and periods. But classicism had only loosened its grip; it would live on as a recurring theme to the present day.

[1] Preface to *Designs for Ornamental Plate many of which have been executed in silver from original drawings* (London, 1806).
[2] Pickett & Rundell 1769–1786, Rundell & Bridge 1787–1804, Rundell, Bridge & Rundell 1804–1834, Rundell, Bridge & Co. 1834–1843.
[3] Jefferys & Jones 1779–1793, Jefferys, Jones & Gilbert 1796–1798, Jefferys & Gilbert 1798–after 1800.
[4] Parker & Wakelin 1760–1776, Wakelin & Tayler 1776–1792, Wakelin & Garrard 1792–1805, Garrard & Co. 1805 to the present date.
[5] Green & Ward 1789–1804, Green, Ward & Green 1804–c. 1818.

113
Inkstand, silver, glass, London, 1833, maker's mark of John Bridge for Rundell, Bridge & Rundell. The form is based on a Greek stemless *kylix*, with delicate flat chased decoration of palmettes. The winged cherub on the cover, however, gives the composition a whiff of romanticism. John Gawler Bridge, a partner in the firm and a skilled artist in his own right, may have designed this. *Lent by a private collector.* Cat. no. 65

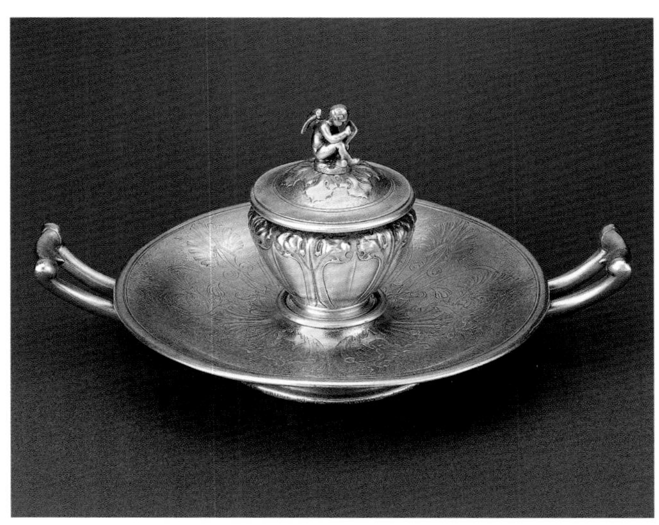

1

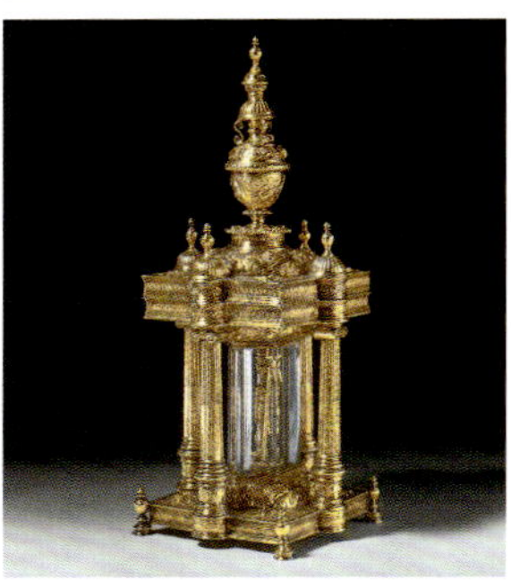

The Gibbon Salt of the Worshipful Company of Goldsmiths
Silver, silver-gilt, rock crystal
Marks: London, 1576–7
Maker's mark: Three trefoils
Jackson, p. 99, line 14
Inscription: "The giuft of Simon Gibbon, Goldsmith, 1632"
Provenance: Presented to the Company by Simon Gibbon in 1632
Published: Jackson, *History*, plate opposite p. 173 and figs. 193–4; Carrington and Hughes, pp. 37–9; Glanville, *Tudor*, fig. 171
H. 12 in. (30.5 cm)
W. 5 in. (12.9 cm)
D. 4 ⅞ in. (12.7 cm)
Wt. 57 oz. 4 dwt. (1779 g)
An electrotype copy of the salt is exhibited, lent by the Trustees of the Victoria and Albert Museum

2

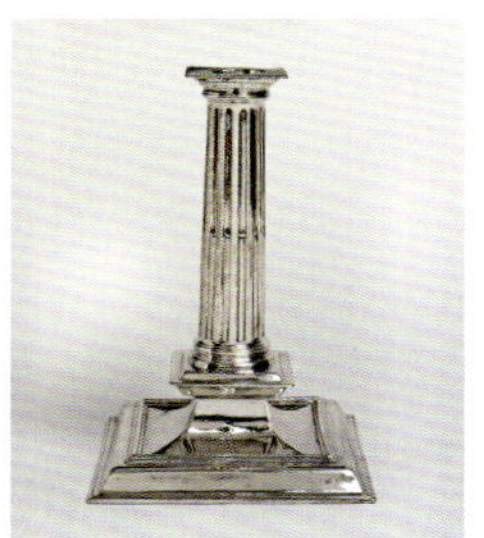

Candlestick
Silver
Marks: London, c. 1682
Maker's mark: RM or RA in monogram
Jackson. p. 134, line 6
Published: Oman, plate 78

H. 7 ⅛ in. (18.1 cm)
W. 5 in. (12.5 cm)
D. 5 in. (12.5 cm)
Wt. 10 oz. 6 dwt. (321.1 g)
Accession no.: M.562-1911
Lent by the Trustees of the Victoria and Albert Museum

3

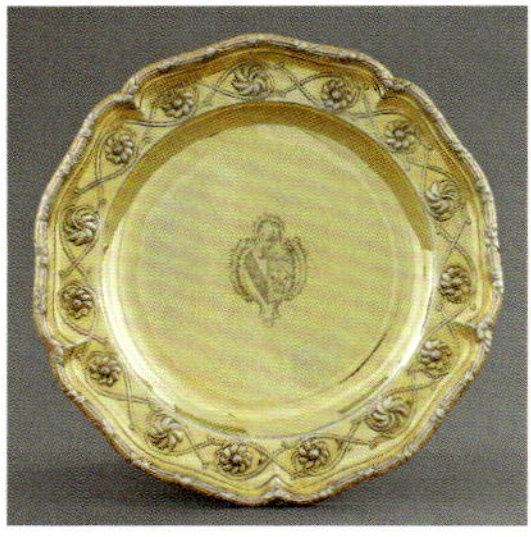

Dessert plate
Silver-gilt
Marks: London, 1758–9
Maker's mark: William Cripps for Phillips Garden
Grimwade, no. 3056
Provenance: Sir Nathaniel Curzon, 5th Bt. and (1761) 1st Baron Scarsdale (1726–1804), by descent to Francis Curzon, 3rd Viscount Scarsdale, the National Trust
Diam. 9 ¾ in. (25 cm)
Wt. 19 oz. 10 dwt. (606 g)
Lent by the National Trust, Kedleston Hall, the Scarsdale Collection (acquired with the help of the National Heritage Memorial Fund and transferred to the National Trust in 1987)

4

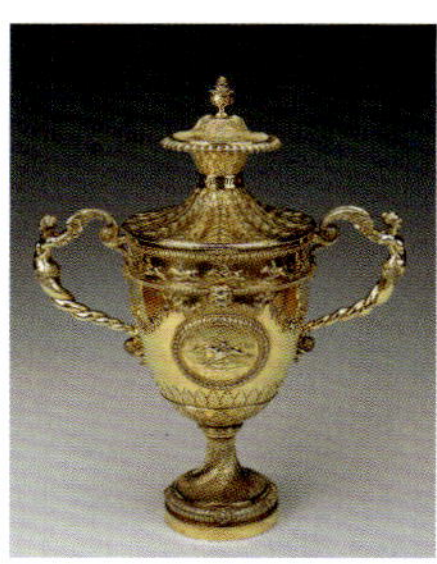

Cup and cover
Silver-gilt
Marks: London, 1764–5

Maker's mark: Daniel Smith & Robert Sharp
Grimwade, no. 3523
Design: Robert Adam (1728–1792)
Inscription: Engraved on cover flange: "HUGH PERCY EARL OF NORTHUMBERLAND LORD LIEUTENANT GENERAL AND GENERAL GOVERNOR OF IRELAND 1764"; on the front elliptical cartouche: "TO THE BEST IN IRELAND"
Provenance: Huttleston Broughton, 1st Lord Fairhaven (1896–1966), bequeathed to the National Trust
Exhibited: Cambridge, 1975, no. 2H11
Published: Crighton, p. 43, 2H11; Ellis, p. 324
H. 19 in. (48 cm)
W. 16 in. (41 cm)
D. 8 ¼ in. (21 cm)
Wt. 142 oz. (4416 g)
Lent by the National Trust, Anglesey Abbey, the Fairhaven Collection

5

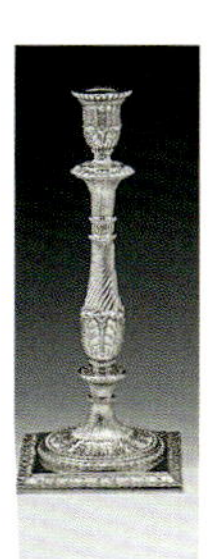

Candlestick
Silver
Marks: London, 1767–8
Maker's mark: John Carter II
Grimwade, no. 1214
Design: Robert Adam (1728–1792)
Inscription: Engraved under base "No. 7"
Heraldry: Engraved crest of Phillips of Picton Castle, Dyfed, Wales
Provenance: Picton Castle, Dyfed; Harrods Silver Department, 1915; Dr H.F. Marshall DSC; sale, Christie's, London, 19 June 1963, lot 152 (a pair)
Exhibited: London, 1972;

Washington DC, 1976; New York, 1982
Published: *Leeds Arts Calendar*, no. 53 (1064), pp. 2–3; Rowe, p. 37, plate 10, 11a and b; Beard, pp. 66, 228; Fergusson, pp. 752–4, fig. 58; Lomax, pp. 158–60, no. 175
H. 13 ¹³⁄₁₆ in. (35.1 cm)
Wt. 37 oz. 6 dwt. (1160 g)
Accession no.: 9/63
Lent by Leeds Museums and Galleries (Temple Newsam House)

6

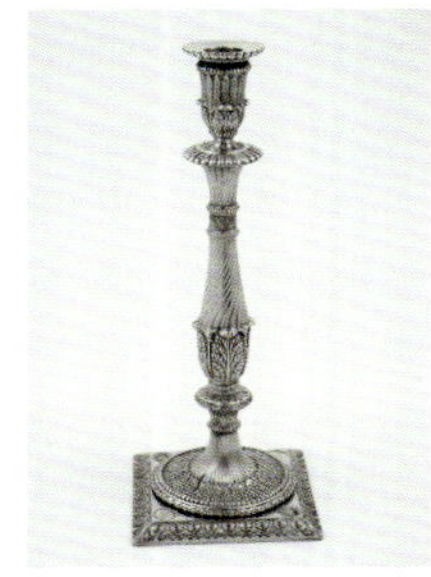

Candlestick
Silver
Marks: London, 1767–8
Maker's mark: David Whyte & William Holmes
Grimwade, no. 3526
Design: Robert Adam (1728–1792)
H. 13 ¹³⁄₁₆ in. (35.1 cm)
Accession no.: 1984.36/4
Lent by Manchester City Galleries

7

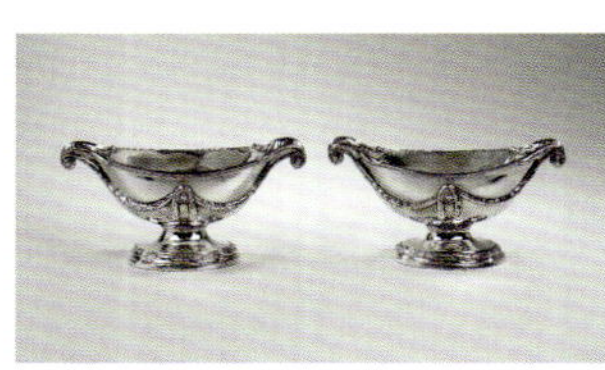

Pair of sauce boats
Silver
Marks: London, 1768–9
Maker's mark: John Parker & Edward Wakelin, made by James Ansill & Stephen Gilbert
Grimwade, no. 1602
Design: John Yenn (1750–1821) after Sir William Chambers (1723–1796)

Heraldry: Later engraved crest of Churchill
Provenance: George, 4th Duke of Marlborough (1738–1817), by descent to John, 10th Duke of Marlborough; Christie's, London, 12 July 1989, lot 157 (a set of six)
Published: Young, "Chambers", pp. 31–5; Young, "Marlborough", pp. 396–400; Harris and Snodin, p. 152
H. 4 ¾ in. (12 cm)
W. 9 ½ in. (24 cm)
D. 4 ½ in. (11.4 cm)
Wt. 57 oz. (1772 g)
Lent by Koopman Rare Art

8

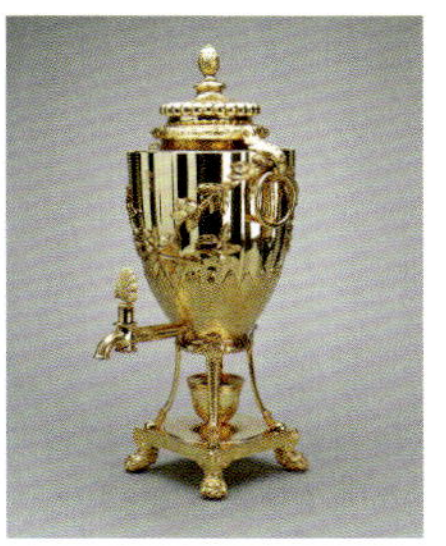

Tea urn
Silver-gilt
Marks: London, 1768–9
Maker's mark: Thomas Heming
Grimwade, no. 3828
Heraldry: Engraved cipher and crown of Queen Charlotte
Provenance: Queen Charlotte (1744–1818), consort of George III
Exhibited: London, 2004, no. 371
Published: Garrard, 1914, no. 306; Roberts, no. 371, p. 331
H. 20 in. (51 cm)
W. 10 ¼ in. (26 cm)
D. 9 ½ in. (24 cm)
Wt. 149 oz. 15 dwt. (4657 g)
Inventory no.: RCIN 49823
Lent by Her Majesty The Queen

9

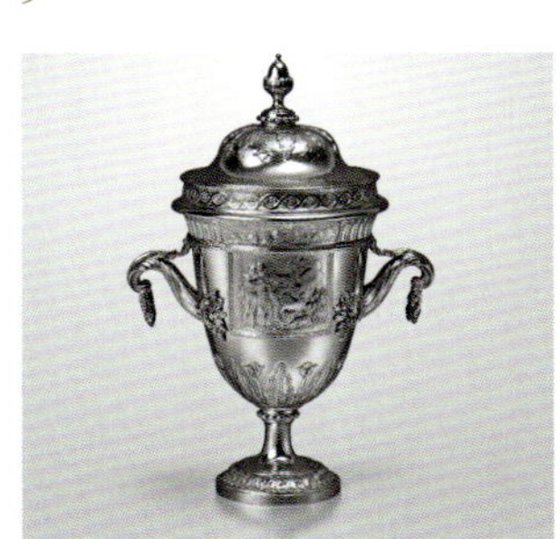

Cup and cover
Silver
Marks: London, 1770–1
Maker's mark: Louisa Courtauld & George Cowles

Grimwade, no. 1907
Design: Possibly by William Chambers (1723–1796)
Published: Hayward, p. 59, plate 32; Harris and Snodin, p. 153, fig. 227; Braham, p. 47, no. B10
H. 11 ¾ in (29.5 cm)
W. 8 ¼ in. (21 cm)
D. 5 ¾ in. (14.7 cm)
Wt. 50 oz. 8 dwt. (1567 g)
Accession no.: LO.1990.CS.1009
Lent by the Azko Nobel Corporation, on loan to the Courtauld Institute of Art

10

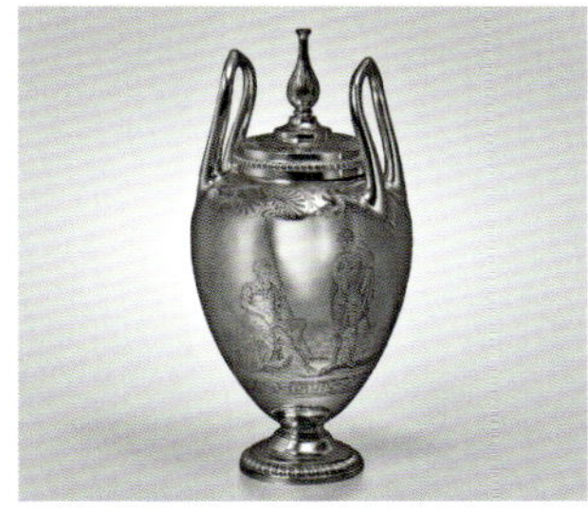

Condiment vase
Silver
Marks: London, 1771–2
Maker's mark: Louisa Courtauld & George Cowles
Grimwade, no. 1907
Heraldry: Engraved arms of Charles Birch (d. 1780) of Woodford, Essex, and his wife Sarah Creed
Exhibited: London, 1985, no. 28
Published: Hayward, p. 60, plate 33; Hatfield, p. 16; *Courtauld*, no. 28; Braham, p. 44, no. D3
H. 7 ½ in. (19.3 cm)
Diam. 3 ¾ in. (9.6 cm)
Wt. 13 oz. 2 dwt. (407 g)
Accession no.: LO.1990.CS.2901
Lent by the Azko Nobel Corporation Collection, on loan to the Courtauld Institute of Art

11

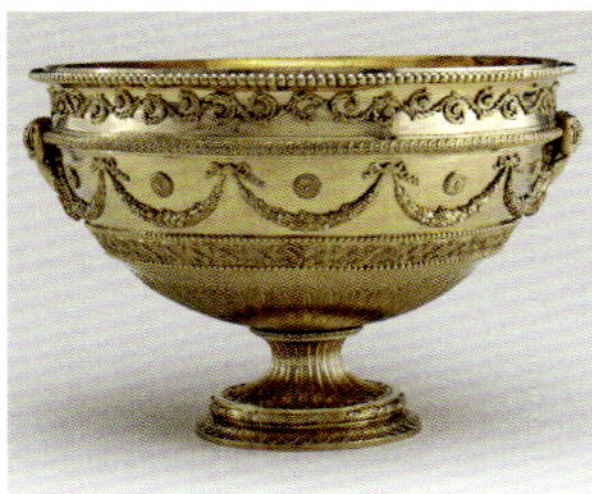

Punch-bowl
Silver-gilt
Marks: London, 1771–2
Maker's mark: Thomas Heming

Grimwade, no. 3828
Design: Robert Adam (1728–1792)
Inscription: "Chester Plate Won by Fop in the years 1769 and 1770"
Heraldry: Sir Watkin Williams-Wynn, 4th Bt.
Provenance: Sir Watkin Williams-Wynn, 4th Bt., by descent to Sir Watkin Williams-Wynn, 8th Bt., sale, Sotheby's, London, 10 October 1946; anonymous sale, Sotheby's, London, 18 May 1967, lot 102
Published: Hughes, "Punch", p. 646; Brett, no. 990; Fairclough, p. 377, fig. 24
H. 10 ¼ in. (26.2 cm)
Diam. 15 ¾ in. (40 cm)
Wt. 194 oz. 19 dwt. (6062 g)
Accession no.: NMWA 50455
Lent by Amgueddfa Cymru – National Museum Wales

12

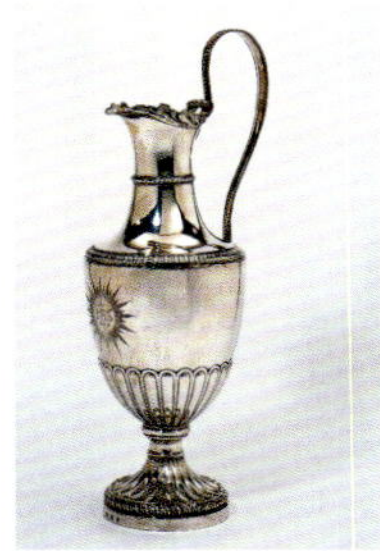

Communion flagon
Silver
Marks: Birmingham, 1773–4
Maker's mark: Matthew Boulton & John Fothergill
Jones, p. 357, col. 2, no. 3
Design: Possibly by James Wyatt (1746–1813)
Provenance: Given by the Earl of Hertford to the parishes of Sudborne and Orford, Suffolk
Published: Hopper, p. 49
H. 15 in. (38 cm)
Accession no.: Loan: OrfordPCC.1-2005
Lent by St Bartholomew's Church, Orford, Suffolk, on loan to the Victoria and Albert Museum

13

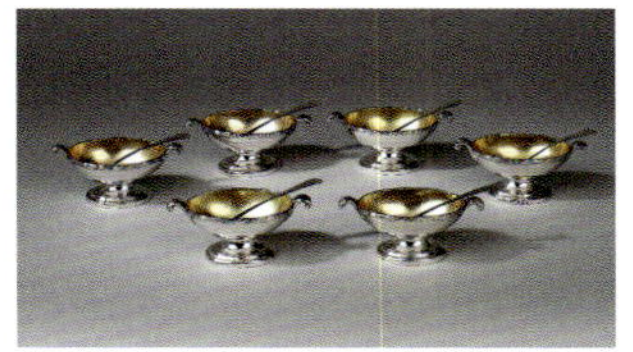

Six salts
Silver
Marks: Birmingham, 1773–4

Maker's mark: Matthew Boulton & John Fothergill
Jones, p. 357, col. 2, no. 3
Heraldry: Engraved crest of a martlet
H. 2 in. (5 cm)
W. 4 ¾ in. (12 cm)
D. 2 ½ in. (6.5 cm)
Lent by a private collector

14

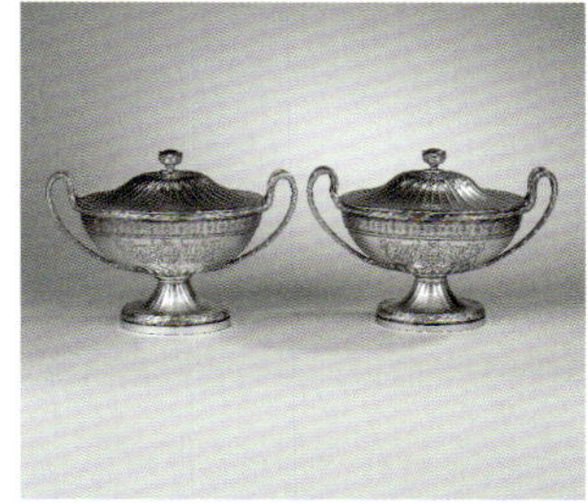

Pair of sauce tureens and covers
Silver
Marks: Birmingham, 1773–4
Maker's mark: Matthew Boulton & John Fothergill
Jones, p. 357, col. 2, no. 3
Design: possibly by James Wyatt (1746–1813)
Heraldry: Engraved arms of Vere impaling those of Lucas, as borne by Charles Vere, who married Martha Lucas on 4 June 1771
H. 6 ¾ in. (17.2 cm)
W. 9 ½ in. (24 cm)
D. 5 ¼ in. (13.2 cm)
Wt. 50 oz. (1555 g)
Lent by a private collector

15

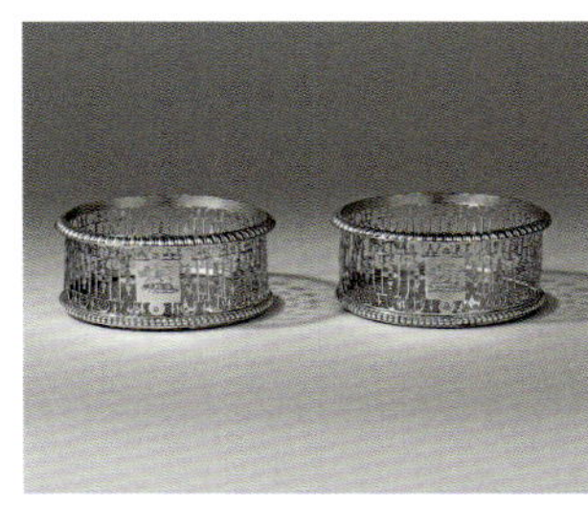

Pair of wine coasters
Silver, fruitwood, felt
Marks: Birmingham, 1773–4
Maker's mark: Matthew Boulton & John Fothergill
Jones, p. 357, col. 2, no. 3
Heraldry: Engraved crest of Vere, as borne by Charles Vere who married Martha Lucas on 4 June 1771
H. 2 in. (5 cm)
Diam. 4 ⅞ in. (12.5 cm)
Lent by a private collector

16

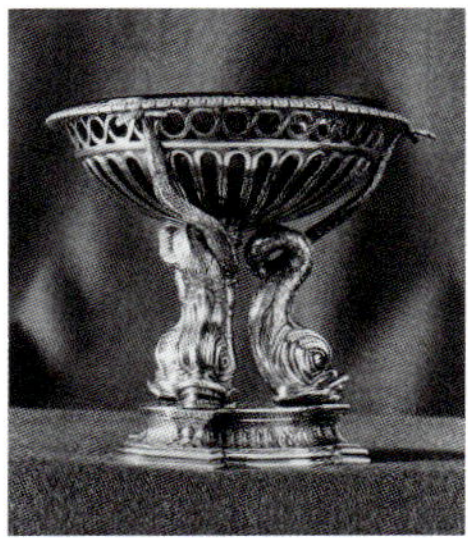

Pair of salts
Silver, glass
Marks: London, 1773–4 and 1774–5
Maker's mark: Probably John Carter
II for Joseph Creswell
Grimwade, no. 1214
Design: Robert Adam (1728–1792)
Heraldry: Engraved arms of Sir
Watkin Williams-Wynn, Bt.
Provenance: Sir Watkin Williams-
Wynn, 4th Bt., of Wynnstay, Wales,
by descent to Sir Watkin Williams-
Wynn, 8th Bt., sale, Sotheby's,
London, 10 October 1946, (a set of
six); Christie's, London, 11 March
1959, lot 172 (a set of six); a pair
acquired by Nottingham Castle
Museum in 1968
Published: Fairclough, p. 84, fig. 38
Diam. 4 ¼ in. (10.7 cm)
Accession no.: NCM 1968–107
Lent by Nottingham Castle
Museum

17

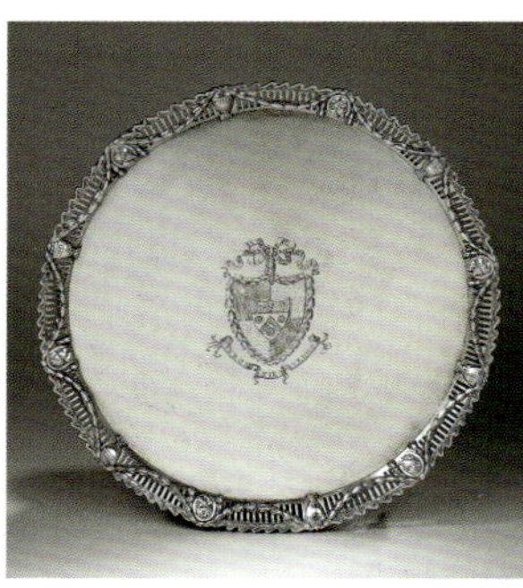

Salver
Silver
Marks: London, 1773–4
Maker's mark: John Carter II
Grimwade, no. 1214
Heraldry: Engraved arms of Vere
impaling those of Lucas, as borne by
Charles Vere, who married Martha
Lucas on 4 June 1771
H. 12 in. (30.5 cm)
Diam. 16 in. (40.5 cm)
Wt. 65 oz. (2021 g)
Lent by a private collector

18

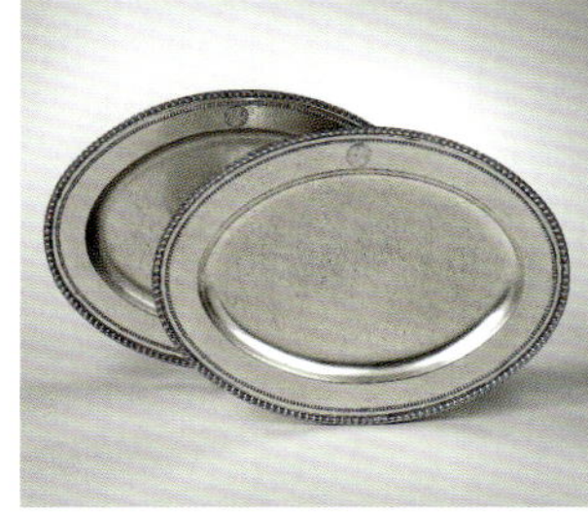

Pair of meat dishes
Silver
Marks: London, 1773–4
Maker's mark: Probably John
Carter II for Joseph Creswell
Grimwade, no. 1214
Design: Robert Adam (1728–1792)
Heraldry: Engraved arms of Sir
Watkin Williams-Wynn, Bt.
Provenance: Sir Watkin Williams-
Wynn, 4th Bt., of Wynnstay, Wales,
by descent to Sir Watkin Williams-
Wynn, 8th Bt., sale, Sotheby's,
London, 10 October 1946
H. 1 in. (2.4 cm)
W. 18 in. (46 cm)
Wt. 134 oz. (4152 g)
Lent by a private collector

19

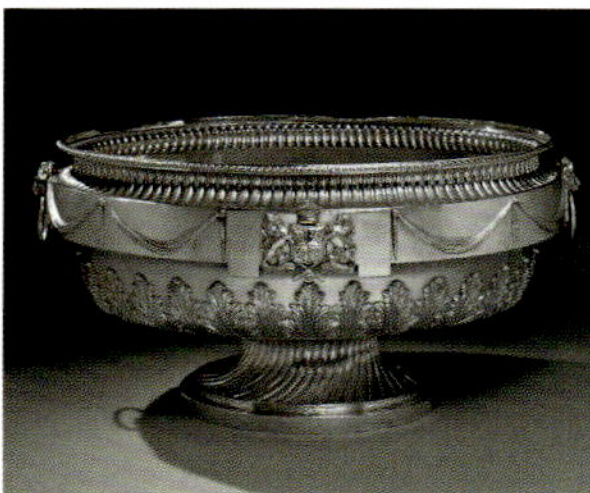

Wine cistern
Silver
Marks: London, 1773–4
Maker's mark: Daniel Smith &
Robert Sharp
Grimwade, no. 506
Heraldry: Applied arms of
Primrose quartering those of
Cressy, for Neil, 3rd Earl of
Rosebery (1729–1814)
Provenance: Neil, 3rd Earl of
Rosebery (1729–1814); Property of a
Gentleman, sale, Sotheby's, London,
10 March 1977, lot 205
Exhibited: Sydney, Australia, 1980,
no. 10; London, 1989, no. 105
Published: Penzer, "Wine Coolers";
Hawkins, *Masterpieces*, p. 36, no. 10;
Hawkins, *Al Tajir*, vol. I, pp. 72–3;
Brett, no. 1013, Truman, p. 143, no.
105
W. 34 in. (86 cm)

Wt. 470 oz. (14618 g)
Lent by His Excellency Mohamed
Mahdi Altajir

20

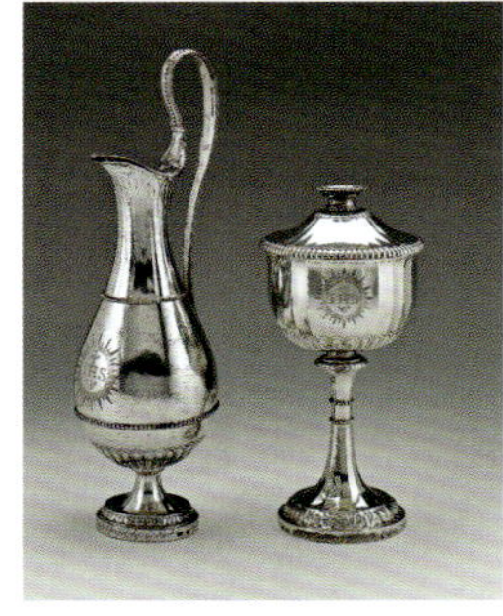

**Communion cup, paten cover
and flagon**
Silver
Marks: Birmingham, 1774–5
Maker's mark: Matthew Boulton &
John Fothergill
Jones, p. 357, col. 2, no. 3
Design: Probably by James Wyatt
(1746–1813)
Provenance: Given to St Andrew's
Church, Gunton, by Sir Harbord
Harbord, 2nd Bt., later (1786) 1st
Baron Suffield (1734–1810)
Exhibited: London, 2008, no. 86
Published: Schroder, *Treasures*, p.
76, fig. 86; Brett, *Church*, p. 38,
no. 132
H. of flagon 16 ½ in. (42 cm)
Lent by St Andrew's Church,
Gunton, Norfolk

21

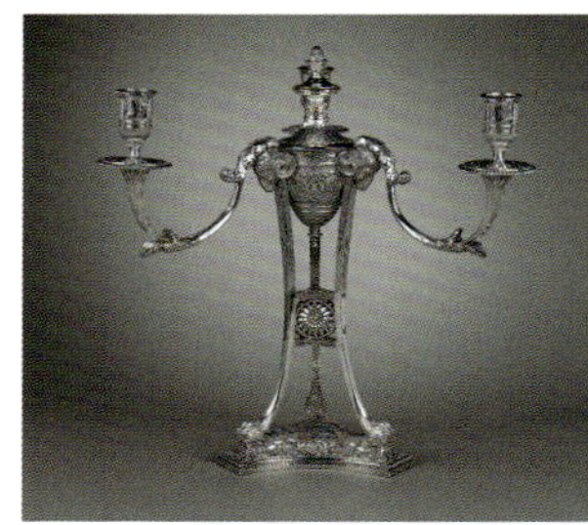

Three-light candelabrum
Silver
Marks: London, 1774–5
Maker's mark: Probably John Carter
II for Joseph Creswell
Grimwade, no. 1214
Design: Robert Adam (1728–1792)
Heraldry: Engraved arms of Sir
Watkin Williams-Wynn, 4th Bt.
Provenance: Sir Watkin Williams-
Wynn, 4th Bt., of Wynnstay, Wales,
by descent to Sir Watkin Williams-
Wynn, 8th Bt, sale, Sotheby's,

London, 10 October 1946; presented
to Lloyds of London by Lloyds
Insurance Brokers Association in
1956
Published: Rowe, plate 12;
Fairclough, p. 383, fig. 34
H. 14 ¾ in. (37.5 cm)
W. 14 ¾ in. (37.5 cm)
D. 14 ¾ in. (37.5 cm)
Lent by Lloyds Corporation

22

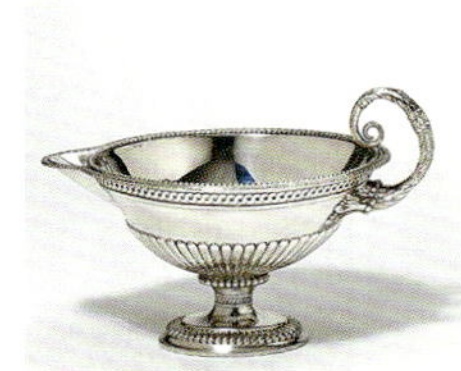

Sauce boat
Silver-gilt
Marks: London, 1774–5
Maker's mark: Probably John Carter
II for Joseph Creswell
Grimwade, no. 1214
Design: James Wyatt (1746–1813)
Heraldry: Engraved arms of Sir
Watkin Williams-Wynn, 4th Bt.
Provenance: Sir Watkin Williams-
Wynn, 4th Bt., of Wynnstay, Wales,
by descent to Sir Watkin Williams-
Wynn, 8th Bt, sale, Sotheby's,
London, 10 October 1946;
anonymous sale, Sotheby's, London,
20 November 1986, lot 173
Published: *The Burlington Magazine*,
CXXXI (1989), p. 389
H. 5 ⅜ in. (13.7 cm)
W. 8 ⅝ in. (21.9 cm)
D. 5 ⅝ in. (14.1 cm)
Wt. 22 oz. (684 g)
Accession no.: M.13-1987
Lent by the Trustees of the Victoria
and Albert Museum

23

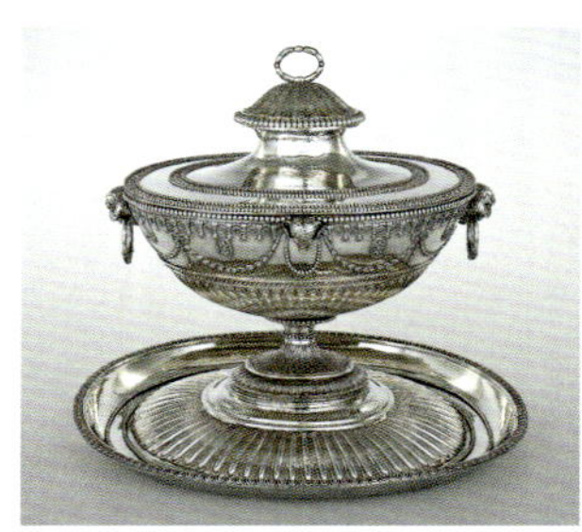

Soup tureen and cover
Silver
Marks: London, 1774–5
Maker's mark: Probably John Carter
II for Joseph Creswell

Grimwade, no. 1214
Design: Robert Adam (1728–1792)
Heraldry: Engraved arms of Sir
Watkin Williams-Wynn, 4th Bt.
Provenance: Sir Watkin Williams-
Wynn, 4th Bt., of Wynnstay, Wales,
by descent to Sir Watkin Williams-
Wynn, 8th Bt., sale, Sotheby's,
London, 10 October 1946; Alfred J.
Moran, sale, Sotheby's, New York,
2–3 November 1989, lot 358, bt. S.J.
Phillips for Amgueddfa Cymru –
National Museum Wales
Published: Fairclough, p. 381, fig.
28
H. 12 in. (30.5 cm)
Accession no.: NMWA 50509
Lent by Amgueddfa Cymru –
National Museum Wales

24

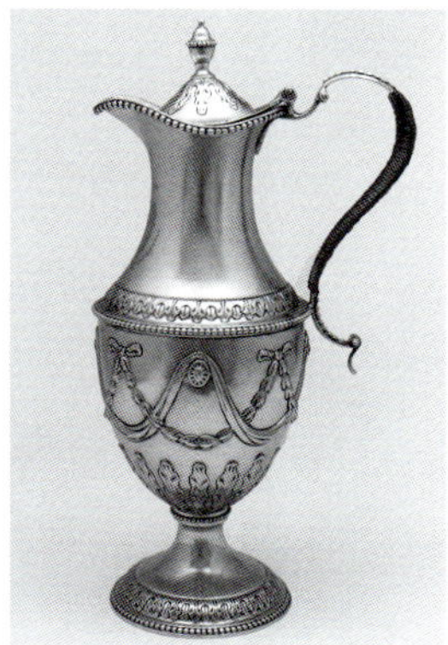

Hot-water jug
Silver, raffia
Marks: London, 1774–5
Maker's mark: John Denziloe
Grimwade, no. 1255
H. 12 ¼ in. (31 cm)
W. 6 ½ in. (16.5 cm)
D. 4 ½ in. (11.5 cm)
Wt. 27 oz. 10 dwt. (855 g) gross
Lent by a private collector

25

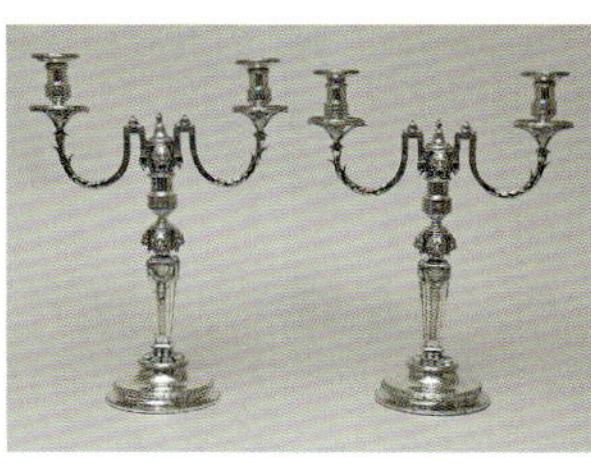

A pair of candelabra
Silver
Marks: London, 1774–5
Maker's mark of Thomas Heming
Grimwade, no. 3828
Heraldry: Engraved arms of
Lascelles impaling those of

Colman, for Edwin Lascelles, Ist
and last Baron of Harewood
(1712–1795), who married in 1770,
as his second wife, Jane, daughter of
William Colman
Provenance: Edwin Lascelles, Ist
and last Baron of Harewood
(1712–1795, by descent
H. 18 ⅞ in. (48 cm)
Inventory no.: HHTM:2006.44a–b
Lent by the Earl and Countess of
Harewood and the Trustees of the
Harewood House Trust

26

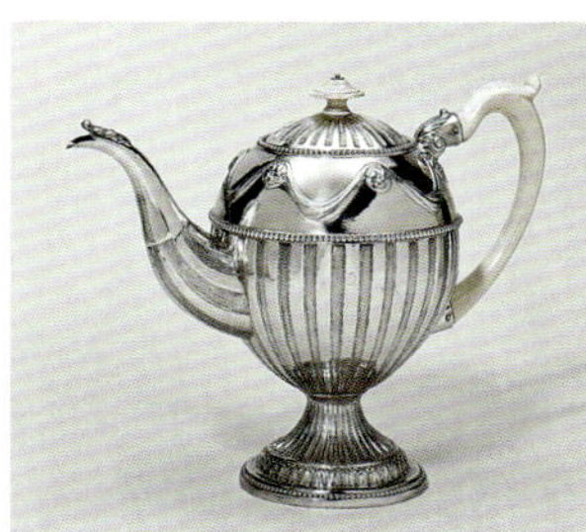

Teapot
Silver-gilt, ivory
Marks: London, 1774–5
Maker's mark: James Young &
Orlando Jackson
Grimwade, no. 1767
Heraldry: Engraved arms of
Garrick impaling those of Veigel
Provenance: David Garrick
(1717–1779) and his wife, Eva Maria
Veigel (d. 1822), by descent to
Lieutenant-Colonel R. Solly, sale,
Sotheby's, London, 19 October 1961,
lot 95
Published: Brett, p. 233, no. 1038
H. 8 ½ in. (21.5 cm)
Accession no.: M.24C-1973
Lent by the Trustees of the Victoria
and Albert Museum

27

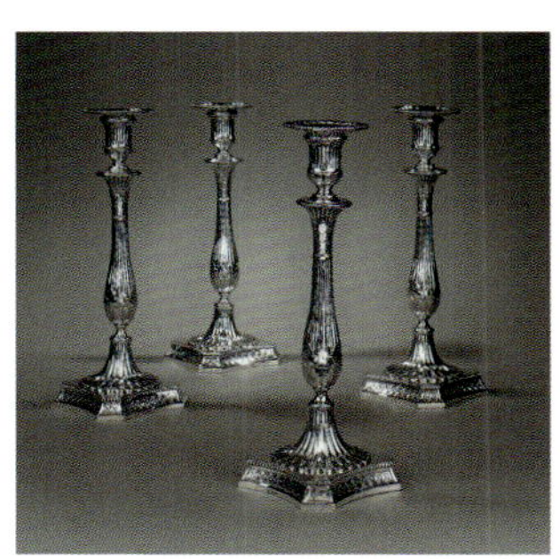

Four candlesticks
Silver
Marks: Birmingham, 1776–7
Maker's mark: Matthew Boulton &
John Fothergill

Designed by James Wyatt
(1746–1813)
Jones, p. 357, col. 2, no. 3
Heraldry: Engraved crest
H. 12 in. (30.5 cm)
Diam. 4 ¾ in. (12 cm)
Lent by an American charitable
trust

28

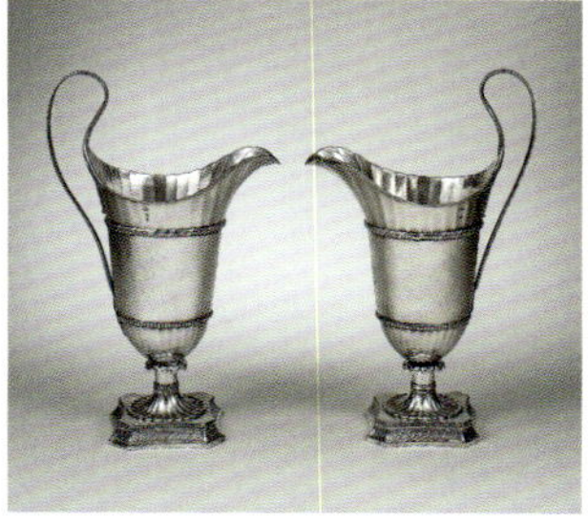

Pair of ewers
Silver
Marks: Birmingham, 1776–7
Maker's mark: Matthew Boulton &
John Fothergill
Jones, p. 357, col. 2, no. 3
Design: Possibly by James Wyatt
(1746–1813)
Heraldry: Engraved arms of Tighe
Provenance: Anonymous sale,
Phillips, London, 30 May 1980, lot
193, Australian private collection,
acquired by Leeds Museums and
Galleries for Temple Newsam in
honour of Robert Rowe, 2010
Published: Alcorn, p. 222
H. 15 in. (38 cm)
Wt. 72 oz. 6 dwt. (2250 g)
Lent by Leeds Museums and
Galleries (Temple Newsam House)

29

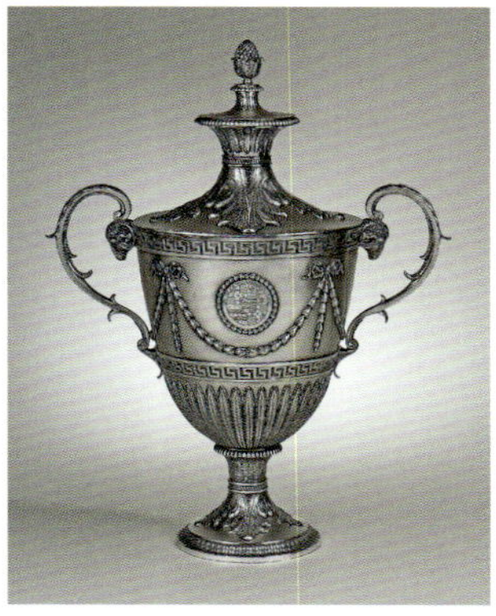

Cup and cover
Silver
Marks: London, 1776–7
Maker's mark: John Carter II
Provenance: Won at Aylesbury,
1776, by Sir John Rous, Bt.; by

descent until 1982; sale, Sotheby's,
New York, 18 October 2001, lot 283
H. 19 in. (48 cm)
W. 15 in. (38 cm)
D. 8 ⅞ in. (22.5 cm)
Wt. 94 oz. 10 dwt. (2940 g)
Lent by the Alan and Simone
Hartman Collection

30

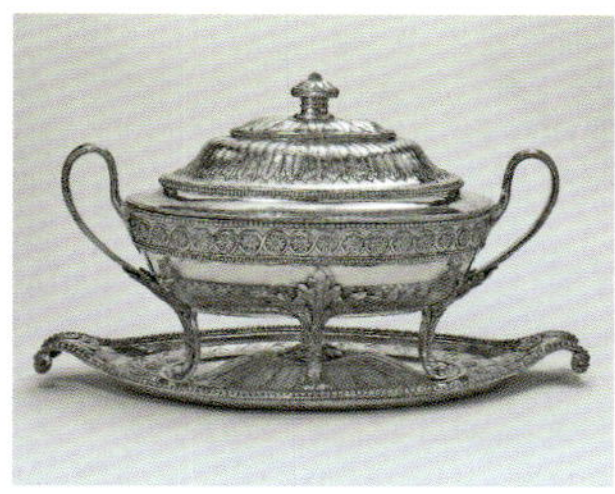

Soup tureen, cover and stand
Silver
Marks: London, 1776–7, also struck
with French importation hallmarks,
c. 1893
Maker's mark: Thomas Heming
Grimwade, no. 3828
Inscription: Engraved underneath:
"No. 2 – 146"
H. 11 in. (28 cm)
W. 17 ¼ in. (45.25 cm)
D. 9 in. (22.9 cm)
Accession no.: M.17&A-1972
Lent by the Trustees of the Victoria
and Albert Museum

31

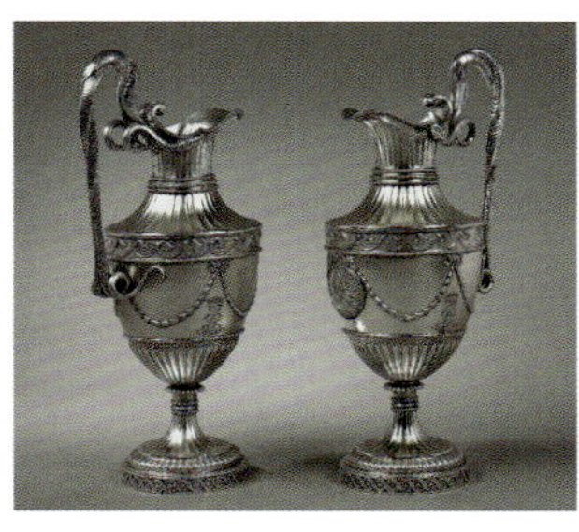

Pair of ewers
Silver
Marks: London, 1776–7
Maker's mark: William Holmes
Grimwade, no. 3161
Heraldry: Engraved after 1837 with
interlaced Ls and earl's coronet
Provenance: Thomas William Coke
(1754–1842), created Earl of
Leicester in 1837, by descent
H. 16 ¼ in. (42.5 cm)
W. 8 ½ in. (21.6 cm)
D. 6 ½ in. (16.5 cm)
Wt. 161 oz. 17 dwt. (5035 g)
Lent by Viscount Coke and the
Trustees of the Holkham Estate

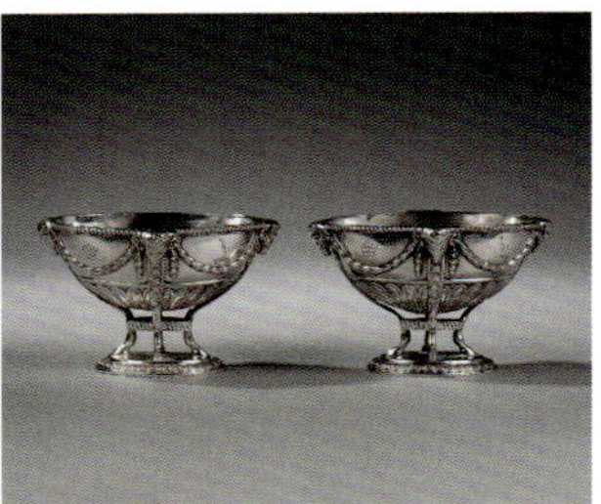

Pair of salts
Silver
Marks: London, 1776–7
Maker's mark: Robert Hennell
Grimwade, no. 2331
Heraldry: Engraved after 1837 with
crest and earl's coronet
Provenance: Thomas William Coke
(1754–1842), created Earl of
Leicester in 1837, by descent
H. 2 ½ in. (6.4 cm)
W. 4 ½ in. (11.4 cm)
D. 3 ⅜ in. (8.6 cm)
Wt. 13 oz. 2 dwt. (407 g)
Lent by Viscount Coke and the
Trustees of the Holkham Estate

33

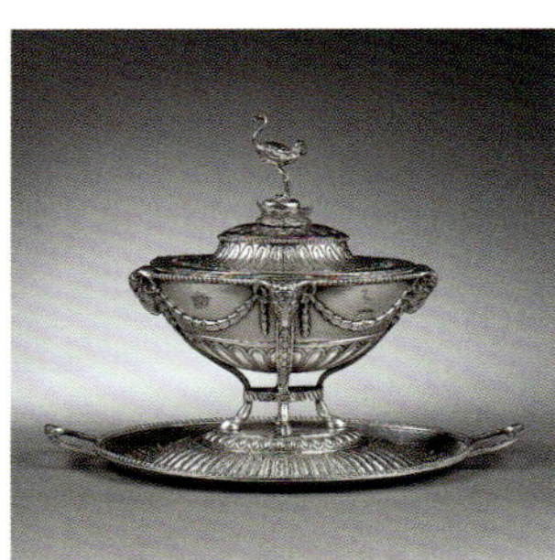

Sauce tureen, cover and stand
Silver
Marks: London, 1776–7
Maker's mark: Robert Hennell
Grimwade, no. 2331
Heraldry: Engraved after 1837 with
crest and earl's coronet; the crest
finial 1843, maker's mark of
Mortimer & Hunt
Provenance: Thomas William Coke
(1754–1842), created Earl of
Leicester in 1837, by descent
H. 9 in. (22.9 cm)
W. 12 in. (30.5 cm)
D. 7 ½ in. (19 cm)
Wt. 53 oz. 5 dwt. (1656 g)
Lent by Viscount Coke and the
Trustees of the Holkham Estate

34

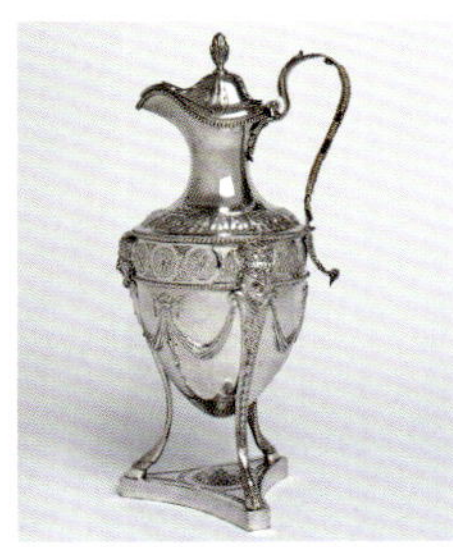

Chocolate pot
Silver, raffia
Marks: London, 1777–8
Maker's mark: Henry Greenway
Grimwade, no. 996
Published: Oman, plate 163, Rowe,
plate 25
H. 12 ¾ in. (32.4 cm)
Accession no.: 460-1875
Lent by the Trustees of the Victoria
and Albert Museum

35

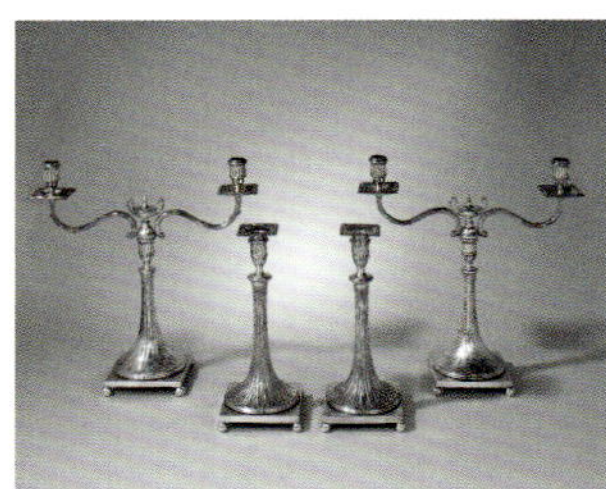

**Pair of two-light candelabra
and pair of candlesticks**
Silver
Marks: London, 1777–8
Maker's mark: John Wakelin &
William Taylor
Grimwade, no. 1764
Heraldry: Engraved crest and
baron's coronet
H. 16 ½ in. (42 cm) and 13 ¼ in. (33.5
cm)
W. 16 ½ in. (42 cm) and 13 ¼ in. (33.5
cm)
D. 6 in. (15.2 cm)
Diam. 5 ¾ in. (14.5 cm)
Wt. 169 oz. (5280 g)
Lent by the Alan and Simone
Hartman Collection

36

Pair of ewers and six goblets
Silver-gilt
Marks: London, 1780–1
Maker's mark: Andrew Fogelberg &
Stephen Gilbert
Grimwade, no. 37
The medallions based on designs by
James Tassie (1735–1799)
Heraldry: Engraved arms of

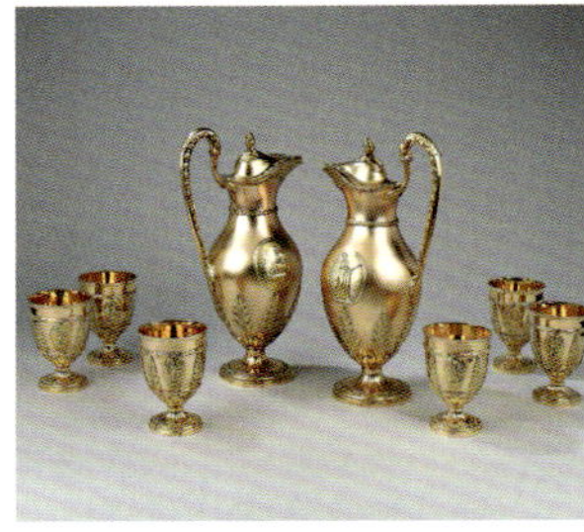

FitzMaurice impaling those of
O'Brien, for the Hon. Thomas
FitzMaurice (1742–1794) of
Llewenny Hall, Denbighshire,
second son of John, 1st Earl of
Shelburne, and his wife Mary,
Countess of Orkney (1755–1831),
whom he married on 21 December
1777
Provenance: The Hon. Thomas
FitzMaurice (1742–1794);
anonymous sale, Sotheby's, London,
30 November 1972, lot 165, S.J.
Phillips; D.S. Lavender; His
Excellency Mahdi Mohamed Altajir,
London
Exhibited: New York, 1974–5;
Sydney, Australia, 1980, no. 11;
London, 1989, no. 107
Published: Hawkins, *Masterpieces*, p.
38, no. 11; Hawkins, *Al-Tajir*, vol. I,
pp. 74–7; Brett, p. 231–2, no. 1027;
Truman, p. 145, no. 107
H. ewers 15 in. (38 cm); goblets 5 ¼
in. (13.5 cm)
Wt. 209 oz. 10 dwt. (6515 g)
Lent by a private collector

37

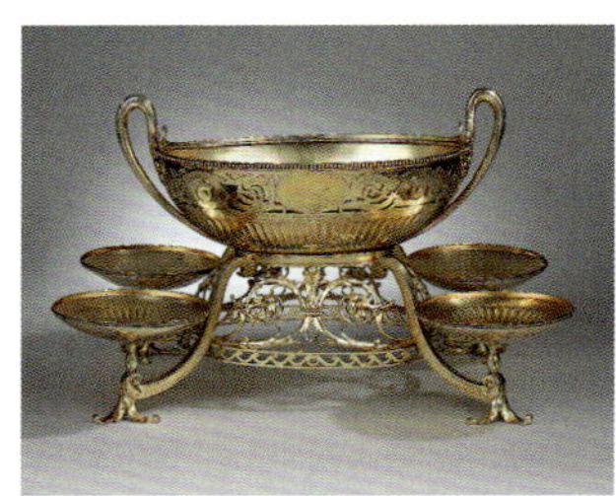

Epergne
Silver-gilt
Marks: London, 1782–3
Maker's mark: John Wakelin &
William Taylor
Grimwade, no. 1764
Inscription: On side: "Col.
Thornton received this Piece of
Plate of Sir Harry Featherstone and
Sir John Ramsden, Barts., as a
compromise to a Bett made in
honour of a Hambleton Fox. Col.
Thornton by his original Bett
engaged for 300 Guineas to find a
Fox at Hunt's Whint or in the

Easingwold Country, that after
Christmas 1779 should run Twenty
Miles. The Day to be fix'd and
Morning approved by Col. Thornton
and to be determined by Sir J.
Ramsden and Sir H. Featherstone, or
the Company up." Under base:
"Certificate. We the under-
mentioned do Declare that on a day
appointed for the decision of a Bett
made by Col. Thornton with Sir J.
Ramsden and Sir H. Featherstone,
that a Fox broke off in view of the
Hounds and Company which Fox
was killed after a continued Burst
(there not being one Check) by the
different Watches for two Hours and
Thirty Eight Minutes. And we being
the only Gentlemen up, do believe
that the said Fox ran at least Twenty
Eight Miles. Col. T. being a party
concerned gave no Vote. Lascelles
Lascelles, Henry Hitchinson, Val.
Hitchinson, Wm. Dawson, Ran.
Marriott. N.B. There were only
Eight Horsemen out of Seventy up."
Heraldry: Engraved arms of
Thornton
Provenance: Colonel Thomas
Thornton (1757–1823) of Falconers'
Hall and Thornville Royal,
Yorkshire, by descent to Colonel
Thornton Wodehouse, Royal
Artillery, sale, Christie's, London, 11
June 1884, lot 17; anonymous sale,
Christie's, London, 25 March 1953,
lot 153, Thomas Lumley Ltd.
Published: Rowe, plate 37A, Young,
"Chambers resumé", 1995, p. 341
H. 10 ½ in. (26.5 cm)
W. 18 in. (45.5 cm)
D. 13 in. (33 cm)
Wt. 108 oz. (3359 g)
Lent by an American private
collector

38

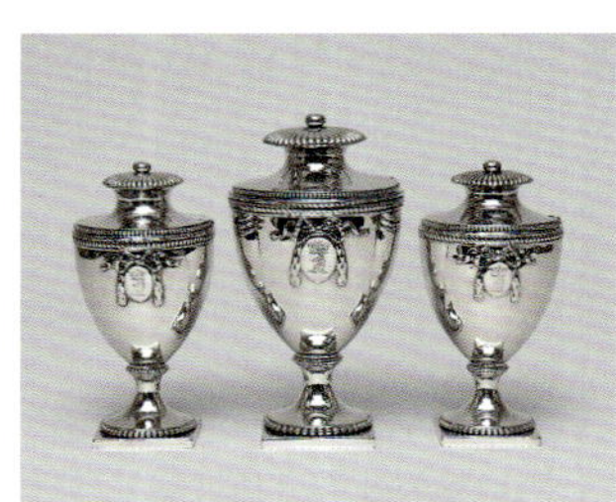

Three condiment vases
Silver
Marks: London, 1783–4
Maker's mark: Daniel Smith and
Robert Sharp
Grimwade, no. 506
Heraldry: Engraved crest and
coronet

Provenance: Probably Edwin Lascelles, 1st and last Baron of Harewood (1712–1795), by descent to the 7th Earl of Harewood
H. 7 in. (18 cm) and 8 ¼ in. (21 cm)
Wt. 41 oz. 9 dwt. (1289 g)
Inventory no.: HHTM:2008.112a–c
Lent by the Earl and Countess of Harewood and the Trustees of the Harewood House Trust

39

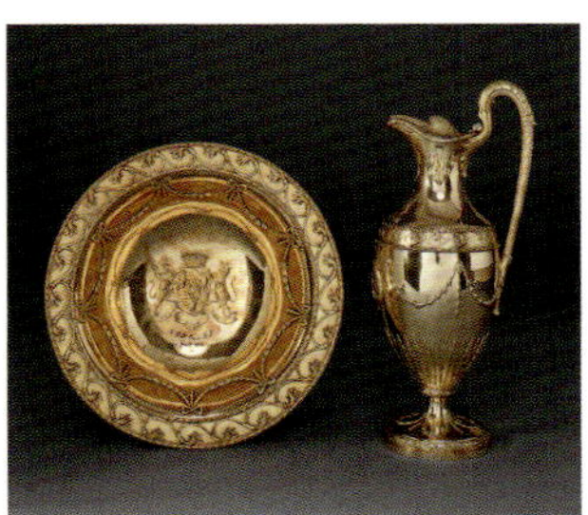

Ewer and basin
Silver-gilt
Marks: London, 1783–4
Maker's mark: Daniel Smith & Robert Sharp
Grimwade, no. 506
Heraldry: Engraved arms of Fane with those of Child in pretence, for John, 10th Earl of Westmorland and Sarah Anne, daughter of Robert Child of Osterley Park, whom he married in 1782
Provenance: John, 10th Earl of Westmorland (1759–1841), by descent to George, 9th Earl of Jersey (1910–1998), the National Trust
Published: Schroder, "Osterley", p. 25
H. ewer 12 in. (30.3 cm)
Diam. basin 14 ½ in. (36.8 cm)
Lent by the National Trust, Osterley Park, the Jersey Collection

40

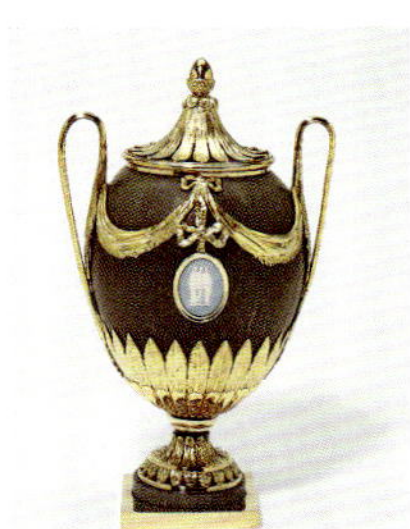

Vase and cover
Silver-gilt, coconut, wood, Jasper ware, c. 1785
The plaque by Josiah Wedgwood and Sons, probably designed by

John Flaxman
Provenance: Given by Lord Frederick Campbell to Assheton, Viscount Curzon (1730–1820)
Published: Oman, plate 166
H. 7 ¾ in. (19.7 cm)
W. 4 ¾ in. (12.1 cm)
D. 4 ¾ in. (12.1 cm)
Accession no.: 815:1,2-1891
Lent by the Trustees of the Victoria & Albert Museum

41

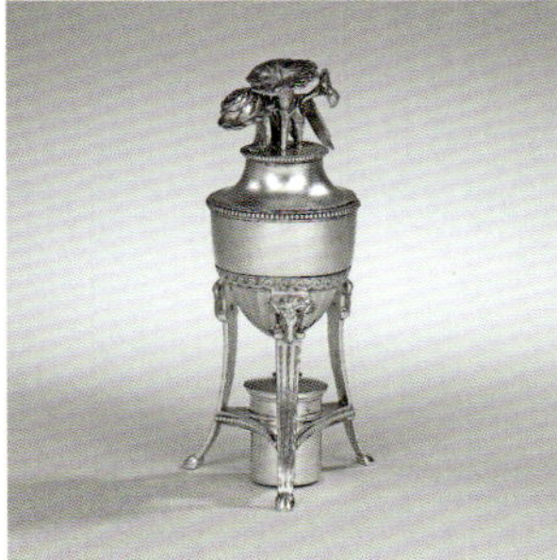

Perfume burner
Silver
Marks: London, 1785–6
Maker's mark: Andrew Fogelberg & Stephen Gilbert
Grimwade, no. 37
Design: Possibly be James Wyatt (1746–1813)
Published: Hernmarck, p. 211, plate 557
H. 6 ¼ in. (16 cm)
Diam. 3 in. (17.5 cm)
Wt. 7 oz. 5 dwt. (226 g)
Lent by a private collector

42

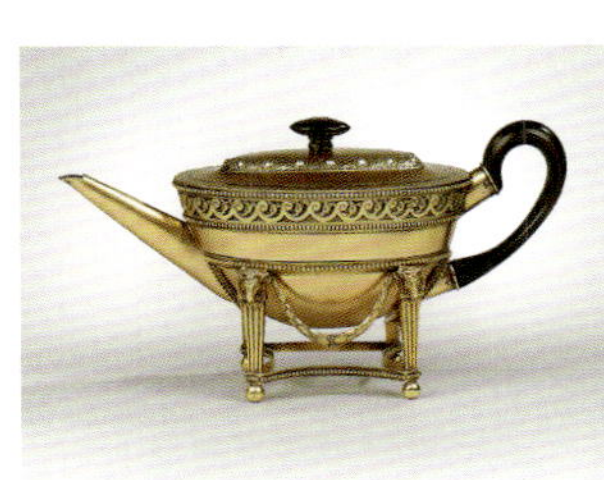

Teapot on stand
Silver-gilt, ebony
Marks: London, 1785–6
Maker's mark: Andrew Fogelberg & Stephen Gilbert
Grimwade, no. 37
Heraldry: Engraved crest of a martlet
H. 5 ¾ in. (14.5 cm)
W. 10 ¾ in. (17 cm)
D. 4 ½ in. (11.5 cm)
Wt. 23 oz. 3 dwt. (720 g) gross
Lent by Koopman Rare Art

43

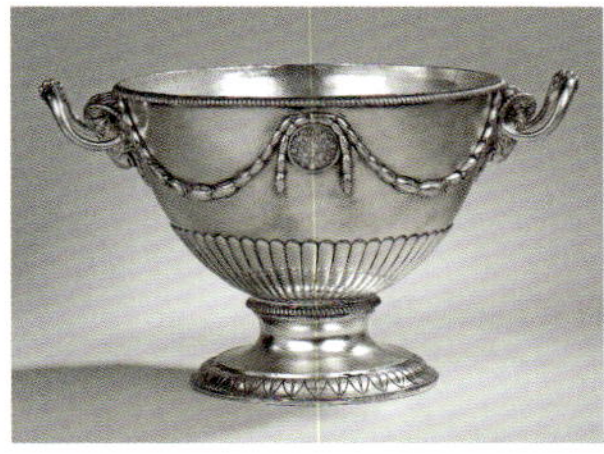

Punch-bowl
Silver
Marks: London, 1785–6
Maker's mark: William Holmes
Grimwade, no. 3161
H. 8 ½ in. (21.5 cm)
Diam. 11 in. (28 cm)
Wt. 86 oz. 2 dwt. (2680 g)
Lent by a private collector

44

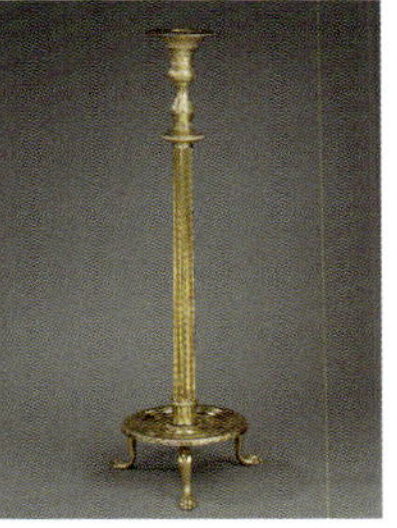

Pair of candlesticks
Silver-gilt
Marks: London, 1787–8
Maker's mark: Charles Aldridge
Grimwade, no. 3263
Provenance: William Beckford (1760–1844), Magnificent Efects at Fonthill Abbey, Wilts., sale, Christie's, 8–17 October 1822, either lot 44 or 45 (sale cancelled), The Unique and Splendid Effects of Fonthill Abbey, sale, , Mr. Phillips, 23 September – 22 October 1823, Thirty-second day's sale [22 October], either lot 1544 or 1545, both pairs purchased by Broadway; [one pair Richard Plantagenet Temple-Nugent-Brydges-Chandos-Grenville, 2nd Duke of Buckingham (1822–1889), The Contents of Stowe, sale, Christie's, 15 August – 30 September 1848, Twentieth day's sale [8 September], lot 783, purchased by S.M. Peto M.P.; anonymous sale, Christie's, London, 17 November 2009, lot 277, Koopman Rare Art
H. 21 ⅜ in. (54.3 cm)
Wt. 85 oz. 10 dwt. (2020 g)
Accession no.: M.5-2010, M.6-2010
Lent by the Trustees of the Victoria and Albert Museum

45

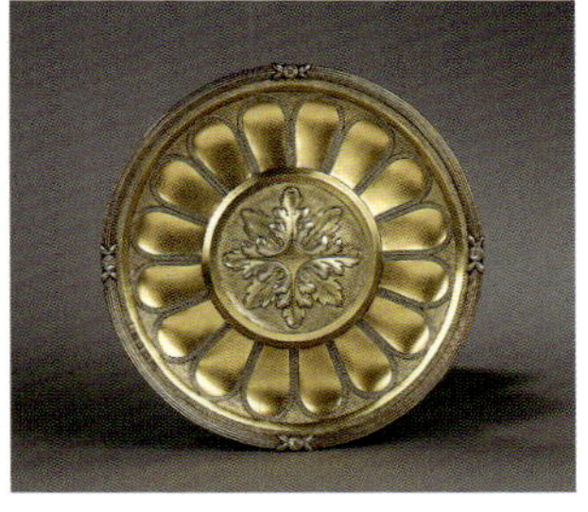

Dish
Silver-gilt
Marks: London, 1787–8
Maker's mark: William Pitts
Grimwade, no. 3263
Published: Clayton, Dictionary, p. 155, fig. 238A
H. ½ in. (1.2 cm)
Diam. 7 ½ in. (19 cm)
Wt. 10 oz. 18 dwt. (340 g)
Lent by Timothy Schroder, Esq.

46

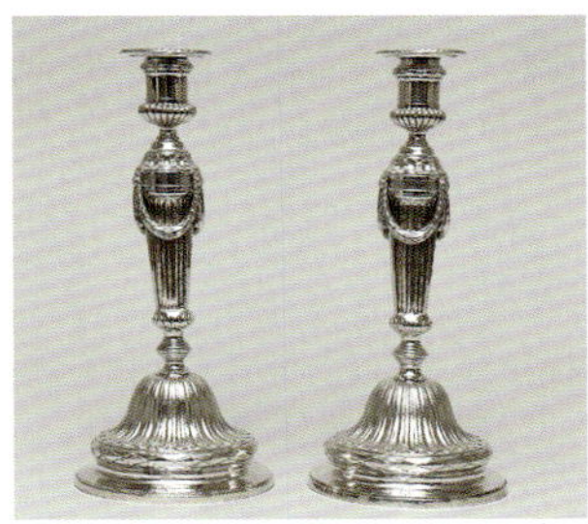

Pair of candlesticks
Silver
Marks: London, 1789–90
Maker's mark: John Scofield
Grimwade, no. 1670
H. 12 ¼ in. (31 cm)
Inventory no.: HHTM:2006.45a–b
Lent by the Earl and Countess of Harewood and the Trustees of the Harewood House Trust

47

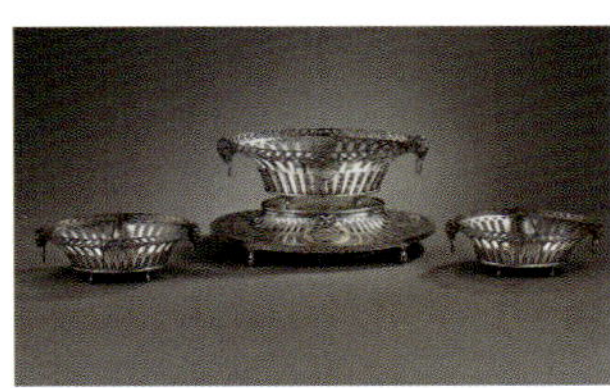

Centrepiece and pair of fruit dishes
Silver, glass
Marks: London, dishes 1789–90; centrepiece 1793–4
Maker's mark: The dishes John Wakelin & William Tayler; the

centrepiece John Wakelin & Robert Garrard I
Grimwade, nos. 1764 and 1760
Heraldry: The centrepiece with engraved arms of Sir Peter Burrell, Bt (1754–1820)
H. dishes 7 ½ in. (19 cm); centrepiece 4 in. (10 cm)
W. dishes 15 ½ in. (39 cm); centrepiece 10 ¼ in. (26 cm)
D. dishes 11 in. (28 cm); centrepiece 6 ¼ in. (15.7 cm)
Wt. 178 oz. 10 dwt. (5552 g)
Lent by a private collector

48

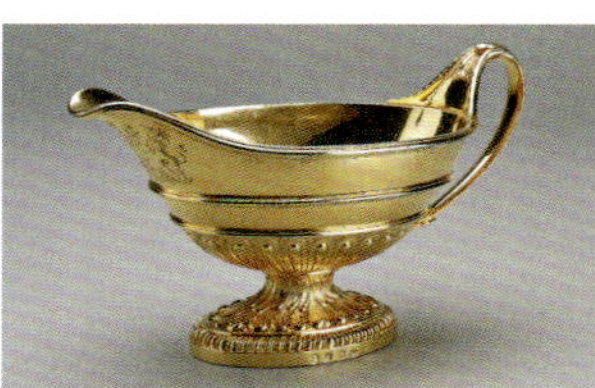

Pair of sauce boats
Silver-gilt
Marks: London, 1789–90
Maker's mark: John Wakelin & William Taylor
Grimwade, no. 1764
Heraldry: Engraved Royal arms
Provenance: Commissioned to commemorate George III's recovery from illness
Exhibited: London, 2004, no. 365
Published: Garrard, 1914, no. 229; Roberts, *George III*, p. 329, no. 365
H. 5 ½ in. (14 cm)
W. 9 ¹¹⁄₁₆ in. (24.6 cm)
D. 4 ⁵⁄₁₆ in. (11 cm)
Inventory no.: RCIN 51841.1-2
Lent by Her Majesty The Queen

49

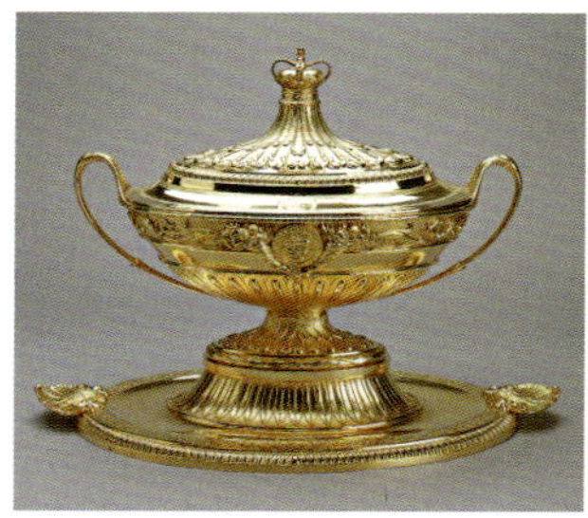

Soup tureen, cover and stand
Silver-gilt
Marks: London, 1789–90
Maker's mark: John Wakelin & William Taylor
Grimwade, no. 1764
Heraldry: Applied Royal badge and Garter motto
Provenance: Commissioned to

celebrate George III's recovery from illness
Exhibited: London, 2004, no. 363
Published: Roberts, *George III*, p. 329, no. 363
H. 12 ⅝ in. (32 cm)
W. 18 ⁵⁄₁₆ in. (46.5 cm)
D. 10 ⁹⁄₁₆ in. (26.8 cm)
Inventory no.: RCIN 50631.1
Lent by Her Majesty The Queen

50

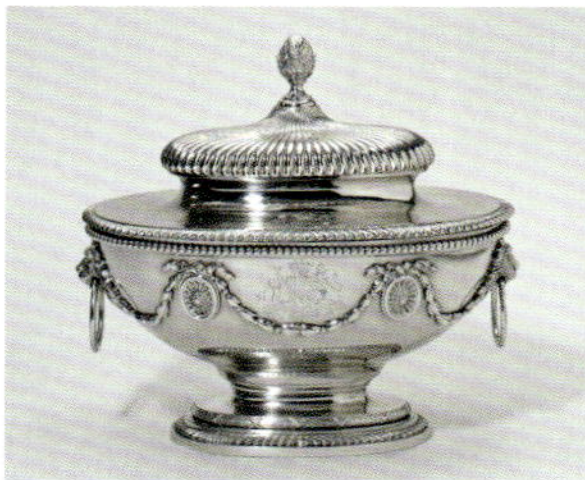

Soup tureen and cover
Silver
Marks: London, 1792–3
Maker's mark: Daniel Smith & Robert Sharp
Grimwade, no. 506
Design: John Yenn (1750–1821) after Sir William Chambers (1723–1796)
Heraldry: Engraved arms of William, 4th Earl Fitzwilliam (1748–1833)
Provenance: William, 4th Earl Fitzwilliam (1748–1833)
Published: Harris and Snodin, p. 151, fig. 217
W. 13 ¾ in. (35 cm)
Wt. 142 oz. (4416 g)
Accession no.: Loan: Metanon.1:15B/1-1996
Lent by the Trustees of the Victoria and Albert Museum, accepted by H.M. Government in lieu of Inheritance Tax from the Whiteley family and allocated to the Victoria and Albert Museum

51

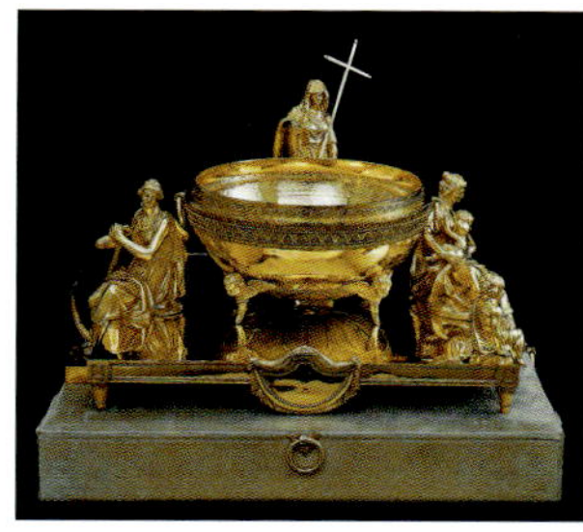

The Portland Font
22-carat gold
Marks: London, 1797–8

Maker's mark: Paul Storr
Grimwade, no. 2234
Design: Humphry Repton (1752–1818)
Provenance: Made for the christening of William Henry, Lord Woodstock (b. 1796), eldest son of William Henry, Marquess of Titchfield, afterwards 4th Duke of Portland (1768–1854), by descent to Lady Anne Bentinck, sale, Christie's, London, 11 July 1985, lot 347, Armitage, Sheika al Altas, acquired by the British Museum in 1986
Published: Jones, *Gold*, plate XXVIII; Jones, *Welbeck*, p. 4, plate I; Jones, *Windsor*, pp. li–lij; Penzer, *Storr*, p. 100; Grimwade, "Gold", p. 89; Clayton, *Dictionary*, p. 191; *Country Life*, 5 September 1985, p. 606; Gough, p. 143; Fothringham, p. 314, fig. 17
H. 7 ¼ in. (18.3 cm)
W. 13 ¾ in. (34.9 cm)
D. 13 ¾ in. (34.9 cm)
Wt. 222 oz. 16 dwt. (6929 g)
Accession no.: 19,860,403.10
Lent by the Trustees of the British Museum

52

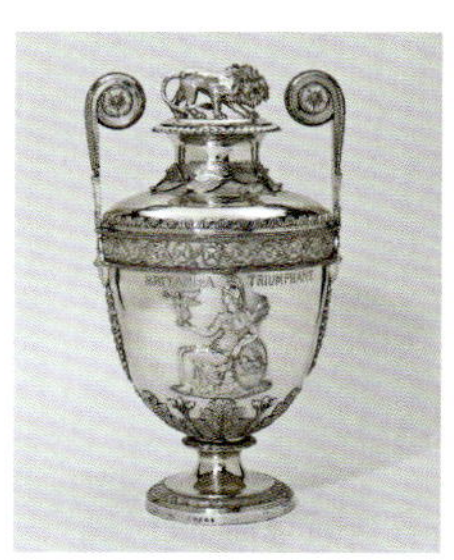

Trafalgar Vase
Silver
Marks: London, 1805–6
Maker's mark: Digby Scott & Benjamin Smith II for Rundell, Bridge & Rundell
Grimwade, no. 505
Design: John Shaw (1745–1829)
Inscription: "BRITONS STRIKE HOME" and "BRITAIN TRIUMPHANT"
Provenance: Joseph Bond (d. 1886), give to the Victoria and Albert Museum, 1890
Exhibited: Moscow and Leningrad, 1978; Belgrade, 1980; London, 2005
Published: Oman, plate 186; Berkowitz, fig. 16; Southwick, "Patriotic Fund", p. 37, fig. 13; Hartop, *Rundell*, p. 149, no. 14
H. 17 in. (43.2 cm)
W. 10 ¼ in. (23.5 cm)

Accession no.: 803:1,2-1890
Lent by the Trustees of the Victoria and Albert Museum

53

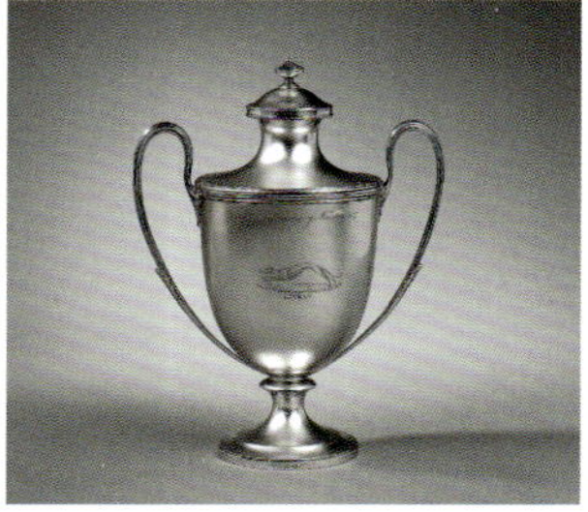

Cup and cover
Silver
Marks: London, 1806–7
Maker's mark: John Emes
Grimwade, no. 1807
Inscription: "Swaffham Coursing Meeting 1807"
H. 12 in. (30.5 cm)
W. 9 ½ in. (24 cm)
D. 5 ½ in. (14 cm)
Wt. 37 oz. 10 dwt. (1166 g)
Lent by a Private Collector

54

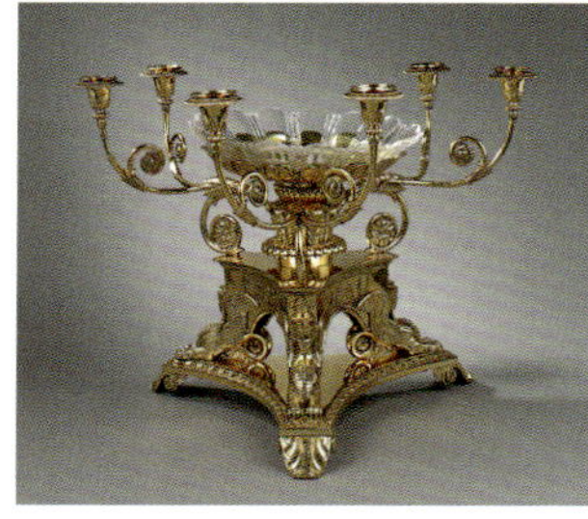

Epergne
Silver-gilt, glass
Marks: London, 1806–7
Maker's mark: Philip Cornman for Rundell, Bridge & Rundell
Grimwade, no. 2148
Design: Charles Heathcote Tatham (1772–1842)
Signature: "RUNDELL BRIDGE & RUNDELL AURIFICES REGIS FECERUNT"
Heraldry: Engraved arms of Beaumont
Provenance: Colonel Thomas Beaumont (1758–1829) by descent to A Nobleman, sale, Christie's, London, 24 June 1981, lot 22; The Property of a Lady, sale, Christie's, London, 9 July 1997, lot 77
Published: Clayton, *History*, p. 219, no. 4
H. 17 in. (43 cm)
W. 24 in. (61 cm)

D. 21 in. (53 cm)
Lent by a private collector, courtesy
of Philip Hewat-Jaboor

55

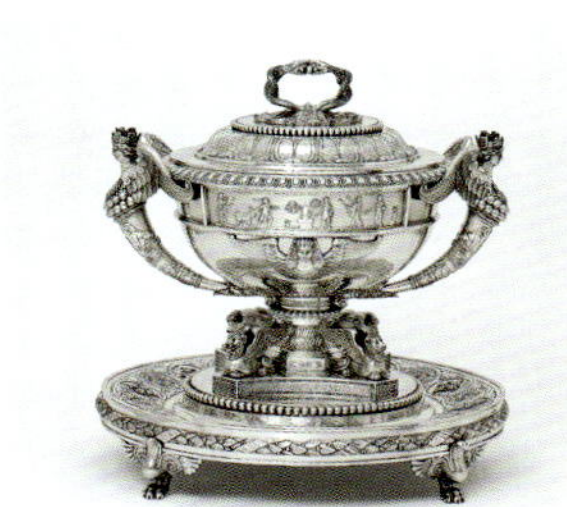

Soup tureen, cover and stand
Silver
Marks: London, 1806–7
Maker's mark: Paul Storr
Grimwade, no. 2234
Design: probably by Jean Jacques
Boileau (*fl.* c. 1787–after 1851)
Signature: "RUNDELL BRIDGE
ET RUNDELL AURIFICES
REGIS ET PRINCIPES WALLAE
LONDINI FECERUNT"
Heraldry: Engraved crest and
insignia of Ernest Augustus, Duke
of Cumberland and later King of
Hannover
Provenance: Ernest Augustus, Duke
of Cumberland (1771–1851) and,
after 1837, King of Hanover, by
descent to the Duke of Brunswick,
sold privately 1923, Glückselig,
Vienna, Crichton Bros., London;
The Plohn Collection, New York,
Mrs Fay Plohn, sale, Sotheby's,
London, 15 October 1970, part of lot
89; Lillian and Morrie A. Moss,
Memphis, Tennessee, David Orgell
Inc., Beverly Hills, 1975, Rosalinde
and Arthur Gilbert
Exhibited: Los Angeles County
Museum of Art, Los Angeles,
1975–1998; Gilbert, 1998–1999;
Somerset House, London,
2000–2008
Published: Jones, "Cumberland",
pp. 679–85; Tipping, p. 681; Honour,
p. 226; Moss, pp. 254–6; Hillier, pp.
118–19; Brett, no. 1130; Schroder,
Gilbert, pp. 358–63; no. 95, Schroder,
Heritage, pp. 58–59
H. 17 in. (43.2 cm)
Diam. 18 ½ in. (47 cm)
Wt. 323 oz. 8 dwt. (10057 g)
Accession no.: Loan: Gilbert.786:1-
2008
Lent by the Rosalinde and Arthur
Gilbert Collection on loan to the
Victoria and Albert Museum (with
support from the Heritage Lottery
Fund)

56

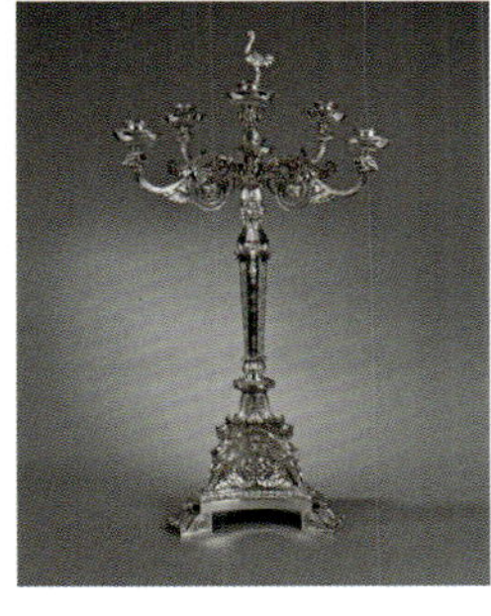

Six-light candelabrum
Silver
Marks: London, 1811, the central
finial and some sockets 1843,
maker's mark of Mortimer & Hunt
Maker's mark: Paul Storr for
Rundell, Bridge & Rundell
Grimwade, no. 2234
Heraldry: Applied in 1842 with
interlaced Ls and earl's coronet
Provenance: Thomas William Coke
(1754–1842), created Earl of
Leicester in 1837, by descent
H. 40 ¼ in. (102 cm)
W. 22 in. (56 cm)
D. 22 in. (56 cm)
Lent by Viscount Coke and the
Trustees of the Holkham Estate

57

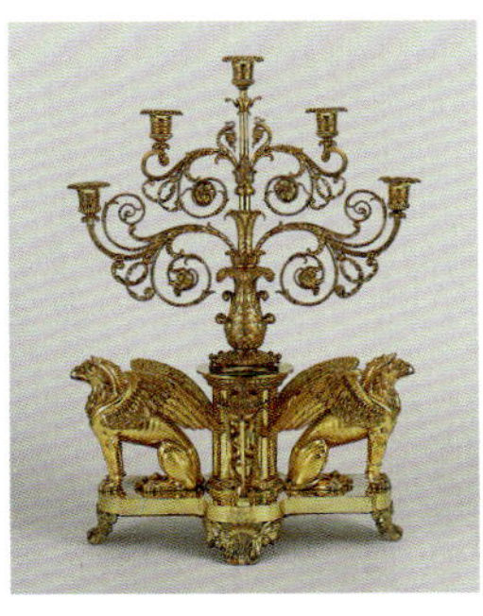

Five-light candelabrum
Silver-gilt
c. 1812–20
Maker's mark: Paul Storr for
Rundell, Bridge & Rundell
Grimwade, no. 2234
Heraldry: Engraved Royal Arms
within Garter motto
Provenance: Supplied to the Prince
Regent soemtime between 1812 and
1820
Exhibited: London, 1991, no. 89
Published: Roberts, *Carlton*, p. 129,
no. 89
H. 32 ½ in. (82.5 cm)
W. 23 ⁷⁄₁₆ in. (59.5 cm)
D. 11 in. (28 cm)
Inventory no.: RCIN 51104
Lent by Her Majesty The Queen

58

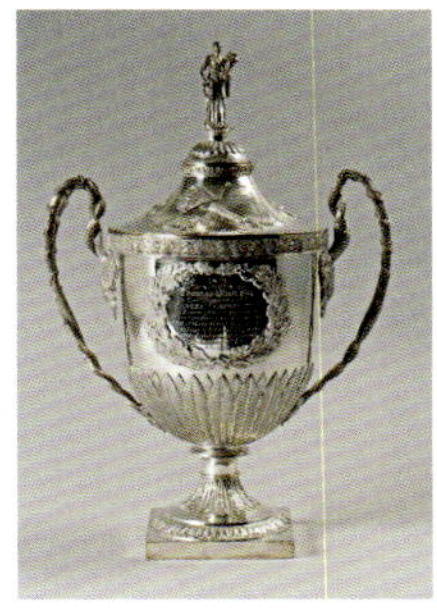

Cup and cover
Silver
Marks: London, 1814–15
Maker's mark: Thomas Wallis &
Jonathan Hayne
Grimwade, no. 2978
Design: James Bennett (1760–1845)
Inscription: "1814/PRESENTED
TO/Thomas Back Esqr./by the
Members of the/CASTLE
CORPORATION/As a Token of
their Approbation/of his Conduct
as a Magistrate/and of their
Gratitude for his/zealous and
liberal support/of the loyal and
constitutional/principals of
that/Society"
Heraldry: Engraved arms of Back
Provenance: Presented in 1814 to
Thomas Back (Lord Mayor in
1809), by descent to Major D.H.L.
Back, sale, Knight, Frank and
Rutley, 29 January 1970, lot 148, bt.
Spink & Son Ltd. for Friends of
Norwich Museums
Published: Osborne, p. 62
H. 17 ½ in. (44.5 cm)
Accession no.: 1970.1
Lent by Norfolk Museums &
Archaeology Service (Norwich
Castle Museum & Art Gallery)

59

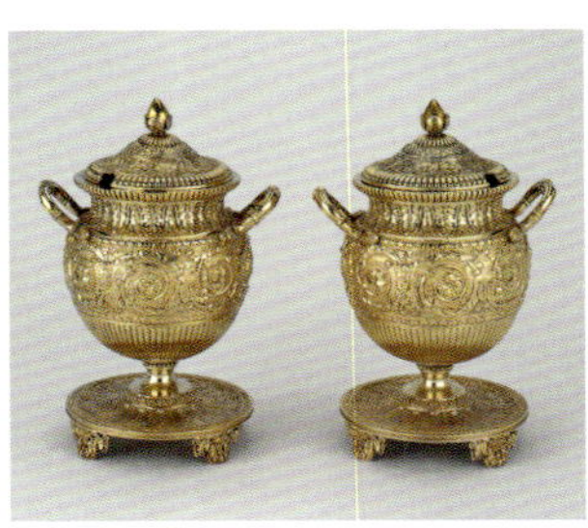

Pair of sugar vases
Silver-gilt
Marks: London, 1814–15
Maker's mark: Paul Storr for
Rundell, Bridge & Rundell
Grimwade, no. 2234
Signature: "RUNDELL BRIDGE
ET RUNDELL AURIFICES
REGIS ET PRINCIPIS
WALLIAE LONDINI
FECERUNT"
Provenance: The Niederhoffer
Collection
Exhibited: London, 2005, no. 30
Published: Hartop, *Rundell*, p. 151,
no. 30
H. 7 ¾ in. (19.5 cm)
Wt. 62 oz. (1928 g)
Lent by the Alan and Simone
Hartman Collection

60

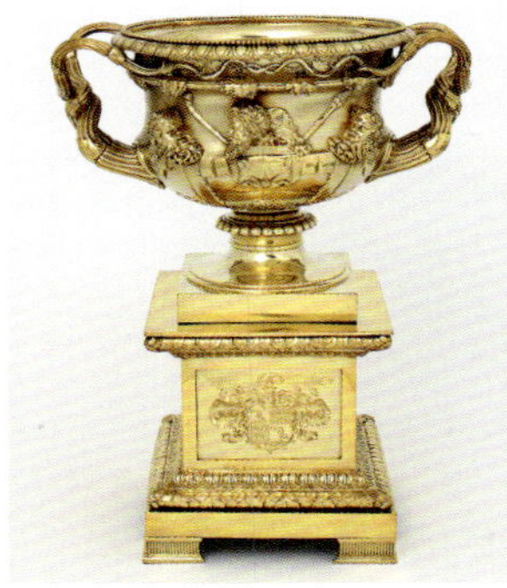

**Copy of the Warwick Vase on
stand**
Silver-gilt
Marks: London, 1814–15
Maker's mark: Paul Storr for
Rundell, Bridge & Rundell
Grimwade, no. 2234
Signature: "RUNDELL BRIDGE
ET RUNDELL AURIFICES
REGIS ET PRINCIPES
WALLIAE REGENTIS"
Inscription: The Latin inscription is
translated: "To James McGrigor,
Knight, Doctor of Medicine, Fellow
of the Royal Edinburgh College of
Medicine, Fellow of the Royal
Society of Edinburgh, and Inspector
General of the Royal Hospitals; a
wholly distinguished man whether
you consider the sharpness of his
mind or the enormous and
unflagging effort he put into his
duties as inspector; when
performing these duties far and
wide, in Portugal, Spain, and
France, he would never fail to
attend to the public with a singular
integrity but also to his fellow
workers with a distinct friendliness
and a kindness that was all his own;
to the man who had every success in
opening up the sacred springs of
Hygeia and in advancing the studies
of the divine art of healing by
arousing a zealous energy for the
noble sciences. The General

Hospital Staff of the Duke of] Wellington intends this as a monument — ah, what a token of esteem! — both sacred and eternal to his outstanding devotion to his most worthy commander, A.D. 1814"
Heraldry: Engraved arms of McGrigor quartering those of Grant, for Sir James McGrigor, M.D. (1771–1858)
Provenance: Sir James McGrigor, M.D. (1771–1858), by descent to Sir James McGrigor, sale, Christie's, London, 26 April 1967, lot 98; David Orgell Inc., Beverly Hills, Rosalinde and Arthur Gilbert
Exhibited: Los Angeles, 1974, no. 16; Los Angeles 1974A; Los Angeles, 1977, no. 28
Published: Hillier, p. 121; Schroder, *Gilbert*, p. 402, no. 107
H. 17 ¹³⁄₁₆ in. (45.2 cm)
Wt. 282 oz. 4 dwt. (8,777 g)
Accession no.: Loan: Gilbert.829-2008
Lent by the Rosalinde and Arthur Gilbert Collection on loan to the Victoria and Albert Museum (with support from the Heritage Lottery Fund)

61

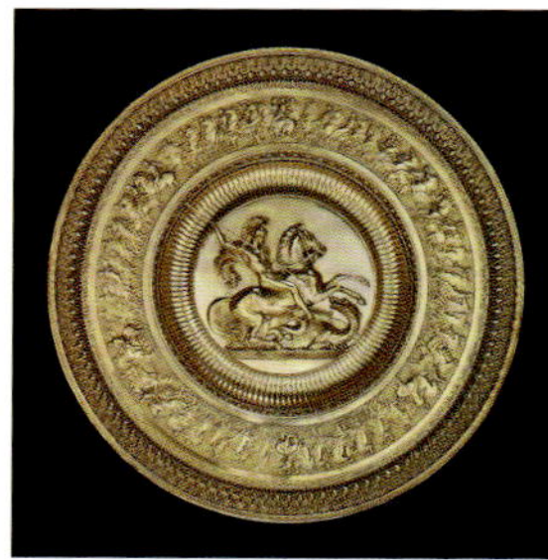

Sideboard dish
Silver-gilt
Marks: 1822–3
Maker's mark: Philip Rundell for Rundell, Bridge & Rundell Grimwade, no. 2228
Design: Benedetto Pistrucci (1784–1855)
Signature: "RUNDELL BRIDGE ET RUNDELL AURIFICES REGIS LONDINI"
Heraldry: Engraved arms of Neeld, for Joseph Neeld (1789–1856)
Provenance: Bequeathed by Philip Rundell to his great-nephew Joseph Neeld (1789–1856)
Published: Oman, plate 207
Diam. 28 in. (71 cm)
Accession no.: M.67-1950
Lent by the Trustees of the Victoria and Albert Museum

62

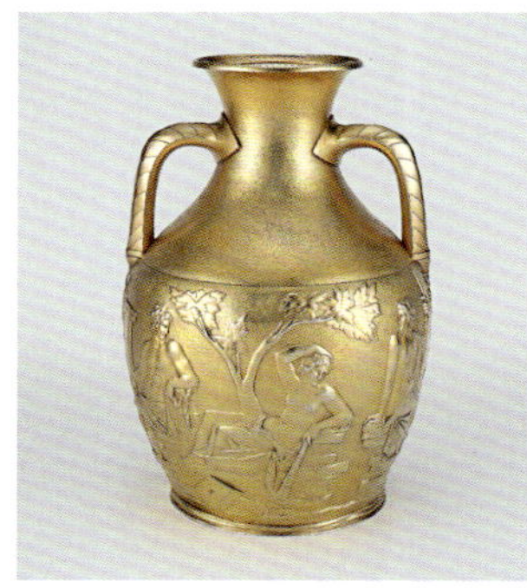

Wine cooler in the form of the Portland Vase
Silver-gilt
Marks: 1823–4
Maker's mark: Philip Rundell for Rundell, Bridge & Rundell Grimwade, no. 2228
Signature: "RUNDELL BRIDGE ET RUNDELL AURIFICES REGIS LONDINI"
Provenance: Anonymous sale, Christie's, London, 19 June 1913, lot 74 (a pair 1820 and 1823); Baroness Burton (1873–1962); anonymous sale, Christie's, London, 27 November 1991, lot 78, Collection of Alan and Simone Hartman, sale, Christie's, New York, 20 October 1999, lot 176; private collection
Exhibited: London, 2005, no. 51
Published: Clayton, *Dictionary*, p. 453, fig. 708; Hartop, *Rundell*, p. 118
H. 9 ⅞ in. (25 cm)
Wt. 82 oz. (2560 g)
Lent by Koopman Rare Art

63

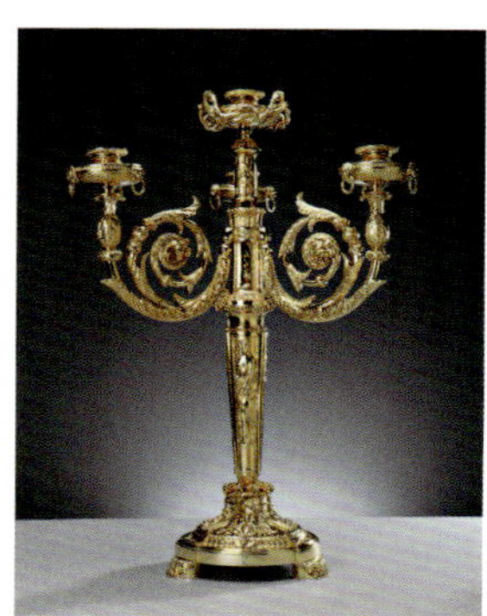

Four-light candelabrum
Silver-gilt
Marks: 1828–9
Maker's mark: John Bridge for Rundell, Bridge & Rundell Grimwade, no. 2228
Signature: "RUNDELL BRIDGE ET RUNDELL AURIFICES REGIS LONDINI"
Heraldry: Engraved Royal badge within Garter motto
Provenance: Purchased by George IV
Exhibited: London, 2002, no. 191
Published: Roberts, 2002, p. 269, no. 191
H. 25 in. (63.4 cm)
W. 16 ¾ in. (42.3 cm)
D. 14 ⅝ in. (37.2 cm)
Inventory no.: RCIN 51102
Lent by Her Majesty The Queen

64

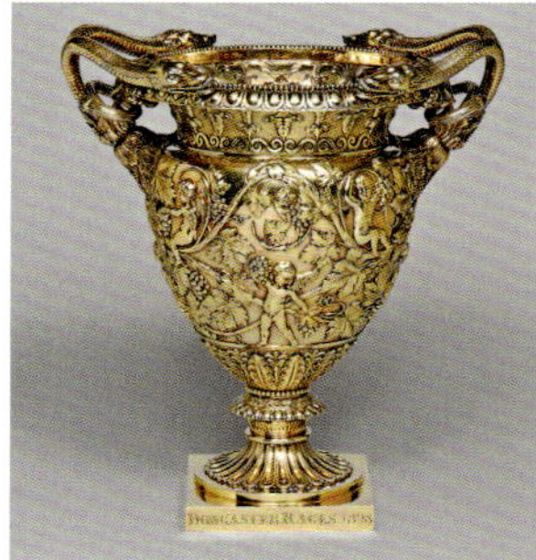

Cup in the form of the Buckingham Vase
Silver-gilt
Marks: 1828–9
Maker's mark: Rebeccah Emes & Edward Barnard I Grimwade, no. 2310
Inscription: "DONCASTER RACES 1828/WON BY MAJOR YARBURGH'S BAY HORSE LAUREL/STEWARDS The Rt. Honble Lord Viscount Morpeth The Honble John Stuart Wortley MP/P. BRIGHT DONCASTER FECT."
Provenance: Won by Major Nicholas Edmund Yarburgh of Heslington, Yorkshire, his nephew Yarburgh Graeme of Sewerby, Yorkshire, his nephew George Yarburgh, , his daughter Mary Elizabeth who married George William Bateson de Yarburgh, later 2nd Baron Deramore, by descent to the 6th Baron Deramore; How (of Edinburgh) Ltd., David Udy, from whom purchased by Leeds Museums and Galleries in 1966
Exhibited: London, 1972, no. 1742; London, 1978, no. 316; Washington DC, 1985, no. 464; Harrogate, 1989
Published: Lomax, no. 16, pp. 27–9; Newman, p. 110
H. 15 ½ in. (39.4 cm)
Wt. 169 oz. 8 dwt. (5270 g)
Accession no.: 13/66
Lent by Leeds Museums and Galleries (Temple Newsam House)

65

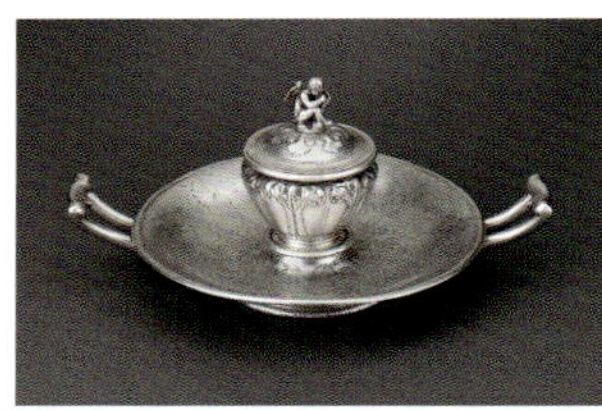

Inkstand
Silver
Marks: 1833–4
Maker's mark: John Bridge for Rundell, Bridge & Rundell Grimwade, no. 2228
H. 4 in. (10 cm)
W. 9 ½ in. (24 cm)
D. 6 ¾ in. (17.1 cm)
Wt. 18 oz. (560 g)
Lent by a private collector

66

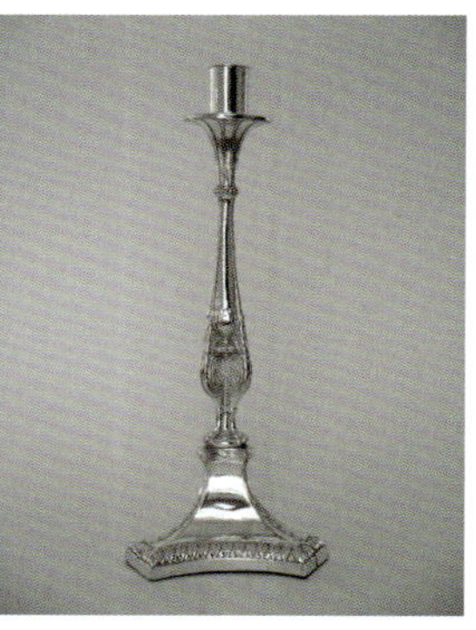

Candlestick
Fused plate
Marks: None, c. 1775
Design: James Wyatt (1746–1813)
H. 12 ⅝ in. (32 cm)
W. 5 ½ in. (14 cm)
D. 5 ½ in. (14 cm)
Lent by Dr David Needham

67

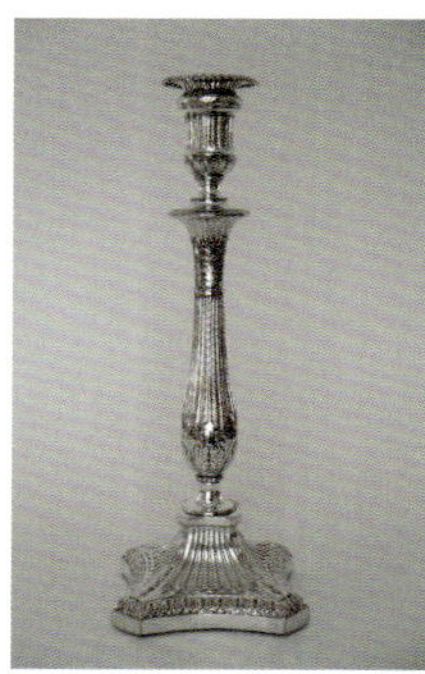

Candlestick
Fused plate
Marks: None, c. 1775
Design: James Wyatt (1746–1813)

H. 12 ¼ in. (31 cm)
W. 5 ½ in. (14 cm)
D. 5 ½ in. (14 cm)
Lent by Dr David Needham

68

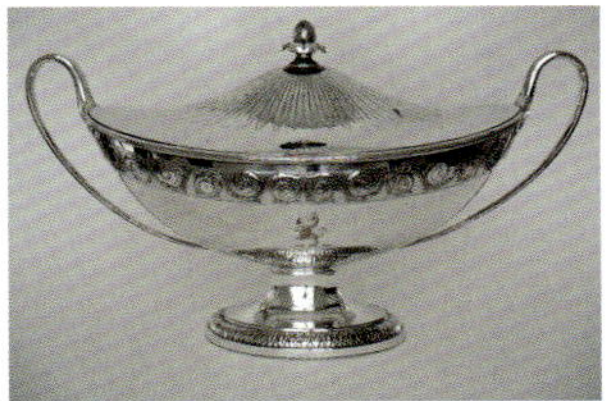

Soup tureen and cover
Fused plate
Marks: None, c. 1775–80
Provenance: Phillips, New York, 28
October 1982, lot 236A
H. 11 ⅜ in. (29 cm)
W. 19 in. (48.2 cm)
D. 9 ⅛ in. (23 cm)
Lent by Dr David Needham

69

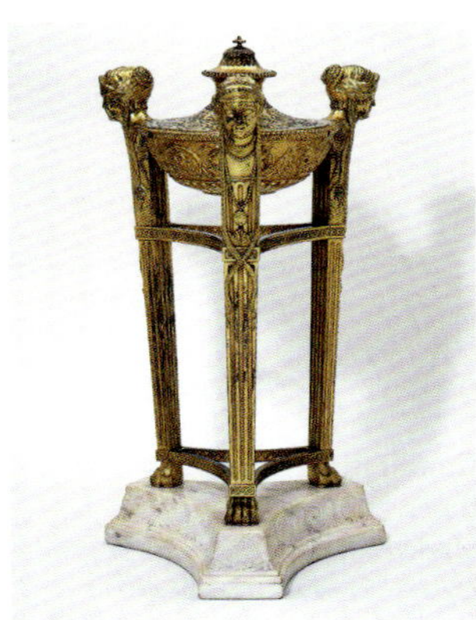

Perfume burner
Gilt bronze, marble
Maker: Probably made by
Diederich Nicolaus Anderson
c. 1760
Design: James "Athenian" Stuart
(1713–1788)
Provenance: Charles, 2nd Marquess
of Rockingham (1730–1782), by
descent until 1946
Exhibited: Stuart, 2005, no. 40
Published: Snodin, "Athenian", p.
471, fig. 11-7
H. 21 ¼ in. (53.97 cm)
W. 10 ⅝ in. (27 cm)
D. 11 ¼ in. (28.8 cm)
Accession no.: M. 46:1,2-1948
Lent by the Trustees of the Victoria
and Albert Museum

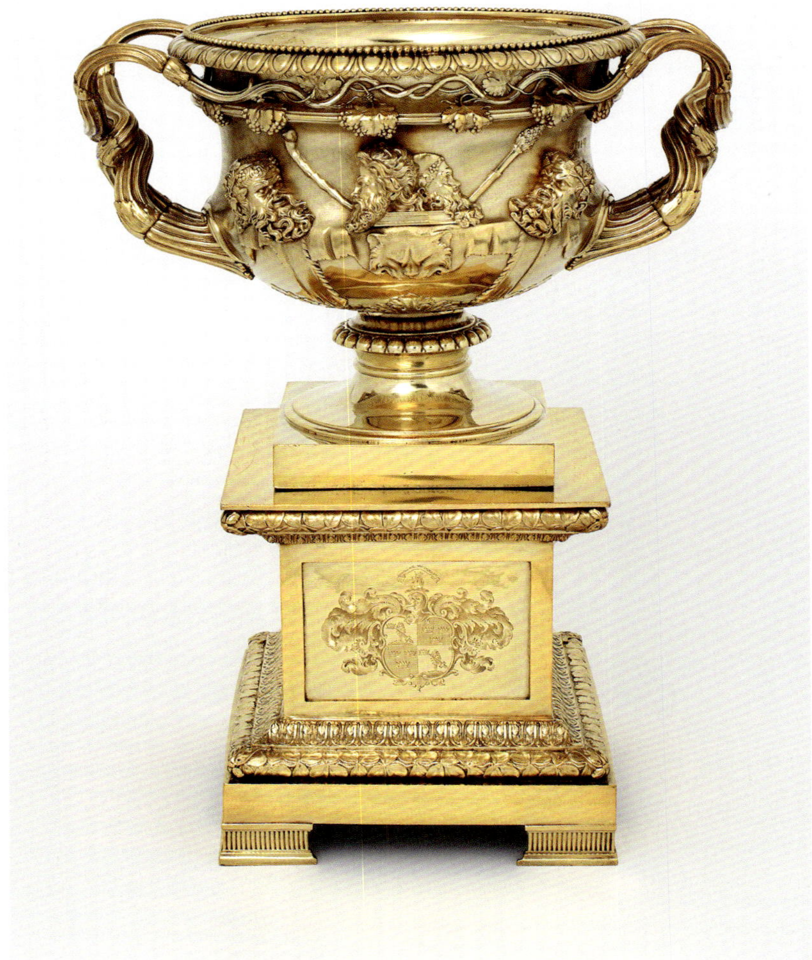

Cat. no. 60

Alcorn
Ellenor M. Alcorn, *English Silver in the Museum of Fine Arts, Boston*, vol. 2: *Silver from 1697*, Boston, 2000

Bailey
Peter Bailey, "Scott & Smith: Further Light on the Greenwich Silversmiths", unpublished paper, 2004

Beard
Geoffrey Beard, *The Work of Robert Adam*, London, 1978

Berkowitz
Roger Berkowitz, *Benjamin Smith Sr, Regency Silversmith*, unpublished Ph.D. thesis, University of Michigan, 1977

Bindman
David Bindman, ed., *John Flaxman*, exh. cat., Royal Academy, London, 1979

Bird
Clifford and Yvonne Bird, *Norfolk and Norwich Clocks and Clockmakers*, Chichester, 1996

Brett
Vanessa Brett, *The Sotheby's Directory of Silver*, London, 1986

Brett, *Church*
Vanessa Brett, ed., *Church Plate in England*, special issue of *Silver Studies: The Journal of the Silver Society*, 24 (2009)

Bury, "Rundell's", 1
Shirley Bury, "The Lengthening Shadow of Rundell's: Part 1: Rundell's and their silversmiths", *The Connoisseur*, CLX (February, 1966), pp. 79–85

Bury, "Rundell's", 2
Shirley Bury, "The Lengthening Shadow of Rundell's: Part 2: The substance and growth of the Flaxman tradition", *The Connoisseur*, CLX (March, 1966), pp. 152–8

Bury, "Rundell's", 3
Shirley Bury, "The Lengthening Shadow of Rundell's: Part 3: The Rundell influence on the Victorian trade", *The Connoisseur*, CLX (April, 1966), pp. 218–22

Carrington and Hughes
John Bodman Carrington and Graham Hughes, *The Plate of the Worshipful Company of Goldsmiths*, London, 1926

Clayton, *History*
Michael Clayton: *The Christie's Pictorial History of English and American Silver*, Oxford, 1985

Clayton, *Dictionary*
Michael Clayton, *The Collectors' Dictionary of the Silver and Gold of Great Britain and North America*, rev. edn, Woodbridge, 1985

Clifford, *Garrard*
Helen Clifford, *Garrard, Royal Goldsmiths*, Garrard's, London, 1991

Clifford, *Parker and Wakelin*
Helen Clifford, *Silver in London: the Parker and Wakelin Partnership 1760–1776*, New York, 2004

Clifford, "Richmond"
Helen Clifford, "The Richmond Gold Cup: social, sporting and design history", *Apollo*, CXXXVII, no. 372 (1993), pp. 102–6

Clifford, *Vulliamys*
Helen Clifford, "The Vulliamys and their silversmiths 1793–1817", *The Silver Society Journal*, 10 (1998), pp. 96–101

Cornforth
John Cornforth, "On his own legs", *Country Life*, CLXXXIX, no. 39 (28 September 1995), pp. 71–3

Courtauld
The Courtauld Family, exh. cat., Goldsmiths' Hall, London, 1985

Crighton
R.A. Crighton, *Cambridge Plate*, exh. cat., Fitzwilliam Museum, Cambridge, 1975

Culme
John Culme, *The Directory of Gold & Silversmiths, Jewellers & Allied Traders 1838–1914 From the London Assay Office Registers*, Woodbridge, 1987

Dale
Anthony Dale, "An Album of Wyatt Drawings", *The Architect and Building News*, CXCIV, no. 4175 (24 December 1948), pp. 526–9

Davidson
Simon Davidson, "John Denziloe of London. A goldsmith working in Aldersgate 1774–1805", *Silver Studies: the Journal of the Silver Society*, 16 (2004), pp. 125–9

Delieb
Eric Delieb, *The Great Silver Manufactory: Matthew Boulton and the Birmingham Silversmiths 1760–1790*, London, 1971

Dickinson
H.W. Dickinson, *Matthew Boulton*, Cambridge, 1937

Dommisse
Jet Pijzel-Dommisse, "Aan tafel: De collectie Europees serviesgoed en zilver", in Annette de Vries, ed., *Duivenvoorde: Bewoners, landgoed, kasteel, interieur en collectie*, Zwolle, 2010

Ellis
Myrtle Ellis, "Huttleston Broughton, 1st Lord Fairhaven (1896–1966) as a collector of English silver", *Apollo*, 446 (1999), pp. 38–44

Eriksen
Svend Eriksen, *Early Neo-classicism in France*, London, 1974

Fairclough
Oliver Fairclough, "Sir Watkin Williams-Wynn and Robert Adam: commissions for silver 1768–80", *The Burlington Magazine*, CXXXVII (1995), pp. 55–9

Fergusson
Frances Fergusson, "Wyatt Silver", *The Burlington Magazine*, CXVI (December, 1974), pp. 751–5

Fergusson, "Chairs"
Frances Fergusson, "Wyatt Chairs: Rethinking the Adam Heritage", *The Burlington Magazine*, (July, 1977)

Fothringham
Henry [Steuart] Fothringham, "Silver appearing before the Reviewing Committee on the Export of Works of Art from 1953 to 1993", *The Silver Society Journal*, 6 (Winter, 1994), pp. 302–22

Fox MS
George Fox: Untitled MS account of Rundell and Bridge, written between 1843 and 1846, presented to the Baker Library, Harvard Business School by Fox's great-granddaughter, Lydia Burgess Brownson (*née* Phinney) in 1949 (597 1843). A typed transcription done in the 1950s is in the Metalwork Department, Victoria and Albert Museum and the Library, Goldsmiths' Hall. The transcription contains a number of misreadings.

Glanville, *Tudor*
Philippa Glanville, *Silver in Tudor Early Stuart England: A Social History and Catalogue of the National Collection, 1480–1660*. London, 1990

Goodison, *Ormolu*
Nicholas Goodison, *Matthew Boulton: Ormolu*, rev. edn, London, 2002

Goodison, "Tripod"
Nicholas Goodison, "Mr Stuart's Tripod", *The Burlington Magazine*, CXIV (October, 1972), pp. 695–704

Gore and Carter
Ann Gore and George Carter, ed., *Humphry Repton's Memoirs*, Norwich, 2005

Gough
S. Gough, ed., *Treasures for the Nation*, exh. cat., National Heritage Memorial Fund, London, 1988

Grimwade, "communion"
Arthur Grimwade, "New Light on Canadian Treasure: the royal communion service of Quebec", *Country Life*, CLXIII (31 January 1985), pp. 268–73

Grimwade
Arthur Grimwade, *London Goldsmiths 1697–1837: their Marks and Lives from the Original Registers at Goldsmiths' Hall and Other Sources*, London, rev. edn, 1990

Harris, Adam
Eileen Harris, *The Genius of Robert Adam*, London, 2001

Harris, Kedleston
Leslie Harris, *Robert Adam and Kedleston*, exh. cat., Kedleston Hall, Derbyshire, 1987

Harris and Snodin
John Harris and Michael Snodin, *Sir William Chambers, Architect to George III*, exh. cat., The Courtauld Gallery, London, 1997

Hartop, "Empire"
Christopher Hartop, "Empire Silver: a Gilded Age", in Eleanor Delorme, ed., *Joséphine and the Arts of France*, J. Paul Getty Museum, Los Angeles, 2005

Hartop, *Geometry*
Christopher Hartop, *Geometry and the Silversmith, The Domcha Collection*, Cambridge, 2008

Hartop, *Rundell*
Christopher Hartop, *Royal Goldsmiths: The Art of Rundell & Bridge 1797–1843*, exh. cat., Koopman Rare Art, London, 2005

Haskell and Penny
Francis Haskell and Nicholas Penny, *Taste and the Antique*, New Haven, 1981

Hatfield
Leslie Campbell Hatfield, "A Set of English silver Condiment Vases from Kedleston Hall", *Bulletin of the Museum of Fine Arts, Boston*, 79 (1981), pp. 4–19

Hawkins, *Al-Tajir*
J.B. Hawkins, *The Al-Tajir Collection of Silver and Gold*, London, 1983

Hawkins. *Masterpieces*
J.B. Hawkins, *Masterpieces of English and European Silver and Gold*, exh. cat., The Art Gallery of New South Wales, Sydney, Australia, 1980

Hayward
J.F. Hayward, *The Courtauld Silver: An Introduction to the Work of the Courtauld Family of Goldsmiths*, London, 1975

Hillier
Bevis Hillier, "The Gilbert Collection of Silver", *The Connoisseur*, 192 (June, 1976), pp. 114–21

Honour
Hugh Honour, *Goldsmith and Silversmiths*, New York, 1971

Honour, *Neo-Classicism*
Hugh Honour, *Neo-Classicism*, London, 1968

Hope
Thomas Hope, *Household Furniture and Interior Decoration*, reprint, New York, 1971

Hopper
Rev. E.C. Hopper *et al.*: "Church Plate in Suffolk", *Suffolk Institute of Archaeology and Natural History*, 8 (1894), pp. 279–333

Hughes, "Punch"
Peter Hughes, "An Adam Punch Bowl", *The Burlington Magazine*, CIX (1967), p. 646

Irwin, *Flaxman*
David Irwin, *John Flaxman 1755–1826, Sculptor, Illustrator, Designer*, London, 1979

Irwin, *Neoclassicism*
David Irwin, *Neoclassicism*, London, 1997

Jackson
Ian Pickford, ed., *Jackson's Silver and Gold Marks of England*, Woodbridge, 1989, an updated edition of Sir Charles Jackson's *English Goldsmiths and their Marks*, London, 1921

Jackson, *History*
Sir Charles Jackson: *An Illustrated History of English Plate*, London, 1911

Jackson-Stops
G. Jackson-Stops, ed., *The Treasure Houses of Britain*, exh. cat., National Gallery of Art, Washington DC, 1985

Jenkins and Sloane
Ian Jenkins & Kim Sloane, *Vases and Volcanoes: Sir William Hamilton and his Collection*, exh. cat., British Museum, London, 1996

Jones
Kenneth Crisp Jones (ed.), *The Silversmiths of Birmingham and their Marks 1750–1980*, London, 1981

Jones, "Cumberland"
E. Alfred Jones, "The Duke of Cumberland's Collection of Old English Plate", *National Review*, January, 1920, pp. 679–85

Jones, *Gold*
E. Alfred Jones, *Old English Gold Plate*, London, 1907

Jones, *Welbeck*
E. Alfred Jones, *Catalogue of Plate belonging to the Duke of Portland, K.G., G.C.V.O. at Welbeck Abbey*, London, 1935

Jones, *Windsor*
E. Alfred Jones, *The Gold and Silver of Windsor Castle*, Letchworth, 1911

Lomax
James Lomax, *British Silver at Temple Newsam and Lotherton Hall*, Leeds, 1992

Lomax, "Jewel House"
James Lomax, "Royalty and silver: the role of the Jewel House in the eighteenth century", *The Silver Society Journal*, 11 (Autumn, 1999), pp. 133–9

Lovett, "Rundell"
Robert W. Lovett, "Rundell, Bridge and Rundell
– An early Company History", *Bulletin of the
Business Historical Society*, 23 (September, 1949),
pp. 150–65

Mason
Shena Mason, ed., *Matthew Boulton: Selling what
all the world desires*, exh. cat., Birmingham
Museum & Art Gallery, 2009

McCormick and Ottomeyer
Heather Jane McCormack and Hans Ottomeyer,
*Vasmania: Neo-classical Form and Ornament in
Europe*, exh. cat., New Haven, 2004

Mortlock
D.P.Mortlock, "Thomas Coke and the family
silver", *The Silver Society Journal*, 9 (Autumn,
1997), pp. 552–8

Moss
Morrie A. Moss, *The Lillian and Morrie Moss
Collection of Paul Storr Silver*, Miami, 1972

Oman
Charles Oman: *English Silversmiths' Work Civil
and Domestic: an Introduction*, Victoria & Albert
Museum, London, 1965

Oman, "Rundell"
Charles Oman, "A Problem of Artistic
Responsibility: The Firm of Rundell, Bridge and
Rundell", *Apollo*, LXXXIII (March, 1966), pp.
174–83

Parissien
Steven Parissien, *Adam Style*, London, 1992

Parker
R.A.C. Parker, *Coke of Norfolk: A Financial and
Agricultural Study 1707–1842*, Oxford, 1975

Penzer, "Coolers"
N.M. Penzer, "The Great Wine Coolers", *Apollo*,
September, 1957

Penzer, *Storr*
Norman M. Penzer, *Paul Storr 1771–1844,
Silversmith and Goldsmith*, London, 1954

Phillips and Sloane
Anthony Phillips and Jeanne Sloane, *Antiquity
Revisited: English and French Silver-Gilt from the
Audrey Love Collection*, London, 1997

Quickenden, "Boulton"
Kenneth Quickenden, "Boulton and Fothergill's
Silversmiths", *The Silver Society Journal*, 7 (1995),
pp. 324–56

Quickenden, "Chippendall"
Kenneth Quickenden, "Richard Chippendall
and the Boultons", *Silver Studies: The Journal of
the Silver Society*, 22 (2007), pp. 51–66

Quickenden, "Epergne"
Kenneth Quickenden, "Boulton and Fothergill
silver: an epergne designed by James Wyatt",
The Burlington Magazine, CXXVIII, no. 999
(June, 1986), pp. 417–21

Quickenden, "Lyon"
Kenneth Quickenden, "'Lyon-faced'
candlesticks and candelabra", *The Silver Society
Journal*, 11 (Autumn, 1999), pp. 196–210

Quickenden, "Montagu"
Kenneth Quickenden, "Elizabeth Montagu's
service of plate", Part 1, *Silver Studies: The
Journal of the Silver Society*, 16 (2004), pp.
131–41, and Part 2, *Silver Studies: The Journal of
the Silver Society*, 19 (2005), pp. 19–37

Ransome-Wallis
Rosemary Ransome-Wallis, *Matthew Boulton
and the Toymakers, Silver from the Birmingham
Assay Office*, exh. cat., Goldsmiths' Hall,
London, 1982

Roberts, *Carlton*
Hugh Roberts, ed., *Carlton House: The Past
Glories of George IV's Palace*, exh. cat., The
Queen's Gallery, London, 1991

Roberts, *George III*
Jane Roberts, ed., *George III & Queen Charlotte:
Patronage, Collecting and Court Taste*, exh. cat.,
The Queen's Gallery, London, 2004

Roberts, *Treasures*
Jane Roberts, ed., *Royal Treasures: a Golden
Jubilee Celebration*, exh. cat., The Queen's
Gallery, London, 2002

Roberts, *Windsor*
Sir Hugh Roberts, *For the King's Pleasure: The
Furnishing and Decoration of George IV's
Apartments at Windsor Castle*, London, 2001

Rowe
Robert Rowe, *Adam Silver 1765–1795*, London,
1965

Rykwert
J. and A. Rykwert, *The Brothers Adam: the Men
and the Style*, London, 1985

Schrager
Luke Schrager, "The royal and aristocratic
patronage of Wakelin & Tayler, 1776–92", *Silver
Studies: The Journal of the Silver Society*, 21
(2006), pp. 87–104

Schroder, Ashmolean
Timothy Schroder, *British and Continental Gold
and Silver in the Ashmolean Museum*, Oxford,
2009

Schroder, *Domestic*
Timorthy Schroder, *The National Trust Book of
English Domestic Silver, 1500–1900*, London,
1988

Schroder, *Gilbert*
Timothy Schroder, *The Gilbert Collection of
Gold and Silver*, Los Angeles, 1988

Schroder, *Heritage*
Timothy Schroder, *Heritage Regained: Silver
from the Gilbert Collection*, exh. cat., London,
1998

Schroder, "Osterley"
Timothy Schroder, "The silver at Osterley",
Apollo, CXXXI (new series, April, 1995), pp.
23–6

Schroder, *Treasures*
Timothy Schroder, *Treasures of the English
Church, A Thousand Years of Sacred Gold and
Silver*, exh. cat., The Goldsmiths' Company,
London, 2008

Silferstolpe
Susann Silferstolpe, "Swedish or English?
Another look at the work of Andrew
Fogelberg", *The Silver Society Journal*, 6 (Winter,
1994), pp. 290–295

Smith, "Vulliamy"
Roger Smith, "Vulliamy and the Kinnaird
candelabra: Craftsmanship and patronage in
Regency London", *Apollo*, January, 1997, pp.
30–4

Snodin, "Adam"
Michael Snodin, "Adam Silver Reassessed", *The
Burlington Magazine*, CXXXIX (January, 1997),
pp. 17–25

Snodin, "Adam into Context"
Michael Snodin, "Putting Adam into Context",
in K. and N.A. Quickenden, eds., *Silver &
Jewellery: Production and Consumption since 1750*,
Birmingham, 1995, pp. 13–20

Snodin, "Athenian"
Michael Snodin, "James 'Athenian' Stuart's
Metalwork", in S. Soros, ed., *James 'Athenian'
Stuart, 1713–1788: The Rediscovery of Antiquity*,
exh. cat., New Haven, 2005, pp. 466–493

Snodin, "Boileau"
Michael Snodin, "J.J. Boileau: A Forgotten
Designer of Silver", *The Connoisseur*,
CLXXXVIII (June, 1978), pp. 124–133

Snodin, "Sheffield Plate"
Michael Snodin, "Matthew Boulton's Sheffield
Plate Catalogues", *Apollo*, CXXVI, no. 305, pp.
25–32

Southwick, "Patriotic Fund"
Leslie Southwick, "The silver vases awarded by the Patriotic Fund", *The Silver Society Journal*, 1 (Winter, 1990), pp. 27–49

Stirling
A.M.W. Stirling, *Coke of Norfolk and his Friends*, London, 1908

Thomason
Sir Edward Thomason, *Memoirs during a half-century*, 2 vols, London, 1845

Tipping
H. Avray Tipping, "The Silver Plate of the Duke of Cumberland", Parts 1 and 2, *Country Life*, 56 (1, 8 November 1924), pp. 681–83, 701–3

Truman
Charles Truman, ed., *The Glory of the Goldsmith: Magnificent Gold and Silver from the Al-Tajir Collection*, exh. cat., London, 1989

Udy, "Adam's Vase"
David Udy, "Neo-Classicism and the Evolution of Adam's Vase Designs in Silver", *The Antique Collector*, LXIII (August, 1972), pp. 192–7

Udy, "Piranesi"
David Udy, "Piranesi's 'Vasi', the English Silversmith and his Patrons", *The Burlington Magazine*, CXX (December, 1978), no. 909, pp. 820–37

Wade Martins
Susannah Wade Martins, *Coke of Norfolk 1754–1842, a Biography*, Woodbridge, 2009

Watkin
David Watkin, *Thomas Hope 1769–1831 and the Neo-classical Idea*, London, 1968

Watkin and Hewat-Jaboor
David Watkin and Philip Hewat-Jaboor, *Thomas Hope: Regency Designer*, exh. cat., New Haven, 2008

Wood
Robert Wood, *The Ruins of Palmyra*, London, 1753, reprinted Farnborough, 1971

Young, "Boileau"
Hilary Young, "A Further Note on J.J. Boileau, A Forgotten Designer of Silver", *Apollo*, 1986

Young, "Chambers"
Hilary Young, "Sir William Chambers and John Yenn: Designs for Silver", *The Burlington Magazine*, CXXVIII (January, 1986), pp. 31–5

Young, "Chambers resumé"
Hilary Young, "The silver designs of Sir Wiilliam Chambers: a resumé and recent discoveries", *The Silver Society Journal*, 7 (Autumn, 1995), pp. 335–41

Young, "Cornman"
Hilary Young, "Philip Cornman: a biographical note", *The Silver Society Journal*, 8 (Autumn, 1986), pp. 481–6

Young, "Drawings"
Hilary Young, "Neo-Classical Silversmiths' Drawings in the Victoria & Albert", *Apollo*, CXXIX, no. 328 (new series, June, 1989), pp. 384–8

Young, "Marlborough"
Hilary Young, "Sir William Chambers and the Duke of Marlborough's Silver", *Apollo*, CCCIV (June, 1987), pp. 396–400

Exhibitions cited

London, 1972
The Age of Neo-classicism, The Royal Academy and Victoria & Albert Museum, London, 1972

Los Angeles, 1974
Monumental Silver: The Gilbert Collection, Los Angeles County Museum of Art, Los Angeles, 1974

Los Angeles, 1974A
Monumental Silver and Mosaics: The Gilbert Collection, Los Angeles County Museum of Art, Los Angeles, 1974

New York 1974–5
The Grand Gallery, the Metropolitan Museum of Art, New York, 1974–5

Cambridge 1975
Cambridge Plate, Fitzwilliam Museum, Cambridge, 1975

Washington DC, 1976
The Eye of Thomas Jefferson, National Gallery of Art, Washington DC, 1976

Los Angeles, 1977
Monumental Silver and Mosaics: Selections from the Gilbert Collection, Los Angeles County Museum of Art, Los Angeles, 1977

London, 1978
Piranesi, Hayward Gallery, London, 1978

London, 1979
John Flaxman, Royal Academy, London, 1979

Sydney, Australia, 1980
Masterpieces of English and European Silver and Gold, The Art Gallery of New South Wales, Sydney, Australia, 1980

New York, 1982
Robert Adam and his Style, Cooper Hewett Museum, New York, 1982

Washington DC, 1985
The Treasure Houses of Britain, National Gallery of Art, Washington DC, 1985

London, 1989
The Glory of the Goldsmith: Magnificent Gold and Silver from the Al-Tajir Collection, Christie's, London, 1989

Harrogate, 1989
The Northern Antique Dealers' Fair, Harrogate, 1989

Garrard's, 1991
Garrard, Royal Goldsmiths, Garrard's, London, 1991

London, 1991
Carlton House: The Past Glories of George IV's Palace, exh. cat., The Queen's Gallery, London, 1991

Gilbert, 1998–9
Heritage Regained: Silver from the Gilbert Collection, London, Glasgow, Manchester, York, Birmingham, Leeds and Cardiff, 1998–9

London, 2002
Royal Treasures: a Golden Jubilee Celebration, The Queen's Gallery, London, 2004

London, 2004
George III & Queen Charlotte: Patronage, Collecting and Court Taste, The Queen's Gallery, London, 2004

New York, 2005
James 'Athenian' Stuart, 1713–1788: The Rediscovery of Antiquity, Victoria and Albert Museum and Bard Garduate Centre, New York, 2005

London, 2005
Royal Goldsmiths: the Art of Rundell & Bridge, 1797–1843, Koopman Rare Art, London, 2005

London, 2008
Treasures of the English Church, A Thousand Years of Sacred Gold and Silver, The Goldsmiths' Company, London, 2008

Birmingham, 2009
Matthew Boulton: Selling what all the world desires, Gas Hall Exhibition Gallery, Birmingham, 2009

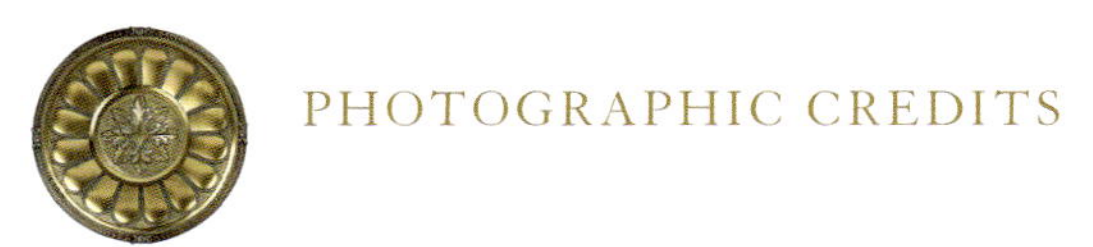

His Excellency Mohamed Mahdi Altajir, fig. 5
ADC Heritage, fig. 53
Martin Charles for Sir John Soane's Museum, image for foreword
Viscount Coke and the Trustees of the Holkham Estate, fig. 67
Courtauld Institute of Art, London, figs. 14, 94
Birmingham Archives and Heritage, fig. 51
The Trustees of the British Museum, fig. 89
The Syndics of Cambridge University Library, fig. 96
Shelagh Collingwood, fig. 76
Kasteel Duivenvoorde, figs. 74–5
Leeds Museums and Galleries (Temple Newsam House), figs. 29, 59, 102
Manchester City Galleries, fig. 28
The Metropolitan Museum of Art, New York, fig. 108
The National Museum and Gallery of Wales, Cardiff, figs. 33, 35
© The National Portrait Gallery, London, fig. 19
The National Trust, Anglesey Abbey, the Fairhaven Collection, © NTPL/James Austin, fig. 25
The National Trust, Kedleston Hall, the Scarsdale Collection, © NTPL/John Hammond, figs. 20–1
Dr David Needham, figs. 52, 62–5
Norwich Castle Museum and Art Gallery, figs. 90–2
Nottingham Castle Museum and Art Gallery, fig. 42
The Royal Collection © 2010, Her Majesty The Queen, figs. 15, 17–18, 110, 112
The Trustees of Sir John Soane's Museum, figs. 22–4, 26–7. 30, 32, 34, 36, 39, 41, 43–4
V&A Images/Trustees of the Victoria and Albert Museum, figs. 3–4, 12–13, 16, 37, 46, 76–7, 80, 83, 85, 100, 103–4, 107, 111
Simon Warner for the Harewood House Trust, figs. 9–10, 87
© The Worshipful Company of Goldsmiths, London, figs. 2, 54

COVER ILLUSTRATIONS
Front cover:
Ewer, one of a pair, silver, London, 1776–7, maker's mark of William Holmes. *Viscount Coke and the Trustees of the Holkham Estate*

Inside front flap:
Teapot and stand, silver-gilt, London, 1785–6, maker's mark of Andrew Fogelberg and Stephen Gilbert. *Private collection*

Back cover:
Soup tureen, cover and stand, silver-gilt, London, 1789–90, maker's mark of John Wakelin and William Tayler. *The Royal Collection © 2010 Her Majesty Queen Elizabeth II*

Candlestick for Sir Watkin Wynn, Bart, Adelphi, 18th January 1773, pen, pencil and wash, Robert Adam. *Sir John Soane's Museum*

Inside back flap:
Candlestick, one of a pair made for William Beckford, silver-gilt, London, 1787–8, maker's mark of Charles Aldridge. *V&A Images/Trustees of the Victoria and Albert Museum*

Detail of the design for a pair of Roman lamp stands from Herculaneum. Engraving from *Le Antichità di Ercolano Esposte*, vol. 8, Naples, 1782, p. 330. *Syndics of Cambridge University Library*

The roundel motif that adorns this book is taken from a silver-gilt dish of 1787–8, maker's mark of William Pitts, lent by Timothy Schroder, Esq. (Cat. no. 45)